MAKING PEACE LAST

MAKING PEACE LAST

A Toolbox for Sustainable Peacebuilding

Robert Ricigliano

Paradigm Publishers

Boulder • London

Published in the United States by Paradigm Publishers, 2845 Wilderness Place, Boulder, CO 80301 USA.

Paradigm Publishers is the trade name of Birkenkamp & Company, LLC, Dean Birkenkamp, President and Publisher.

Library of Congress Cataloging-in-Publication Data
Ricigliano, Rob.
  Making peace last / Robert Ricigliano.
      p. cm.
  Includes bibliographical references and index.
  ISBN 978-1-59451-994-9 (hbk. : alk. paper) — ISBN 978-1-59451-995-6 (pbk. : alk. paper)
  1. Peace-building. 2. Peace-building—Methodology. I. Title.
  JZ5538.R54 2012
  303.6'6—dc23

2011024726

Printed and bound in the United States of America on acid-free paper that meets the standards of the American National Standard for Permanence of Paper for Printed Library Materials.

Designed and Typeset by Straight Creek Bookmakers.

16 15 14 13 12   1 2 3 4 5

CONTENTS

LIST OF ILLUSTRATIONS

FIGURES

TABLES

BOXES

ACKNOWLEDGMENTS

If it takes a village to raise a child, it takes multiple systems to write a book. As such, I need to thank those people who make up the systems around me. First, there is my most important system, my family: my mom and dad; my wife, Kris; and our kids, Will, Greta, and Annie. Without this system, I would not be here.

I also depend on and benefit from multiple and overlapping professional networks. First, I need to thank Julilly Kohler and the J. M. Kohler Foundation, which provided a generous writing grant. Quite simply, this book would not exist without Julilly.

Without the cooperation and support of my colleagues at the University of Wisconsin, Milwaukee (UWM), my writing leave would not have happened. Specifically, Susan Yelich Biniecki, Doug Savage, Nicole Palasz, and Rachel Schrag all did double duty for the seven months I was away from the Institute of World Affairs. Also instrumental were Patrice Petro, vice provost for International Education, Sara Tully, Larry Borchardt, and Bob Beck at the Center for International Education. In addition, Patrice was a wise counselor who helped me get through my toughest writing challenges. I also needed the advice and support of Nancy Burrell, chair of the Communication Department at UWM (my academic home), and Mike Allen. Nathan England and Drew Zoromski, graduate students in the department, and Ellen Lindeen, a former student, were also instrumental in producing this book.

Last, but not least, dozens of colleagues tolerated, supported, and instructed me as I learned many lessons about peacebuilding. I apologize for only being able to single out a few of these people. I especially need to thank Roger Fisher of Harvard Law School, who ignited my interest in negotiation and started my career in peacebuilding. Mary Anderson, founder of the Collaborative for Development Action, is also an inspiration. Mary's willingness to confront, reasonably and intelligently, potentially unpleasant truths about our field set me on the path to writing this book.

I owe a debt to David Stroh, who introduced me to systems thinking. Diana Chigas and Peter Woodrow instructed, assisted, and sustained me through this journey. Similarly, I relied on advice and support from Doug Stone, Sheila Heen, Michael Moffitt, Andrea Schneider, Chip Hauss, and Dan Snodderly. Cynthia Irmer (US Department of State) and Tjip Walker (US Agency for International Development), as well as Peter and Diana, were instrumental in developing many of the ideas in this book. Chic Dambach, former president of the Alliance for Peacebuilding, is a great friend—'nuf said. I am particularly indebted to Ambassador Peter Galbraith for coming up with the title of this book. Lastly, I need to thank my colleagues from Harvard Negotiation Project, Conflict Management Group, and Mercy Corps.

And there could be no book without a publisher, and I am grateful for Jennifer Knerr and her colleagues at Paradigm Publishers, who saw the distinctive aspects of this book and were creative in accommodating and capitalizing on them. Also, thanks to the Rishi Tea Company of Milwaukee, which provided most of the caffeine I ingested during my hours of writing.

This book is far from perfect, but if it helps make peace last, I owe it to all of you.

PART I

UNLOCKING THE POWER OF PEACEBUILDING

Chapter 1

WE NEED TO DO BETTER, AND WE CAN

✎

The fault, dear Brutus, is not in our stars,
But in ourselves, that we are underlings.
                        —Cassius, *Julius Caesar* (I, ii, 140–141)

This book is an attempt to apply insights from systems thinking to spark a revolution in the sustainability and cost-effectiveness of efforts to build a more peaceful, just, and secure world. It represents a personal journey as much as an intellectual one. I will try to limit the personal stories to those that make the intellectual argument more comprehensible and to discuss the technical side in ways that are accessible to those outside these specific fields. I am sure I will at times fail at both, but bear with me as I pick up the journey ...

In the summer of 1995, in the middle of a crowded airplane traveling toward a destination halfway around the world, I spotted a young woman nuzzling her infant son. Most people would smile at this. I cried. Two months earlier, my wife and I had had our first child. When I saw the woman and her son on the plane, I realized that I was speeding away from the two people I loved the most.

Why was I doing this? Traveling abroad was a regular feature of my job doing conflict resolution work, or what some might call peace work, but now it seemed too great a sacrifice. Then I thought about others I have worked with in places like Colombia or the former Soviet Union and what they had sacrificed to improve their lives and their societies. I thought about the activist in South Africa in 1993 who was assassinated simply for attending a workshop on negotiation that I helped conduct. What motivates people to make these sacrifices? I thought about the fact that what kept me going was a belief that the great problems of the world—war, poverty, and injustice—were formidable, but they were within our grasp as humans to affect. Cassius's lament in *Julius Caesar* is both a criticism and an opportunity—because the current situation is our fault and not our fate; we have the power to change it. This was what I needed to be able to say to my family. We can make the world a better, more peaceful place.

Unfortunately, events of the late twentieth and early twenty-first centuries have provided ample evidence to prove my optimism unfounded. In July 2004, the US government took the unprecedented step of labeling the violence in Darfur, Sudan, as a genocide. Still, the suffering there continued. The Democratic Republic of Congo witnessed what has been labeled the world's worst humanitarian tragedy (5.4 million dead between 1998 and 2007). Wars raged in Iraq (over 2 million displaced people, perhaps 1 million dead) and Afghanistan against the backdrop of an increasing global terrorist threat. These followed on the heels of 800,000 killed in the Rwandan genocide (1994) and ethnic cleansing in Bosnia (early 1990s) and Kosovo (1999). Suffering continues in Somalia, Haiti, Israel-Palestine, Colombia, Zimbabwe, and elsewhere. This history provides ample support for the view that the prospect of "peace in our time" is as bleak as ever.

In stark contrast, however, there are credible claims that the decades after 1989 have witnessed a level of success in ending violent conflicts that is unprecedented in human history:

- After peaking in 1991, the number of civil wars had dropped 40 percent by 2003.[1]
- The number of wars ended through a negotiated settlement has increased dramatically. During the Cold War, "the number of civil wars ending in military victory (by the government or the rebels) was twice as large as the number that were concluded by negotiated settlements."[2] In the 1990s this trend was reversed, and almost twice as many wars ended in negotiated settlements versus military victories.[3]
- In the fifteen years between 1988 and 2003, more wars ended through negotiated settlement than had in the previous two centuries.[4]

These trends are a cause for celebration and have led many to tout the impact of organizations like the United Nations and its member governments along with the growing number and diversity of nongovernmental organizations (NGOs).

So, which is it: inexorable slide toward doom or accelerating trend toward peace? Asked another way, if the patient is planet Earth and the malady is violent conflict, is the patient terminal or on the road to recovery? As unsatisfying as it sounds, the answer lies somewhere in between. While it may be very difficult to ascribe specific causation to any one group, the positive trends cited above indicate that the international community, practitioners, and academics have learned important lessons about ending wars and building peace. The wealth of reports, books, and papers on postconflict reconstruction, war-to-peace transitions, and conflict resolution testify to this fact.[5]

The impressive statistics cited above are tempered, however, by the reality that almost 25 percent of wars that end in a negotiated settlement relapse into violence within five years.[6] And much of this improved peacebuilding batting average must be ascribed to factors other than increased skill or organizational effectiveness. For example, many of the Cold War conflicts were sustained in large part by military subsidies from one or both superpowers. In some cases, the end of those subsidies after 1989 may have had as big an influence on achieving negotiated settlements as the actions of interveners like the United Nations or the efforts of NGOs.

Although we have no statistic from the Cold War period for how many of the wars that ended through means other than negotiation relapsed into war, the five-year relapse rate of negotiated settlements means that the international community's batting average for settling wars through negotiation is only marginally better than it was during the Cold War. Further, the rate of negotiated peace relapsing into violence shows that the international community is better at stopping violence than building or consolidating peace. This statistic exemplifies the heart of the problem: *The challenge is not making peace, at least in some partial sense; rather, the difficulty is making peace last.* Several studies have concluded that the track record of peacebuilding is "quite mixed."[7] Nicolas Sambanis and Michael Doyle looked at 124 peacebuilding initiatives from 1945 to 1997.[8] Their study concluded that peacebuilding initiatives were successful in 43 percent of the cases, using a lenient definition of peace, and in only 35 percent of cases, using a "stricter" definition of peace. More troubling are cases where peace processes may have contributed to even greater violence. For example, in Rwanda (1994) and Angola (1993) more people died after peace agreements failed than died in the previous civil wars.[9]

In addition to the difficulty of consolidating peace, the international community has not necessarily shown a markedly increased ability to prevent the outbreak of wars. The post–Cold War period has not seen a reduction in the rate at which new civil wars begin.[10] Prevention is a critical challenge because states that have had one civil war are "far more likely" to experience additional violent conflict.[11]

The difficulty that the international community faces in preventing the outbreak of wars and consolidating peace has gained importance with the changing nature of war from predominately interstate to predominately intra-state wars. Civil wars are proving more destructive than interstate wars.[12] And the longer a war continues, the more likely it is to exacerbate the structural factors that supported the outbreak of the war in the first place, lead to additional grievances, and make peace more difficult to consolidate.[13] Studies show that a main determinant of whether there will be a recurrence of a civil war is the duration and destructiveness of the preceding violence.[14]

The challenge is much larger than just stopping violent conflict. It also entails creating the conditions for a sustainable peace or redressing the conditions that may lead to future conflict. Definitions of peace vary, but most would agree that it means more than just the absence of violence. Inextricably interconnected with peace are issues of chronic poverty, state weakness or failure, environmental degradation, health crises, food shortages and other resource conflicts, and recurring human rights violations. For example, while poverty alone may not necessarily spark violence, it is hard to imagine that there could be sustainable peace when about 1 billion people are living in extreme poverty with another 1.5 billion living just above the subsistence level.[15]

In addition, a 2001 report by the Council on Foreign Relations finds a correlation between a country's poor health status and "a decline in state capacity, leading to instability and unrest."[16] Dr. Michael Ryan, global alert and response coordinator for the World Health Organization (WHO), estimates that 50 to 75 percent of WHO responses to epidemics are in conflict-affected countries, considered "zones of emergence" for diseases that spread to non-conflict areas. Many of the last cases of diseases eradicated in other parts of the world remain in violence-affected areas.[17]

There is also a strong link between violence and state failure, either as a driver or consequence of state collapse.[18] Violent conflict has many well-established impacts on the environment.[19] In addition, there is a growing link between climate change, instability, and conflict. A report on the connection between climate change and national security found that "climate change acts as a threat multiplier for instability in some of the most volatile regions of the world."[20]

There are two critical implications of this link between peace and the many social problems identified above. First, whatever the particular cause—reversing global warming, ending poverty, protecting human rights—building peace is certainly going to be part of the solution. Second, and perhaps most profoundly, the interconnectedness of the issues peacebuilding affects raises the fundamental question of how the world is going to finance efforts to deal with all these problems. When one aggregates the costs—not just of peacekeeping or peacemaking operations but of dealing with poverty, humanitarian crises, weak states, and the like—it is clear that the demand for resources to address these problems will easily and permanently outstrip the resources dedicated to alleviating them. Aaron Salzberg, special coordinator for water resources at the US State Department, said that "even if we took all the world's official development assistance together and applied it to water [issues], it would not be enough."[21]

This changes the problem from one of absolute resources to one of efficiency in using them. The international community has to get much more productive, by several orders of magnitude, in how it spends funds dedicated to peace, justice, development, and the environment. Unfortunately, the international community is not using its resources wisely. The inefficiency in how the international community spends its money on peacebuilding in conflict zones is a good case in point. It is not hard to find examples of peacebuilding funds being wasted. An audit by the special inspector general for Iraq reconstruction found $9 billion in unaccounted-for funds.[22] In Afghanistan, $300 million was spent on a presidential election in 2009 in order to strengthen governance as part of rebuilding that country. However, many observers felt the massive fraud in the election further delegitimized the government of Hamid Karzai.[23]

The problem extends beyond these notable examples. William Easterly, a former World Bank economist, argues that the problem is not that the donor countries are stingy but that they are ineffective because their programs are poorly designed and executed.[24] In order to test whether there was a relationship between a country's rate of economic growth and the level of foreign aid it received, Easterly divided the countries in the poorest quintile into two groups: half with highest level of aid and half with the lowest level. The result of his analysis is sobering for those who tout the effectiveness of foreign aid: "There is no significant difference in growth rates between the two groups, despite average aid as a percentage of GDP being two to five times larger in the top group."[25]

WHY AREN'T WE DOING BETTER?
THE MICRO-MACRO PARADOX

Lasting peace will not likely be attained unless peacebuilding undergoes a productivity revolution. The central reason why peacebuilding programs are not more productive, or cost-effective, is that we are not working "smart." This is not to say that we lack smart, hardworking people in the field who are designing and carrying out a myriad of peacebuilding programs. The thousands of peacebuilding practitioners across the world are among the best and the brightest. Rather, the problem is that peacebuilders need the tools to create synergy among their programs in order to make their collective impact much greater than the sum of their individual projects. Michael Lund, a leading evaluator of the effectiveness of peacebuilding programs, explains this phenomenon well: "Energies are dispersed in hundreds of different directions but the myriad of activities is not guided by an underlying grounded theory, or overall strategy, only vague assumptions."[26]

Developing this underlying theory and a practical approach for its implementation is the most urgent task of the peacebuilding community. The starting point is to squarely confront the "micro-macro paradox": Why do we see many programs across conflict zones, diverse in their nature and particulars, that are successful as measured by their ability to achieve immediate program objectives at the local (micro) level in the midst of conflicts that resist systemic (macro-level) change? This dynamic was captured best by Mary Anderson and Lara Olson (2003), who conclude, "From the vantage point of a broad overview of many activities over many locations over a long period of time one overwhelming conclusion emerges: *All the good peace work being done should be adding up to more than it is. The potential of all these efforts is not being realized.*"[27] In terms of cost-effectiveness, one could paraphrase Anderson and Olson to say that the billions of dollars spent on peacebuilding projects should be buying more peace. Resolving the micro-macro paradox holds the key to improving our peacebuilding productivity.

What should we learn from both our successes and our shortcomings in reducing violent conflict and building a more peaceful world? Perhaps the best way to think of it is to return to the medical analogy involving patient Earth and the malady of violent conflict. We have seen real successes, but they have been mostly at the local level—the equivalent of having localized success in treating the symptoms of a disease (the tumor was removed, blood pressure reduced, and an artery opened). We are still unable, however, to return the patients to health or to keep ahead of the disease as it changes and spreads through the body. In more direct terms, the international system has proven it can address the symptoms of violent conflict, but it is still losing too many patients.

Given the mixed track record of peacebuilding, the answer is neither to declare victory over violent conflict nor to give up in despair. Rather, the key to improving our ability to end violent conflict and consolidate peace is to figure out why the macro-micro paradox exists.

The Need for a Holistic Approach

Roger Fisher, a founding figure in the field of negotiation, championed the value of learning from experience and often pointed out that "before autopsies, physicians literally buried their mistakes." People do not like to dwell on their shortcomings. For many years, practitioners in the conflict resolution and development fields resisted even asking why a gap existed between the micro and macro levels. Macro-level peace was a complex endeavor beyond the control of any one intervener, including even large states like the United States and organizations like the United Nations, let alone a small NGO. There are huge hurdles to achieving macro-level peace: chronic poverty, vested self-interests, ancient hatreds, to name a few. So, if the reason for the micro-macro gap is beyond the control of any one intervener, why even ask the question of how to bridge it?

In 2001, when I made the transition from the NGO world, doing applied conflict resolution work, to academia, I could not get the macro-micro paradox out of my head. After lots of reflection, reading, writing, and conversation with colleagues, the reason for its existence was crystallized for me in an unlikely place: the intensive care unit (ICU) of a Florida hospital.[28] In January 2006, my father had a stroke. I was with him for a week in the ICU. My thoughts and prayers dwelt on his survival. However, as my father's condition improved, I began to notice the group of diverse medical practitioners who worked with him and with each other. There were cardiologists, neurologists, general practitioners, nurses, nutritionists, pulmonary specialists, surgeons, physical therapists, and others. They regularly diagnosed my father's condition and coordinated how they could work together to increase his chances of recovery.

They took a holistic approach. Despite the fact that their individual specialties gave them insight into only part of my father's condition, they knew that the success of any one intervention affected, and was affected by, any other intervention. They measured success not just in terms of how their specific procedure went but also by how their procedure improved my father's overall condition. Thanks to the work of this dedicated team of medical professionals, my father went from being on a deathwatch to a making a recovery.

Now, imagine that instead of this holistic approach, there was no coordination among the medical staff. What if the cardiologist worked against the neurologist, the pulmonologist ignored the general practitioner, nurses administered multiple, inconsistent medications, and different teams of surgeons operated all at the same time. Any chances the patient had for recovery would quickly shrink to zero.

Yet, this version of the chaotic ICU is a fair analogy to how the international community treats countries trying to make the transition from war to peace or to deal with the effects of a weak or failing state. When practitioners from various disciplines (conflict resolution, human rights, rule of law, environmental protection, diplomacy, reconciliation, economic development, health care, etc.) intervene in a conflict-affected area, they tend to think in terms of their own discipline, not about what would help the situation as a whole.[29] This is like a heart surgeon only looking at how to perform a bypass operation without concern for whether the patient's lungs can withstand the procedure or the impact of the treatment on the patient's kidney dialysis.

The lack of a holistic approach is also apparent in what is termed a "strategic deficit" on the part of donors and policy makers. After examining 336 projects implemented by the governments of Norway, Germany, the United Kingdom, and the Netherlands, the Utstein Study concludes that 55 percent of the programs reviewed "do not show any link to a broader strategy for the country."[30] As Cedric de Coning points out, this strategic deficit was identified as the "most significant obstacle to sustainable peacebuilding."[31] In the chaotic ICU, this is like different medical specialists conducting their various interventions without referring to whether or not they contribute to the patient's overall health.

Lastly, the lack of a holistic approach also hampers the ability of policy makers and practitioners to work in a more integrated way by crossing bureaucratic and disciplinary boundaries. In working across disciplines, policy makers, practitioners, donors, and academics are frustrated by different vocabularies, interests, experiences, and organizational cultures. As Lund observes, "The discourse one hears at public peacebuilding events is largely a Tower of Babel of differing options being hawked in a sprawling policy bazaar."[32] However, it is a sign of progress that policy makers now recognize the existence of this peacebuilding Tower of Babel and that it has serious consequences in the field. De Coning goes on to write, "There is now broad consensus that inconsistent policies and fragmented programmes entail a higher risk of duplication, inefficient spending, a lower quality of service, difficulty in meeting goals and, ultimately, of a reduced capacity for delivery."[33]

Unfortunately, this recognition has been forced by many stark examples of what de Coning calls "a reduced capacity for delivery." A couple of field examples are illustrative. First is the experience of the World Bank in Cambodia. Following the peace deal in 1991, the Bank insisted on shrinking government spending. However, the peace agreement called for just the opposite: an expansion of government spending to accommodate a larger civil service in order to integrate different, competing groups into the government.[34] In the experience in Bosnia, donors, in a rush to disperse aid, relied on beneficiary lists prepared by local mayors, but these lists were ethnically biased. This had a demoralizing effect on those being coaxed by other international actors into various reconciliation and reconstruction projects and deterred their participation in them.[35] These are just two of dozens of such stories.[36]

To improve our ability to build peaceful societies out of those riven by violence, we will need to turn the peacebuilding Tower of Babel into a field that takes a holistic approach. Without such an approach, diverse actors trying to help the reconstruction and reconciliation process do not even think of themselves as belonging to the same field or discipline. How chaotic and ineffective would medical treatment be if nurses, therapists, and doctors did not regard themselves as belonging to the common field of medicine? Or

recognize their common goal of improving patients' health? Or pool knowle
across specialties? Or recognize the interdependence of their work?

Sadly, among those arguably working toward peace, there is no acknowledgment that this is in fact what they are doing. They do not see themselves
as peace practitioners in the same way that doctors, nurses, and others see
themselves as health professionals. This is not just a matter of semantics.
The absence of that common awareness of themselves as working toward
peace leads to much less coordination, a less holistic approach, insufficient
acknowledgment of how individual disciplines affect each other, and, as a
result, less efficient and less sustainable outcomes.

The lack of a common definition of an integrated field has created structural problems in how the field is organized, leading to reduced efficiency and
squandered resources. For example, one practitioner commented, "Constraints
on integrated programming arise mainly from the hegemony of specialized
expertise and the structural divisions that pervade the humanitarian community.... Further, donors organize grants by sector.... The net result is that
each sector operates as a separate world, having its own norms, values, and
culture."[37] This critique is only amplified when we look at the lack of coordination between human rights, conflict resolution, development, reconciliation, diplomacy, environmental conservation, and so forth. If these various
practitioners cannot even acknowledge that they are, in fact, a field or agree
on basic terminology, then a major fault in the world's ability to bring relief
to troubled countries is indeed in ourselves and not just attributable to the
traditional culprits or immutable problems such as state self-interest, lack of
resources, and bad actors.

Although there are many structural obstacles to building peace in violence-
affected countries, a significant improvement *that it is within our power to make*
is to define a field of peacebuilding capable of bringing together the work
of diverse practitioners in the way that medicine or health is an organizing
rubric for diverse heath-care professionals.

IS THERE A FIELD OF PEACEBUILDING?

During a conference at Brandeis University, a group of us were speaking about
the peacebuilding field when a colleague skeptically asked, "Is there a field of
peacebuilding?" He raised the concern that there was no such field and that
attempting to create one was wasting time playing word games that would
change nothing on the ground. Said another way, the obstacles to building
a more peaceful world are not issues of vocabulary.

Developing new terminology is a waste of time unless it reflects a deeper
change in how we think, how we act, and the results we achieve on the
ground. I contend, however, that defining a field of peacebuilding is necessary

to promote more holistic approaches, bridge the micro-macro gap, and improve our ability to address war-torn and chronically impoverished societies around the world.

Yet, is it possible or realistic to define a field of peacebuilding? Can there be a peacebuilding field analogous to the field of medicine or health care? To answer that question in the affirmative, two basic questions must also be answered in the positive:

1. Are the diverse actors and disciplines pursuing a common, supraordinate goal?
2. Is there interactivity between the work of these diverse practitioners? Do the efforts of practitioners from one discipline to achieve their ultimate end affect, and/or are they affected by, the work of others?

The answer to each of those questions is a resounding yes.

Is There Interdependence?

Perhaps the most apparent evidence of whether peacebuilding is a field is the high degree of interactivity among diverse interventions meant to build more peaceful societies out of ones afflicted by conflict and/or severe underdevelopment. For example, in Afghanistan in 2010, the US counterinsurgency strategy (COIN) melded traditionally separate initiatives such as security, development, and conflict resolution. The strategy was based on an organic connection between these disciplines. David Kilcullen, a senior advisor to Gen. David Petreaus and the authors of the COIN, points out, "A government that is losing a counter-insurgency isn't being outfought, it is being out-governed."[38]

The Utstein Study, cited above, and many more like it have led to a flood of calls for greater policy coherence, integration, coordination, and holism.[39] Consider the following sample:

"Without peace, development is not possible, without development, peace is not durable."[40]

"There is a need for a holistic approach in the planning and execution of peacebuilding missions."[41]

Long before the idea of human security gained currency, the authors of these statements understood well the indivisibility of security, economic development, and human freedom.[42]

Building on these studies and broad policy pronouncements are bureaucratic changes designed to promote more holistic programs, capture the gains of greater policy coherence, and minimize the costs of incoherence. For example, the Conflict Prevention Pools system started by the government of the United Kingdom in 2001 was designed to be holistic by linking previously separated areas of policy and program development (e.g., development, foreign policy, security, law enforcement, and trade).[43] There are many other such developments at many international organizations (e.g., the UN Peacebuilding Commission) and in most donor governments (e.g., the Office of Conflict Management and Mitigation at the US Agency for International Development and the US State Department Office of the Coordinator for Reconstruction and Stabilization).

Nongovernmental organizations and academic programs have also witnessed a greater move to integrated study of previously distinct disciplines—for example, the World Wildlife Fund's Impact of Armed Conflict on the Environment program or the integration of the Conflict Management Group (a conflict resolution NGO) into Mercy Corps (a relief and development NGO). Within the academic world in the United States, there is 3P Human Security (formerly 3D Security), which grew out of the Center for Justice and Peacebuilding at Eastern Mennonite University, the Center for Human Rights and Conflict Resolution of the Fletcher School at Tufts University, and the Institute for Peace and Justice at San Diego University. These are just a few of the many NGO and academic programs in the United States, let alone around the world.[44]

Most importantly, in addition to changes at the level of policy making, organizational structure, and academic centers, the reality of interactivity across disciplines is starkly apparent on the ground. For example, if a program is designed to rebuild a well in a particular village, a micro-level goal, physically building a functioning well may not depend, to any great degree, on human rights, rule of law, trauma healing, and the like. However, as one looks at broader and longer-term impacts, the situation changes: Is the well contributing to improved health conditions in the village? Is that healthy village contributing to higher levels of peace in the society overall? The answer to these questions depends, to an increasing degree, on the work of other disciplines—for example, intergroup reconciliation, governance, and security. As one NGO worker describes it, "Programming needs to be guided by a causal framework that recognizes interactions across sectors. One cannot promote health, for example, by attending to medical issues while ignoring issues of water, sanitation, shelter, and household income."[45] The question is not whether there is interdependence and interactivity among diverse specialties such as development, environmental conservation, reconciliation, justice, and conflict transformation. Rather the hard question is whether these fields can be united in pursuit of a common end. Without that, dealing successfully and proactively with the interactivity among these diverse fields will be difficult.

Can Peace Serve as a Supraordinate Goal?

Despite the interactivity among the various disciplines concerned with building more just and sustainable societies, there is a reluctance to group such endeavors under the label of "peace work." A colleague of mine spends her time bringing together diverse practitioners to discuss the interactivity of their work. Because it is so difficult to get these diverse practitioners to agree on what to call their collective field, she has taken to calling the end to which they are all working "underwater basket weaving." This is her attempt to avoid contentious discussions about terminology—for example, is their common concern peace, justice, coexistence, development, a sustainable environment?

One thing is for sure: If practitioners from these various fields are asked why they do the work that they do or what they hope to accomplish, almost all will articulate an end state that goes beyond their particular specialty. They may be working on a human rights campaign, but they see respect for human rights as essential to a peaceful society. Building schools in Afghanistan is a worthy pursuit in itself, but those working to build these schools do it because it will contribute to a more peaceful future for all Afghans. Anderson and Olson studied a diverse group of "peace practitioners" and found that all aimed to accomplish two basic goals: stopping violence and destructive conflict and building just and sustainable peace.[46] Finding a general consensus that various practitioners are striving for something more than economic growth, rule of law, poverty reduction, or war crimes prosecutions, they labeled this "something more" as Peace Writ Large (PWL).[47]

Is PWL the common end that these diverse fields are all striving toward? Defined in part as "building sustainable peace," PWL begs the question of what "peace" means. The term *peace,* whatever the accompanying modifiers (e.g., just, sustainable, etc.), has proven controversial, and many practitioners would reject it as defining the larger ends to which they are working. This resistance is due, in large part, to how peace has been traditionally defined. The word is criticized as being overly broad, encompassing everything from new age personal spiritual enlightenment to utopian dreams of a perfect world to simply the absence of violence. For many, the term *peace* has not overcome what they perceive as the stigma of being the symbol for softheaded, drug-dependent flower children in the 1960s.

For others, the resistance is based on a reluctance to raise expectations improperly of their work. For example, take a group of development practitioners who specialize in rebuilding agricultural systems. This group might resist calling their efforts "peace work" because they do not want to over-promise: They know that their agricultural work, even if successful, cannot by itself deliver "peace" in some grand sense. I refer to this as the "utopian expectations problem."

These two challenges, peace being an overly broad concept (with many definitions, many with negative associations) and peace being an overly ambitious goal, stand in the way of peace serving as the supraordinate goal or organizing concept for a field of peacebuilding. Although significant, these challenges can be overcome. The first step is to address the fact that peace is typically used only to reference an end state: justice, prosperity, security, or all three. This definition of peace begs the question, How much? How just, prosperous, or secure? But answering this question is fatal. For example, if one says complete justice for all, then one makes peace a utopian standard that can never be attained. If one compromises and says acceptably or tolerably just, then one runs into moral critiques (e.g., why are some only entitled to tolerable justice?). Or one needs to engage in artificial line drawing (how does one measure tolerably just?). The same can be said for other static indicators of peace. The basic problem is that peace is always arriving and never arrives. And because it is defined as an end state, it is defined as an unattainable utopian ideal that no one can ever succeed in delivering.

A second critique of how peace has been defined is that it sets up a fundamental trade-off between peace and justice. If peace is defined as stability and the lack of violence, it is open to the critique that it favors preservation of the status quo and privileges entrenched or dominant interests over marginalized groups. For example, an aid recipient said that she feared that the goal of the international community was merely to "make my poverty more tolerable."[48] Some would argue that justice, an essential ingredient in most formulations of peace, might require significant social upheaval and even the use of violence to redress wrongs imposed on minority or less powerful populations. So, human rights workers may not refer to their work as peace work because they prioritize realizing justice, whether or not it results in peace.

For peace to serve as the supraordinate goal of diverse practitioners, it must be redefined so as to avoid utopian critiques or a trade-off between peace and justice. In this regard, consider the following definition:

Peace is a state of human existence characterized by sustainable levels of human development and healthy processes of societal change.

To be regarded as peaceful, a society needs two things: (1) the capacity to meet the basic needs, at any one time, of the individuals and groups that comprise it, and (2) the ability to change and evolve over time in response to a constantly changing environment. *Sustainable levels of human development* refers to how well people's basic human needs are being met and could be gauged using objective measures of nutrition, infant mortality, poverty, health, security, respect for human rights, and the like.[49] *Healthy processes of change* refers to the ability of individuals and groups in the society to deal with important problems, opportunities, and challenges in ways that improve, or at least do not compromise, their ability to meet basic needs in the future. Healthy processes of change might be gauged in terms of good governance, the degree of social capital, measures of intergroup tensions, levels of violence, effectiveness of dispute resolution processes (formal and informal), and so forth.

Measured at any one point in time, a process of change is healthy if it does not prejudice the ability of the society to coexist tomorrow. A process of change is healthy if the means used for change do not harm, and ideally improve, the ability of groups to make change in the future. Healthy processes of change would rule out most, if not all, forms of violence (though it may be theoretically possible, at least, to think of a situation in which some form of violence actually improved the ability of the polity to meet its basic needs in the future).

This definition of peace recognizes that peace is fundamentally about how people work together (a process measure) to meet the basic needs of a population and how well they are meeting those needs (a substantive measure). Peace is not just a snapshot in time. It is about substantive indicators of human development measured at any one moment (e.g., a snapshot of good governance, rule of law and respect for human rights, security, economic vitality, social capital, etc.), and peace is also about how the society deals with problems or issues on an ongoing basis.

This measure of peace would give a different picture than one that looked at substantive indicators alone. For example, a particular society might do fairly well on most measures of good governance, but if it has no ability to grapple with current governance problems, then it is less healthy, hence less peaceful, than if one looked at the static indicators alone. Similarly, a country might have significant governance problems, but if it is addressing those problems in a positive, inclusive, and productive way, then it would be healthier and more peaceful than if one looked at the static indicators alone.

This definition of peace is better able to serve as the supraordinate goal toward which many diverse fields contribute. Anything that helps build sustainable human development and/or healthy processes of change is peacebuilding. If one defines human rights as a basic human need, then human rights work is a key part of sustainable human development. The same would be true for a healthy environment, a good economy, and adequate health care. If social capital, mechanisms for dispute resolution, and good governance contribute to healthy processes of change, then work in any of these areas is peacebuilding.

Including both process and substantive components in the definition of peace accepts that the ideal of peace (perfect justice, prosperity, or security) will never be reached. However, acceptance of never reaching the ideal is tolerable if there are sufficient processes of change such that tomorrow may bring improvement in any of the substantive indicators. Defining peace this way avoids the problem of overpromising to bring about some utopian state. Similarly, there is no trade-off between peace and justice if one both looks at a snapshot of how just a society is and considers its ability to become more just in the future.

This endorsement of peacebuilding as the overarching goal is bolstered by a report done for the Norwegian government that states, "Peacebuilding is increasingly seen as the collective framework under which these peace, security, humanitarian, rule of law, human rights and development dimensions can be brought together."[50] It does not, by itself, make any place on earth more peaceful, but it does achieve a critical first step. It allows the diverse practitioners critical to the success of peacebuilding to see themselves as an interdependent whole. And recognizing this interdependent whole is the first step toward overcoming the micro-macro gap, increasing the productivity of peacebuilding, and making peace last. Chapters 2 through 4 flesh out systemic peacebuilding as a conceptual approach, Chapters 5 through 7 discuss a practical approach to systemic assessment and planning, and Chapters 8 through 10 provide practical advice on how to begin implementing systemic peacebuilding programs.

CHAPTER 1 SUMMARY

- There is a need to do better at building peace, both for the purposes of reducing the levels and impact of violent conflict and for addressing longer-term costs of state weakness and persistent poverty.
- A key to doing better at building peace is bridging the gap between success at the micro (project) level and the macro level, or what has been termed Peace Writ Large.
- Bridging the micro-macro gap will require interveners to take a more holistic approach.
- We are unlikely to see truly holistic approaches that bridge the micro-macro gap unless we can define a field of peacebuilding that captures the interdependence of diverse practitioners and articulates a common goal toward which they all are working.
- Peace defined as achieving sustainable levels of human development and healthy processes of change is the key to defining a field of peacebuilding that can serve as a uniting rubric for the work of diverse disciplines and organizations.

CHAPTER 2

A SHIFT OF MIND
SYSTEMIC PEACEBUILDING

So it should come as no surprise that the unhealthiness of our world today is in direct proportion to our inability to see it as a whole.

—Peter Senge

Defining peacebuilding as any initiative that contributes to building sustainable levels of human development and/or healthy processes of societal change is a key first step toward making peace last. In order to translate this semantic change into one that makes peacebuilding interventions more productive on the ground, we need to define, in theory and practice, how diverse peacebuilding disciplines and organizations can mesh into a coherent whole.[1] The chief obstacle is neither the fact that these disciplines do not, in fact, form a coherent whole nor the thorny issue of different organizational cultures or bureaucratic turf wars. Rather, as the epigraph to this chapter from Peter Senge indicates, the core challenge to forming a more holistic approach to peacebuilding is that we are not, in general, very good at seeing wholes.

Comprehending wholes is not a new challenge. Remember the Sufi parable about the blind men and the elephant. Several blind men, never having seen an elephant before, rush to find out what this strange creature looks like. Each blind man feels a different part of the elephant and concludes that the part he feels describes the entire animal. So, the blind man who feels its tail concludes that the elephant is long and thin like a snake, the one who feels the leg thinks the elephant is round like a mighty pillar, and so on.

Each individual blind man cannot be faulted for having only a partial view of reality—the truth is that each of us only has such a partial view. In fact, in the Newtonian tradition, we are trained to break reality down into its component parts in order to better understand its complexity. However, we get so good at seeing parts that we lose the ability to see the whole. When we are used to seeing individual trees (or just our own tree), it is very difficult to see the forest. We get into trouble when we think the part we are looking at describes the whole. Similarly, each blind man is wrong to assume that his partial view of the elephant describes the whole beast.

The tale of the blind men and the elephant is a fair description of how diverse actors in the peacebuilding field behave. For example, in 2004 I attended an expert consultation on strengthening conflict prevention in Guinea-Bissau, hosted by the Alliance for Peacebuilding and attended by various peacebuilders: representatives of international development NGOs, human rights organizations, various US government agencies (such as the US Agency for International Development, Department of State, and Department of Defense), various UN agencies (such as the UN Development Programme), conflict resolution groups, and environmental organizations. The centerpiece of the meeting was a panel of three experts from Guinea-Bissau who each gave diverse perspectives on what was currently happening in their country.

Following the reports on Guinea-Bissau, the participants asked questions and offered their opinions about what they saw as the root of the problem and what could be done to lower the threat of violence. I observed the interaction and was startled by how closely the story of the blind men and the elephant was replicating itself. For example, participants who did work setting up electoral systems and holding elections saw the problem as the upcoming elections in Guinea-Bissau. Participants who did dialogue work saw the problem as a lack of communication between key leaders. Those who did market-reform work saw the problem as stagnant economic growth. And so the discussion continued.

As with the blind men, each participant was partly correct; elections, the lack of political dialogue, and the economy were important features of the situation in Guinea-Bissau. However, each made the same error. The orthodox Sufi theologian Muhammad al-Ghazzali concluded his telling of the parable of the blind men this way: "Each was right in a certain sense, since each of them communicated that part of the elephant he had comprehended, but none was able to describe the elephant as it really was; for all three of them were unable to comprehend the entire form of the elephant."[2]

None of the peacebuilders was able to comprehend the whole of what was happening in Guinea-Bissau, but that did not stop them from using their partially valid view to make a prescription that would improve the situation as a whole. For example, understanding the status of human rights in

Guinea-Bissau is important to understanding the conditions there, but the human rights situation is not representative of the whole of Guinea-Bissau, just as the elephant's ear is not representative of the whole of the elephant. Further, we cannot assume that successfully protecting human rights in Guinea-Bissau would, by itself, lessen the potential for violence there. When we assume the contrary and design peacebuilding interventions based on a partial view of reality, we contribute, in Senge's words, to the "unhealthiness of our world."

What we need is the ability to see wholes as well as parts. Fortunately, systems thinking, which was developed as a general science of wholeness, can help.[3] Systems thinking broadly refers to the insights derived from general systems theory and its associated concepts. Ludwig von Bertalanffy coined the term *general systems theory* and began writing about the topic in the 1930s. Von Bertalanffy developed general systems theory as a reaction against "reductionism," or the prevailing methodology in science, which aimed to "break down every problem into as many separate, simple elements as might be possible."[4] As a biologist, von Bertalanffy felt that reductionism was not sufficient for understanding biological organisms. He observed that the whole of an organism was much "more than the sum of its parts," to borrow a phrase generally credited to Aristotle.

For example, reductionism can be helpful in understanding what makes steel, steel; it can be broken down into its component metals, and those can be broken down into basic elements, which can be divided into atoms, each containing some combination of electrons, protons, and perhaps neutrons, and so on. However, it is difficult to understand a complex organism like a person the same way. Examining a person's internal organs, blood type, bone density, and muscle tone might provide insight into his basic health but would not help you understand his personality, values, or behavior. People are much more than the sum of their physical components, and systems thinking is the discipline of understanding how, when you put all the pieces together, they form a different whole.

General systems theory has spawned many related concepts, such as systems dynamics (Jay Forrester), complexity theory (Murray Gell-Mann), cybernetics (Norbert Wiener), dynamical systems theory (Peter Coleman), soft systems methodology (Peter Checkland), and even multitrack diplomacy (Louise Diamond and John MacDonald). It is not necessary to explore the technical aspects of these disciplines to grasp the essence of systems thinking and the basic tools it offers to help people see and understand wholeness. These include

- interaction or relationships among parts;
- interconnectedness of parts;

- feedback and dynamic, as opposed to linear, causality;
- patterns, or holism.

As an illustration of these concepts, take a simplified version of an arms race between two entities, A and B. For ease of understanding, assume that four distinct "parts" make up the arms race:

- A's feeling of being threatened by B;
- A's building arms to protect itself;
- B's feeling of being threatened by A;
- B's building arms to protect itself.

The first step in moving from seeing parts to seeing the whole is to focus on the interactions among, or relationships between, the parts. It may seem obvious, but there is a relationship between A's feeling of threat and A's building of arms to protect itself: The more A feels threatened, the more it builds arms.

If each part in the system is related to at least one other part, this gives rise to the notion of *interconnectedness*; each piece of a system is connected, directly or indirectly, to other parts in the system. Interconnectedness is like a spiderweb: Pulling on any one strand in the web will affect, directly or indirectly, every other strand in the web. In the arms race example, there is no direct relationship between A's feeling threatened and B's feeling threatened (e.g., the fact that A feels threatened does not directly result in B's feeling threatened). However, the two parts are indirectly connected (or interconnected) because A's feeling of threat causes A to build arms to protect itself, which in turn causes B to feel threatened (see Figure 2.1).

Figure 2.1 Systems Thinking Basics

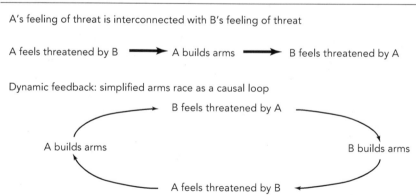

A's feeling of threat is interconnected with B's feeling of threat

A feels threatened by B ⟶ A builds arms ⟶ B feels threatened by A

Dynamic feedback: simplified arms race as a causal loop

B feels threatened by A

A builds arms   B builds arms

A feels threatened by B

Interconnectedness gives rise to the ideas of *feedback* and *dynamic causality.* Think of feedback in terms of the spiderweb: If you pluck a strand in a spiderweb, the vibration will travel around the web until it affects the strand that was initially plucked. It is the same in systems: If one part of the system affects another part, that action will reverberate throughout the system and eventually act on the part that initiated the action. In the arms race, as shown in Figure 2.1, when A responds to its feeling of threat by building arms, this causes B to feel threatened, which in turn leads B to build arms, which actually increases A's feeling of threat! Due to the process of feedback (which works through the phenomenon of interconnectedness), any one part of the system is both a cause (A's feeling of threat causes A to build arms) and an effect (A's feeling of threat is an effect of B's building arms). In systems terms, feedback and dynamic causality are represented by causal loops.

This is a defining feature of wholeness, that causality is dynamic, not linear. Linear and dynamic causality provide two different ways of looking at the world. Both are valid, but they are useful for different purposes. Linear causality looks at discrete causal chains and assumes that causality happens in a line that travels in one direction: If you do A, then B will result; if B happens, then C will result, and so on. Linear thinking can be helpful with more mechanical, short-term tasks—for example, understanding how to use a stove to cook an omelet. If I want to cook an omelet, then I need to know that turning on the stove will cause the burner to heat up, which will cause the pan to heat up, which will cook the egg, and so on.

Dynamic causality assumes that no initial condition exists in isolation; rather, each is part of an interconnected system. Dynamic causality is more helpful when addressing more complex, long-term problems. In the omelet example, dynamic causality asks, What led to the desire to cook the omelet in the first place? Understanding the patterns of behavior that generated my urge to cook and then eat an omelet is much more helpful if my goal is to understand and control my tendency to overeat.

The concept of patterns is a final, important systems thinking tool. George Richardson, a systems thinker at the State University of New York, Albany, defines a "systems view" of the world as one that "stands back just far enough to deliberately blur discrete events into patterns of behavior."[5] For example, in the omelet/overeating example, the mechanics of cooking the omelet (e.g., turning on the stove, putting the pan on the burner, etc.) are a series of discrete events. However, if my goal was to eat more healthfully, understanding the mechanics of cooking any one particular food or the inner workings of a stove is less important than understanding the broader patterns of behavior that contribute to my overeating (e.g., how I respond to stress in the workplace, dynamics within my family, etc.). In Richardson's metaphor, "stepping in" is the equivalent of understanding the details of how the stove works. "Stepping back" is the equivalent of zooming back from a close-up of the stove to see myself (as the cook) and to view my interactions with other members of my family, how I respond to stress in the workplace, and so forth.

The practice of stepping back from the parts far enough to see patterns or wholes is a way of incorporating lots of complexity yet still yielding a manageable and useful narrative. The systems view tells a compelling story about the whole from the perspective of the whole. Standing back, as opposed to studying discrete pieces, allows one to describe the whole elephant rather than its ears, tail, trunk, or legs.

CAN SYSTEMS THINKING REALLY HELP?

Can using systems thinking tools to see wholes really help improve the productivity of peacebuilding initiatives or bridge the micro-macro paradox? It does not provide the entire solution, but it is a critical step. Without adding systems thinking to their toolbox, peacebuilders often end up using the wrong tool for the job: trying to fix complex, long-term problems, like producing Peace Writ Large (PWL), that is, macro-level societal change, with tools better suited for short-term mechanical problems. Said another way, trying to use linear, reductionist thinking to end poverty or build a more peaceful Afghanistan is like trying to use a screwdriver to fix a cloudy day. Former World Bank economist William Easterly points to this phenomenon in his critique of the planning tools used by agencies in the development world:

> Although a large project like a dam or electric plant involves some planning, it takes place on purely engineering grounds. Ending world poverty is not an engineering problem.... It presents many variables of human behavior as well as technical complexity.
>
> Nevertheless, the aid agencies often seem to have in mind the kind of engineering problem that a dam poses when designing planning solutions to the problems of poverty.[6]

Problems arise in the peacebuilding world when we use a linear mind-set to address a systemic problem. For example, holding an election in a village in Afghanistan can be thought of as a mechanical process—so many polling places must be established, with a particular type of voting process, and so on. However, if the goals of an election extend beyond the mere fact of holding it, such as being part of a systemic change in how Afghans create accountable governments that can address the basic human needs of their populations, then this is no longer a mechanical problem. How was the decision made to hold the election? How will local elections in particular or changes to the governance structure in general affect the complex system that is Afghanistan? These are systemic questions that require systems thinking tools.

The overuse of linear thinking and planning tools is not the product of bad intentions or incompetence. Moving from linear to systems thinking can be very difficult and even a bit scary. Peter Senge explains that this difficulty is rooted in how our brains have been trained to work: "Evidence is overwhelming that human beings have 'cognitive limitations.' Cognitive scientists have shown that we can deal with only a small number of separate variables simultaneously. Our conscious information processing circuits get easily overloaded by detail complexity, forcing us to invoke simplifying heuristics to figure things out."[7] Seeing the whole can be maddening or stultifying—it is just too complex. I once worked with a country team from an international NGO working in Afghanistan to draw a causal loop diagram of the conflict in Afghanistan. The picture looked like a plate of spaghetti and meatballs. It was a demoralizing moment when the team looked at the diagram and felt that their individual development programs were insignificant in the face of this complexity.

After an initial feeling of depression, a typical response to this complex systemic view, as Senge explains, is to find some scheme to order the complexity into understandable parts. The problem arises when those ordering schema are based on linear analysis. A good example is the commonly used conflict cycle, also known as the conflict wave or the stages-of-conflict model.[8] The model is a classic attempt to bring order to chaos by positing that conflicts move through a life cycle that starts with low-intensity conflict, rises to active (violent) conflict, and then de-escalates through stages of postconflict settlement and recovery. This typology has been used as the basis for ordering various forms of peacebuilding intervention: Conflict prevention strategies could be used in the early low-intensity phases, peace enforcement or armed intervention could be used during phases of peak intensity or violence, and reconstruction and reconciliation efforts could be used as the intensity curve de-escalates.[9] This thinking has informed policy making that distinguishes between conflict prevention, peacemaking and enforcement, and postconflict reconstruction.

While neat and linear, this model is out of line with reality. In his statement during the UN Security Council's open debate on postconflict peacebuilding, Sir Emyr Jones Parry, the United Kingdom's permanent representative to the United Nations, stated, "There is no regular sequence in which conflict ends, peace is re-established, and stability ensues."[10] Some have tried to warn against a "too-strict" application of the conflict cycle, explaining that conflicts can jump phases or move backward along the conflict wave. But such thinkers neglect "the fact that civil wars and interethnic disputes are made up of a multiplicity of embedded conflicts, which might exhibit properties of several escalation or de-escalation stages simultaneously."[11] As a result, many peace-building practitioners have chafed at the conflict wave and the policies built around it. Participants in dialogue between the US Agency for International Development and representatives of several implementing agencies "concluded that the distinctions between pre, during, and post-conflict are too limiting and do not reflect the reality of conflict situations."[12]

The conflict cycle also promotes approaches to peacebuilding that are disaggregated or tend to treat discrete drivers of a conflict or enablers of peace (e.g., parts of the system) without regard for the impact on the overall system. Rosabeth Moss Kanter observed this phenomenon in the context of organizational change. In arguing against piecemeal approaches to changing discrete parts of complex, interdependent organizations, she concludes that "attempts to carry out programmatic continuing change through isolated single efforts are likely to fail because of the effects of system context."[13] A change in one part of the system is vulnerable to the impact of forces from other parts in the system. In the omelet/overeating example, putting me on a diet may make some short-term improvement in my overeating but will not likely be sustainable. The diet changes one part of the system but does nothing about other factors that contribute to my overeating, such as workplace stresses, which will likely undo any gain a diet may achieve.

Attempts to change a conflict cannot be successful if they focus only on changing a discrete part, or several discrete parts, with no recognition of the dynamic system that these individual pieces comprise. Unfortunately, trends in the peacebuilding field have done just that. From a well-intentioned desire to improve evaluation of peacebuilding programs, donors insist on narrowing their focus to specific "deliverables." This has had the effect of encouraging the disaggregation of a complex conflict into discrete projects with measureable results. The result, however, is to do just what Kanter warns against. Consequently, no one is charged with looking at how the many disparate projects can be reaggregated into a systemic change process.

Linear, reductionist thinking has shaped how peacebuilders define the underlying theories behind the work that they do. Peter Woodrow of the CDA/Collaborative Learning Projects (CDA) pulled together a typology of various theories of change that underlie a large number of peacebuilding interventions (see Box 2.1).[14] These theories were developed out of a study done by CDA's Reflecting on Peace Practice Project (RPP). RPP did in-depth case studies of dozens of diverse peacebuilding programs and found these theories to underlie (explicitly or implicitly) the work of the agencies in the study.

Each of these theories is valid in that it captures a relevant dynamic that can drive a conflict. The partial validity of each theory is also its weakness when looked at systemically. Despite the partial validity of any of these theories, no one of them by itself is sufficient to create systemic change, or PWL.

Box 2.1 Theories of Peacebuilding

Withdrawal of the resources for war theory: Wars require vast amounts of material (weapons, supplies, transport, etc.) and human capital. If we can interrupt the supply of people and goods to the war-making system, it will collapse and peace will break out. [*Methods:* antiwar campaigns to cut off funds/national budgets, conscientious objection and/or resistance to military service, international arms control, arms (and other) embargoes]

Institutional development theory: Peace is secured by establishing stable/reliable social institutions that guarantee democracy, equity, justice, and fair allocation of resources. [*Methods:* new constitutional and governance arrangements/entities; development of human rights, rule of law, anticorruption efforts, economic development, democratization]

Economics of war theory: War is sustained by, among other things, flows of money to fund arms production and purchases; to train, feed, and pay combatants; and to sustain support from key constituencies. Peace can be attained by diverting the flow of resources from making war and, as much as possible, channeling resources to making peace. [*Methods:* use of government or financial institutions to interrupt money streams; examining and controlling incentive and reward systems]

Root causes/justice theory: We can achieve peace by addressing the underlying issues of injustice, oppression/exploitation, threats to identity and security, and peoples' sense of injury/victimization. [*Methods:* long-term campaigns for social change; truth and reconciliation; changes in social institutions, laws, regulations, and economic systems]

Individual change theory: Peace comes through transformative change of a critical mass of individuals, their consciousness, attitudes, behaviors, and skills. [*Methods:* investment in individual change through training, personal-transformation/consciousness-raising workshops or processes, dialogues, and encounter groups]

Healthy relationships and connections theory: Peace emerges out of a process of breaking down isolation, polarization, division, prejudice, and stereotypes between/among groups. [*Methods:* processes of intergroup dialogue; networking; relationship-building processes; joint efforts on substantive problems]

Grassroots mobilization theory: "When the people lead, the leaders will follow." If we mobilize enough opposition to war, political leaders will have to pay attention. [*Methods:* mobilization of grassroots groups either to oppose war or to advocate for positive action; use of the media, nonviolent direct action, education/mobilization efforts, and dramatic events to raise consciousness]

Public attitudes theory: War and violence are partly motivated by prejudice, misperception, and intolerance of difference. We can promote peace by using the media (television and radio) to change public attitudes and build greater tolerance in society. [*Methods:* TV and radio programs that promote tolerance]

Reduction of violence theory: Peace will result as we reduce the levels of violence perpetrated by combatants or their representatives. [*Methods:* cease-fires, creation of zones of peace, withdrawal/retreat from direct engagement, introduction of

(continues on next page)

Box 2.1 (continued)

peacekeeping forces/interposition, observation missions, accompaniment efforts, promotion of nonviolent methods for achieving political, social, and economic ends]

Political elites theory: Peace comes when it is in the interest of political (and other) leaders to take the necessary steps. Peacebuilding efforts must change the political calculus of key leaders and groups. [*Methods:* raising the costs and reducing the benefits of continuing war and increasing the incentives for peace; for political elites, engaging active and influential constituencies in favor of peace, withdrawing international support/funding for warring parties]

For example, if one adopts individual change theory, which says peace is a product of changing individual attitudes, then one has done nothing about "establishing stable/reliable social institutions that guarantee democracy, equity, justice, and fair allocation of resources," which are necessary for building peace under institutional development theory. These theories represent possible ways to change parts of a conflict system, but there is no theory for how to change the system itself.

To be effective and make more effective use of the limited resources dedicated to peacebuilding, the international community needs a systemic theory of peacebuilding: a theory for how to change the overall system that produces problems such as chronic poverty, injustice, global warming, terrorism, and/or violence.

DEVELOPING A SYSTEMIC THEORY OF PEACEBUILDING

To return to Richardson's metaphor of "stepping in" or "stepping back," developing a systemic theory of peacebuilding requires us to step back from looking at one complex system (say, a corporation or Afghanistan) to look at how systemic change happens across different systems. Can we see patterns in how complex systems change? If we see Afghanistan, Nepal, and the Democratic Republic of Congo as systems, can we see patterns common to how each changes?

There are many parallels between the application of systems theory to peacebuilding and the application of systems thinking to other complex problems. For example, systems approaches to organizational change in the corporate world posed a similar challenge: not seeing corporate change just in terms of changing distinct parts of an organization (e.g., marketing, research and development, the "org" chart, etc.) but treating the organization as a whole, addressing the interrelationships between its component parts and its external environment.[15]

Senge (1990), Kanter (1992), and others (Peters 1982; Pascale and Athos 1981; Waterman 1980; Burke and Litwin 1992) point out that large corporations are systems, consisting of interrelated components. This insight had profound implications for those trying to create organizational change intended to improve the corporation. As a result, organizational consultants began to help corporations adopt systemic approaches to critical management problems. For example, McKinsey, one of the most successful management consultant firms, developed its 7S Framework to help corporations understand the basic levers they could use to create systemic change in their organizations.[16]

In *The End of Poverty*, Jeffrey Sachs argues for a more systemic approach to economic development.[17] Starting from the view that economies are complex systems, Sachs argues against treating individual parts of the complex economic system in isolation. He uses a medical analogy to argue for instead making a "differential diagnosis" of the root causes of economic problems that looks at many different factors that can contribute to economic distress. Sachs proposes a checklist of potential contributing factors, from cultural barriers to geography, and urges development practitioners to fashion remedies based on an understanding of the particulars of a specific country's context. Basically, Sachs argues for a complexity of analysis and response equal to the complexity of the problem being addressed. And his checklist for making a differential diagnosis might also be seen as a list of key drivers of systemic economic change.[18]

Just as corporations or economies should be approached as systems, conflicts—indeed whole societies—are systems made up of diverse, yet interrelated components.[19] The challenge now is to build a systemic theory of peacebuilding that incorporates the fundamental insights of systems thinking in order to develop a theory that identifies the drivers of systemic change in conflict-affected or chronically underdeveloped societies.[20] In this, the field of organizational change is again instructive. I am not suggesting that we should apply theories of corporate change to peacebuilding. Any similarity between peacebuilding in Afghanistan and corporate change at General Motors may end at the fact that both involve complex systems. However, I am suggesting that if one can identify the kind of levers used to make systemic change in one kind of large system, then it should be possible to find the levers that could be used to make systemic change in a different kind of complex system.

Daniel Katz and Robert Kahn used open systems theory to understand organizational development. In their study of change across diverse organizations in the 1960s and 1970s, they identified three major components of complex social systems:

- *Norms* are general rules and expectations of individuals working within the system. Norms shape the roles or specific behaviors of people in the system.

- *Values* are "more generalized ideological justifications" for the norms and roles in the system, and they "express the aspirations" that motivate the work of the organization.
- *Roles* are specific forms of behavior "required of all persons playing a part" in the work of the system or organization.[21]

Some congruence exists between the three core system components developed by Katz and Kahn and what Peter Checkland, founder of soft systems methodology in the early 1970s, identified as three domains that required changing in order to effect any significant change in a complex system: *structures, attitudes,* and *processes.*[22] Norms and structures are similar in that they are more tangible elements that give an organization its shape and form the expectations and boundaries for individual behavior. Values and attitudes are similar in that both speak to underlying beliefs that motivate and animate an organization. Lastly, both roles and processes are defined as specific behaviors that are critical to the working of the organization.

A review of other approaches to making systemic change in large organizations reveals a similar, though perhaps more robust, three-part scheme of key drivers of systemic change:

- *Structural:* This refers to systems and policies within the organization, such as an organization chart or an incentive program, designed to facilitate the organization's ability to achieve its goals. This category looks at nonhuman assets that provide a platform to organize and support the work of the organization's people.
- *Cultural:* This includes norms, values, and patterns of shared basic assumptions that promote or guide the successful functioning of the organization. This category refers to implicit or explicit, shared or groupwide attitudes or social capital that hold the organization together and direct its work.
- *Behavioral:* This entails how individuals in the organization act in performing specific functions and pursuing overall organizational goals. This category refers to individuals and their ability to work well together and get things done. This includes both substantive knowledge (e.g., marketing, product development) and process skills (negotiation, communication, relationship management, etc.).

These factors are highly interdependent; they affect, and are affected by, each other. For example, desired behaviors should be consistent with (even inspired by) organizational culture and supported and incented by structures within the organization.

Research and practice in the field of organizational change support this three-part model. W. Warner Burke and George Litwin (1992) propose a model for organizational change that is meant to build on decades of organizational models.[23] Thus, the Burke-Litwin model serves as a good summary of many change models that incorporate, to some degree, a systems approach. The twelve elements of the Burke-Litwin model fit nicely into the behavioral, structural, cultural model. Two of the twelve factors represent the external inputs into the organizational system (the environment) and the output of the system (individual and organizational performance). The remaining ten factors can be grouped into the behavioral, structural, and cultural categories:

- Structural:
  - *Structure:* "the arrangement of functions and people ... to assure implementation of the organization's mission"
  - *Systems (policies and procedures):* "standardized policies and mechanisms that facilitate" the work of the organization
- Cultural:
  - *Mission and strategy:* what top management has declared as, and employees believe to be, the "central purpose of the organization"
  - *Leadership:* "behavioral role models for all employees" (Leadership could also be looked at as a behavioral factor if it is seen as the actions of a key person. As defined here, it references the "role model" aspect of leadership, which is really an embodiment of an organizational value or norm.)
  - *Organizational culture:* "the way we do things around here" or "a collection of overt or covert rules, values and principles that are enduring and guide organizational behavior"
- Behavioral:
  - *Management practices:* "what managers do ... to carry out the organization's strategy"
  - *Task and individuals skills:* the "required behavior for task effectiveness," including relevant skills and knowledge
  - *Work unit climate:* "impressions, expectations and feelings" that affect relations among individuals in the work unit
  - *Motivation:* "aroused behavioral tendencies to move toward goals [and] take needed action"
  - *Individual needs and values:* specific individual "psychological factors that provide desire and worth for individual action"

The basic theory of the Burke-Litwin approach is that for systemic and lasting organizational change to happen, change must take place at each of these three levels. For example, if a company is experiencing declining profits and market position, research might show that it needs to become more customer focused. This systemic change will require different behaviors, structures, and cultural norms. At the behavioral level, sales personnel must switch from focusing on transactions to building longer-term, value-based relationships with clients. Internally, a key behavioral change would be for different divisions of the company to work more collaboratively in cross-functional teams whose objective is to provide integrated, custom-designed products on a timely basis. Structurally, there would need to be a change in incentive and compensation structures from rewarding short-term performance to measuring longer-term relationship building and client loyalty. Bonuses for good performance would go to teams instead of individuals, and organizational reporting lines would need to be adjusted to allow the formation of cross-functional teams.

As Edgar Schein stresses, behavioral and structural changes will be fleeting in the absence of corresponding changes in organizational culture.[24] In this example, the behavioral and structural changes would require cultural norms such as trust between divisions within the company and a willingness to share information. There would need to be strong working relationships between different groups (as opposed to just individuals) in the organization (management and staff, marketing and sales, etc.), as well as a norm of collaboration instead of competition.

One could also think of the behavioral, structural, and cultural categories as the dividers in the toolbox of a systems change specialist. As Burke and Litwin state, their twelve factors are the "primary variables" that can be manipulated in order to make systemic change (e.g., to change individual parts of an organization in order to change the system as a whole). They also advance some hypotheses about how the variables can best be manipulated to make change. Burke and Litwin distinguish between transformational change or change to basic values (culture) and transactional change, which refers to shorter-term behavioral change in how people work together, negotiate, and make decisions.[25] Transformational or cultural change is, in their view, necessary for fundamental, long-term change.[26]

This relationship of behavioral change to the process of structural and cultural change is critical. As a lever for driving systemic change, behavioral change plays a distinctive role. Of the three categories, behaviors can change in the shortest time relative to structures and cultures. As such, behaviors, specifically those pertaining to negotiation, communication, dispute settlement, and problem solving, tend to be the catalysts for producing change at the structural and cultural levels.

Take two organizational change efforts that I have worked on over the last ten years: one for a major financial services firm, the other for a wealthy family that collectively manages billions of dollars in private and philanthropic assets. Both faced major challenges requiring significant change. One needed to distinguish itself in an increasingly competitive marketplace with tighter regulatory demands; the other needed to transition from control by the "first" generation to control by second-generation family members.

Both organizations required behavioral, structural, and cultural change, and, for each, the key to starting that change process was behavioral. In the family, the intervention started with negotiation and communication training for the first and second generations. With some ongoing coaching, the family then went on to do a major restructuring of how it managed its private assets (structural change). Its members also articulated and agreed on a new set of family "principles" for how they would interact with each other (the start of a cultural change process). This, in turn, occasioned the need for specific and more general interventions (mainly training) on the behavioral side as specific key relationships had to be rebuilt or improved, and process help was needed to assist the family in working through and resolving difficult problems.

The family succeeded in reworking the structures for managing its philanthropic assets and created an overall governance structure. Again, there was training, coaching, and facilitation assistance (behavioral work) as the family worked through these issues. The family members talk openly about living their new values (cultural change) as they implement these new systems (structural change), and all have become more skilled at running their own internal negotiation processes (behavioral change). At each critical juncture in the family's change process, structural and cultural change was led by behavioral change (specifically related to negotiation, relationship management, and group problem solving).

Interestingly, the work I have been doing with a large financial services firm mirrors these same core change elements. The firm in question is facing an environmental challenge: how to compete and distinguish itself in a highly competitive industry. To address this task, the firm has employed a three-part strategy with structural, cultural, and behavioral components. In terms of culture, the firm redefined its core mission statement, values, and operating principles. It needed to build a culture that promoted internal cooperation between business areas and geographies (which before had often competed with each other). The firm needed to incent its staff to invest in building deep, long-term relationships with clients and among internal team members. These desired cultural shifts required new structures. The firm conducted a major firmwide reorganization into lines of service and away from primarily geographic boundaries. It reworked its internal performance review and management systems. The firm created a system for selecting out client engagements that were not bringing in high value to the company but demanded lots of resources—bad engagements that represented an old philosophy that said win any business, no matter how bad for the organization in the long term.

To pull these cultural and structural changes together, the firm needed to promote desired behavioral change. I was involved in efforts to build better communication and relationship management skills among new to midlevel partners. The training focused on how to better "share and collaborate" with both clients and internal teams. It prioritized skills like empathy and having tough conversations effectively, and the training helped identify and promote skills for strategic relationship management. The firm saw these three sets of initiatives (cultural, structural, and behavioral) as integral to the success of its change program and particularly saw behavioral skills as key, especially communication and problem-solving skills. If the change process was to take root, the firm would need to use these negotiation skills to honestly reflect on whether the firm was living up to its new values and the new structures were working.

In both the family and the financial services examples, the importance of cultural, structural, and behavioral change to ultimately making systemic change was pronounced.

THE SAT MODEL:
A SYSTEMIC THEORY OF PEACEBUILDING

As noted above, building peace in Afghanistan and effecting corporate change at General Motors entail very different processes. However, because both entities can be thought of as complex systems, a fair question to ask is, Can the same drivers of systemic change in the corporate context help us understand how to drive systemic change in the peacebuilding context?

With a little modification in the terminology, the three-part model of general system change can be transferred from the corporate to the peacebuilding context. Structural factors exist in both environments, but instead of performance and appraisal systems, the peacebuilding context has systems like governance and economy or institutions like courts and police forces. The other main difference is that structures in the peacebuilding context are (or should be) designed to meet the needs of the society, or, more specifically, the basic needs of the people who live in the society, as opposed to achieving corporate objectives.

The label "cultural" is potentially confusing in the peacebuilding context because, in addition to referring to shared norms and values, it might also refer to national cultures (e.g., being Serbian or Chinese) or cultural institutions. A clearer label for this category might be "attitudinal" to capture the importance to the peacebuilding process of large group values and norms as well as to include the state of intergroup relationships and social capital.

"Behavioral factors," as defined in the corporate context, is a manageable label, but it is overly broad in the peacebuilding context. While there may be thousands of people in a corporation, there are often millions of people in a particular society. As the number of people in the system goes up, so do the number and variety of potentially relevant behaviors. A corporation also has a more easily identifiable set of relevant behaviors (e.g., negotiation, communication, marketing, sales, performance review, etc.) as opposed to those in a society like Afghanistan or Colombia. A more effective label for this category is "transactional factors," because the key behavioral element in either context is how people work together to make decisions, build interpersonal relationships, and solve problems effectively. To provide an even clearer focus, attention must be paid to the transactional ability of key people, whether at a national, regional, or local level.[27]

Taken together, the framework for systemic change in the peacebuilding context is as follows[28]:

- *Structural:* This refers to systems and institutions designed to meet people's basic human needs.
  - Structural peacebuilding tools include governance assistance (such as building political parties and holding elections), economic reconstruction programs, rule-of-law programs, security sector reform, and so forth.
- *Attitudinal:* This refers to shared norms, beliefs, social capital, and intergroup relationships that affect the level of cooperation between groups or people.
  - Attitudinal peacebuilding tools include truth-and-reconciliation commissions, trauma-healing initiatives, community-dialogue programs, "peace camps" for youth from divided communities, multiethnic media programs, and so forth.
- *Transactional:* This refers to processes and skills used by key people to peacefully manage conflict, build interpersonal relationships, solve problems collaboratively, and turn ideas into action.
  - Transactional peacebuilding tools include formal mediation initiatives between leaders of combatant parties, cease-fires, negotiation training for representatives of combatants, local development councils, back channel dialogues among leaders, confidence-building measures, and so forth.

The structural, attitudinal, and transactional (SAT) model holds that effecting lasting, systemic change in a social system (PWL) requires change in all three of these domains of the society. Just as in the theory of systems change in the organizational context, the three levels are conceptually distinct but practically interrelated:

- Change at any one level can catalyze or sustain changes at any other level.
- Deterioration in any one level can lead to deterioration at another level.
- Progress at any one level, on its own, is not sufficient to achieve PWL.

Some practical examples can help illustrate this interdependence. In terms of progress at one level spurring progress at another, Lam Akol, who held various posts with the Sudan People's Liberation Movement/Army (SPLM/A), described Operation Lifeline Sudan (OLS) as a case in point.[29] OLS was designed to bring a massive amount of relief supplies to southern Sudan but required the Sudanese government and the SPLM/A to agree to cease-fires along relief routes so that supplies could be delivered. Akol credited the ultimate success of this relief operation (a structural intervention/success) as having spurred success at the negotiation table (a transactional success).

Unfortunately, the positive effect between levels described by Akol can also work in reverse. For example, prior to the first Palestinian intifada, many local peace initiatives were started between Palestinian municipal authorities and their Israeli counterparts to deal with practical structural issues. But as the negotiation process (transactional level) deteriorated and violence increased, these connections between municipalities also collapsed.

Lastly, the Rwandan genocide of 1994 serves as a tragic testament to the inability of progress, or even success, at any one level to create PWL. The peace agreement between the Hutu-led government and the Tutsi leaders of the Rwandan Patriotic Front was hailed as a success when negotiated in 1993. However, many see the peace deal and the threat it posed to more extremist Hutu elements as a major precipitating factor in the mass killings of Tutsis and moderate Hutus a few months later in 1994.[30] The Rwandan case is a classic example of success at the transactional level being insufficient to create lasting peace because of the lack of progress at the attitudinal level (e.g., severe distrust and antagonism in the Hutu-Tutsi intergroup relationship) and the structural level (e.g., a collapsing economy, land conflicts, insecurity, poor governance, etc.).

THE SAT MODEL: A SYSTEMIC THEORY OF CHANGE

This chapter started with idea that in order to make sustainable and systemic change in a society, peacebuilders need tools that allow them to see the world in terms of wholes and not just parts. These tools need to incorporate insights from systems thinking, especially the idea of dynamic causality, and avoid more mechanical or linear-thinking-based tools that focus on affecting only part of the system. The key to making peace last is developing a theory of how to make sustainable peacebuilding change at the macro, or societywide, level. The SAT model makes a key contribution to this effort by identifying three drivers of big systems change that are mutually interdependent. However, what is the theory for how the three SAT domains can be used to achieve Peace Writ Large?

Identifying three key drivers of big systems change does not on its own set out one correct path to building PWL. For example, in a society affected by violent conflict, the particular structural, attitudinal, and transactional initiatives that will be useful and how they should be sequenced will vary depending on the attributes of each social system, the larger political context, and the actors involved in both perpetuating violence and trying to build peace. However, insights from systems thinking can again be helpful. The SAT model makes a key differentiation between transactional factors, on the one hand, and structural and attitudinal peacebuilding factors on the other. Unlike structural and attitudinal factors, transactional factors are "process" factors and can be affected, to a much greater degree, in the short to medium term.

The transactional domain suggests itself as a more accessible place to start a systemic change process than either the attitudinal or structural domains. Any decision to enact attitudinal or structural change must be the product of some transactional activity.

Using the transactional domain as a catalyst for systems change also makes sense from a systems perspective. Donella Meadows, a pioneering systems thinker, identifies three basic ways to create systems change: (1) change the individual parts or elements in the system, (2) change the overall purpose of the system, or (3) change the interconnections between the individual parts of the system.[31] Changing individual parts or elements in the system is perhaps the easiest approach, but this tends to have the least impact on changing the system: "General Motors and the U.S. Congress somehow maintain their identities even though all their members change. A system generally goes on being itself, changing only slowly if at all even with complete substitution of its elements—as long as its interconnections and purposes remain intact."[32]

The US invasion of Iraq in March 2003 was premised in part on the notion that changing a key piece of the system in Iraq, that is, removing Saddam Hussein from power, would change the country for the better. Caught by surprise by the violence that ensued after Hussein's downfall, the US administration learned the hard way that removing him would not change the underlying social dynamics in Iraq, such as the tensions between Sunni and Shia Muslims.

In contrast to the ineffectiveness of trying to change a system by changing discrete elements, changing a system's purpose, such as changing the purpose of a football team from winning to losing, can have the most drastic impact on the system. However, changing the overall purpose of the system is the most difficult change to make. Changing the interconnections or relationships between elements within the system also has the potential to change the system profoundly.[33] Changing interconnections means changing the relationship between parts of the system. Meadows gives the example that a university would be a profoundly different place if one changed the relationship between students and teachers so that students graded their professors and not the other way around.

In the peacebuilding context, important interconnections include those between key actors and how they handle conflict and solve problems collaboratively or the relationships between these key actors and important structural and attitudinal elements of the system. For example, key actors, using their transactional ability, can be instrumental in increasing security (structural change) by agreeing to cease combat between their respective armed groups or by building trust between their respective ethnic groups (attitudinal change) through symbolic public acts of reconciliation. Changing interconnections between parts does not automatically change the system, but it has the potential over time to start a process of change from within the system.

Transactional peacebuilding, using process tools like negotiation, dialogue, facilitation, and mediation, can be a powerful means of changing interconnections between key elements or parts; thus, it can be used as a catalyst for creating change at the structural and attitudinal levels, much as behavioral change is a catalyst in the organizational change models. Therefore, the distinctive role of change in the transactional domain (transactional peacebuilding) gives rise to a systemic theory of change using the SAT model: "Peace Writ Large can be achieved by using transactional peacebuilding (change in the transactional domain) to initiate a dynamic and mutually reinforcing process of change in the structural and attitudinal domains of a society."

The rest of Part I develops the SAT model as a systemic theory of peacebuilding. Chapter 3 investigates the three SAT domains in more detail and evaluates the validity of the domains individually and whether collectively they have the potential to make systemic change in a peacebuilding context. Chapter 4 looks at the practical implications of a systemic theory of peacebuilding for current peacebuilding practice. Because the changes identified in Chapter 4 are so large, Part II gives practical advice for making peacebuilding practice more systemic: changing how peacebuilders do analysis and planning. Part III addresses another key step in making peacebuilding practice more systemic by providing practical advice about how to use transactional peacebuilding as a catalyst for systemic and sustainable peacebuilding change.

CHAPTER 2 SUMMARY

- A key to making peace last is for peacebuilders to develop the skill of seeing wholes instead of just seeing isolated parts.
- Systems thinking requires people to see the interconnections between distinct elements of a system, to see causality in dynamic rather than linear terms, and to look for patterns of behavior.
- Systems thinking, particularly the concept of dynamic causality, is better suited than linear models to longer-term, complex problems (such as ending poverty).
- In order to build a systemic theory of how to create Peace Writ Large (or sustainable macro-level peace), it is helpful to look for patterns in how complex systems change.
- This view produces the SAT model, which holds that sustainable change in complex systems requires change in three domains: the structural, attitudinal, and transactional. Further, transactional peacebuilding serves as the catalyst for structural and attitudinal change.

CHAPTER 3

CAN THE SAT MODEL
REALLY MAKE A DIFFERENCE?

~⊘~

The world we have created is a product of our thinking; it cannot be
changed without changing our thinking.

—Albert Einstein

The above quote from Albert Einstein gives some assurance that changing our
thinking can change the world around us. But when it comes to reforming
how the current peacebuilding system goes about its work or redirecting how
billions of dollars in foreign assistance are spent, is the structural, attitudinal,
and transactional (SAT) model the right change? The SAT model has not been
around long enough to produce a large track record to validate its usefulness.
Despite its grounding in systems theory and approaches to systemic change,
the SAT model needs to overcome two key challenges:

1. Do the SAT domains, taken separately, have an established impact on
   peacebuilding?
2. Is there evidence that, taken collectively, these domains strengthen the
   ability of peacebuilding programs to make lasting systemic change?

PEACEBUILDING IN THE STRUCTURAL DOMAIN

Structural peacebuilding starts from the basic assumption that both peace
and violence are driven, ultimately, by the satisfaction or neglect of people's

basic human needs. There are many ways to label and define these basic needs. The concept of human needs is fundamental and pervasive: "Most intellectual traditions and theories of human behavior are based on fundamental assumptions of human nature and needs."[1] Study of the relationship between human needs theory and conflict dates back to Abraham Maslow and John Burton, and many other authors have elaborated on the subject since then.[2]

Many of these authors acknowledge the centrality of human needs but preface their articulation of them by saying that there is no one schema.[3] For current purposes, I use the following four-part schema of basic needs:

- *Identity* entails the need for a "system of beliefs or way of construing the world" that gives a person a sense of self as a unique entity in relation to the surrounding environment.[4] Identity is often expressed in terms of core values that define who one is.
- *Community* refers to the idea that the need for individual identity creates a need for community, that people can only be who they are by being in relation to others.[5] In addition, community serves the needs for affiliation and recognition. The need for community is based on the view of humans as social beings.[6]
- *Security* encompasses a need for both physical safety (e.g., protection from violence) and psychological safety, or a freedom from fear.
- *Vitality* implies a need for what John Burton describes as "growth and development," as well as for a sense of efficacy (the ability to make choices and affect the environment around oneself), control, and self-actualization.[7]

Just as there are many ways to define basic needs, there are many ways to define the structures (systems and institutions) designed to help people attain them. The SAT framework includes seven fundamental structures:

1. *Governance:* institutions design to manage issues of common concern to people and groups in the society (e.g., electoral systems, legislatures, councils of elders, etc.)
2. *Security:* institutions and infrastructure that provide for the safety of people and groups (e.g., police, military, and security forces)
3. *Economy:* markets, capital, means of production, and other infrastructure needed to allow people to subsist and prosper
4. *Rule of law/human rights:* laws, law enforcement, and judicial institutions designed to protect the basic rights of people and groups
5. *Social services:* institutions and systems that meet predominately non-economic needs, such as health care and education

6. *Environment/natural resources:* systems, policies, and practices that affect the physical environment
7. *Media/civil society:* an independent media and civic organizations (e.g., religious, cultural, community service, labor) that allow people to understand their environment and organize with others in light of it

Taken together, these structures can be either drivers of violent conflict or persistent underdevelopment, or they can be enablers of peace. When structures fail to meet people's basic needs, they tend to do so in two fundamental ways: either by lacking *functionality* (e.g., police are ineffective or the government corrupt) or, even when the structure may be functional, by denying a group or groups *access* (e.g., an ethnic or racial minority is not allowed to vote).

The link between the efficacy of structures designed to meet basic human needs and conflict has been well established in the development literature. Many see persistent poverty and other structural failures as root causes of violent conflict. Paul Collier et al. state flatly that "the key root cause of conflict is the failure of economic development."[8] Consistent with this assertion, a World Bank report cites the fact that "80% of the world's 20 poorest countries have suffered a major war" between 1990 and 2005.[9] Linking conflict to failures in economic and political systems, Veronique Dudouet (2006) cites Ted Robert Gurr and Barbara Harff, who found that "between 1945 and 1980, 80 percent of the 233 ethnic groups which took political action to promote or defend their interests were suffering from 'a systematic and selective limitation of people's access to economic opportunities or political positions based on ascriptive characteristics.'"[10] In addition, several of Peter Woodrow's peacebuilding theories (from Chapter 2) are structural in nature, such as the "withdrawal of resources for war theory," the "institutional development theory," and the "economics of war theory."[11]

PEACEBUILDING IN THE ATTITUDINAL DOMAIN

Structures are not the only drivers of violence or peace. Attitudes also play a key role, specifically attitudes related to relations between groups in the society, the formation of social capital, social grievances, and support for the creation of or participation in critical structures.

Intergroup Relations

John Paul Lederach, an essential voice from the field of conflict transformation, sees social conflict as "a phenomenon of human creation, lodged naturally in relationships."[12] One of the fundamental contributions of the theory and practice of conflict transformation is to establish that conflict is normal in human relationships and that the key to dealing with violent conflict is to "transform" those relationships so that conflict can be dealt with constructively.[13]

Intergroup relationships can turn conflict into a destructive force for structural reasons (e.g., systemic power imbalances) as well as for psychological reasons. Political scientists, cultural anthropologists, and social psychologists describe the psychological dynamics of conflict and the impact of "enemy images," or stereotyped views held by one group about key attributes of another group. These images go to a group's hostile intent, moral unworthiness, and illegitimacy, and they set the context for group action and decision making.[14]

A classic tactic for creating an enemy image is "dehumanization," or creating a belief that members of another group are less than human and thus morally excluded from the norms of justice, fair treatment, or respect for basic needs.[15] Violence against such groups can be seen as necessary and morally justified.[16] The Rwandan genocide and the Holocaust are prominent examples of the tragic consequences of violence propelled by dehumanization. In Rwanda, radio stations controlled by Hutu extremists broadcast messages describing Tutsis as "cockroaches." One human rights worker described how the orchestrators of the genocide persuaded other Hutus to kill Tutsis: "Don't worry, you're not killing humans like you. You are killing some vermin that belongs under your shoe. You're killing cockroaches."[17]

Violence and persistent enemy images can be institutionalized in collective memory and a "conflict ethos."[18] In turn, these form the basis of more institutionalized conflict dynamics such as the victim-oppressor dynamic or an action-reaction cycle of violence and reprisals. Groups can get locked into a zero-sum competition for scarce resources or a dynamic of relative deprivation, where a group sees itself as unfairly less well-off than a rival group.[19] Often the rival group is blamed for this unfair disparity and becomes the target of reprisals. For example, relative deprivation has been cited as a factor contributing to the motivations behind suicide attacks by Palestinians against Israelis.[20]

Social Capital

Another avenue by which societal attitudes impact peace is in the creation or deterioration of social capital, which is defined as "the norms and networks that enable people to act collectively."[21] As with intergroup relations, social capital has structural elements (networks and social institutions like labor unions) but also contains a large attitudinal component, such as the existence of trust or mistrust between groups. Nat Colletta and Michelle Cullen cite

Francis Fukuyama's conception of social capital as hinging mainly on levels of trust between societal groups, or what is defined as "bridging social capital," as opposed to "bonding social capital," which refers to norms and beliefs that tie members of a group more closely together.[22]

According to this school of thought, violent conflict is more likely when low levels of bridging social capital and high levels of bonding social capital exist in a society that has weak structures, such as ineffective, corrupt governance, a poor economy, and insecurity.[23] The result of this dynamic is exclusion, intergroup competition, and oppression, which in turn increase the likelihood of violence. Strong bonding social capital can lead to a perceived incompatibility between loyalty to a government and loyalty to a religious or tribal affiliation. For example, in Iraq, followers of Moktada al-Sadr saw cooperation with the US forces and their allies in Iraq as inconsistent with their Islamic beliefs. In addition, high levels of trust within a group coupled with low levels of trust across groups can foster a distrust of centralized government where power is shared between groups. Extremist Hutus in Rwanda were more threatened by the existence of the Hutu-Tutsi power-sharing government called for in the 1993 peace accords than they were by the war between the groups.[24]

These insights into the psychological dimensions of conflict, the centrality of intergroup relationships, and social capital have given rise to many approaches to peacebuilding. Conflict transformation has built a substantial repertoire of approaches to create "right relationships" as a powerful engine of peaceful change.[25] As noted in Woodrow's typology of peacebuilding theories, the "public attitudes theory" and the "healthy relationships and connections theory" are based on countering enemy images and misperceptions and building trust between groups. Successful truth-and-reconciliation tribunals and intergroup dialogues provide prime examples of strategies that work primarily on changing a conflict ethos and building bridging social capital.

Core Grievances

The Interagency Conflict Assessment Framework (ICAF) adopted by the US Agency for International Development (USAID), the US Department of State, and the US Department of Defense sees the existence of core grievances as a root cause of violent conflict. According to ICAF, core grievances are defined as "the perception, by various groups in a society, that their needs for physical security, livelihood, interests or values are threatened by one or more other groups and/or social institutions."[26] Core grievances are the product of intergroup relations (such as a perceived conflict between the interests, needs, or aspirations of different identity groups) and societal patterns (such as elitism, group exclusion, disillusionment, and alienation).[27]

TRANSACTIONAL FACTORS AS A CATALYST

As noted above, structural factors affect attitudinal factors (e.g., structurally entrenched power imbalances between groups give rise to enemy images), just as attitudinal factors affect structural ones (e.g., the lack of bridging social capital impedes the development of governance structures). Mari Fitzduff puts this relationship at the center of her theory of "meta-conflict resolution," which she defines as addressing "the many facts of a conflict whether these be structural (political or constitutional arrangements, legislation, economic and aid factors, etc.) or psycho-cultural (attitudes, relationships, divided histories) in a comprehensive and complementary manner."[28]

However, structural and attitudinal factors are not sufficient to explain their link to promoting or ameliorating violent conflict without a third key variable: transactional factors. To borrow an analogy from chemistry, structural and attitudinal factors are more or less inert unless mixed with transactional factors that serve as a catalyst. For example, take Collier's link between conflict and economic underdevelopment. Underdevelopment itself does not necessarily cause violence (e.g., many areas of intense poverty do not see major outbreaks of organized violence). Violence occurs when people decide to take armed action in response to that underdevelopment. The transaction leading to that decision is the catalyst. The decision is precipitated by one or more transactions: some form of negotiation among group members, which is often preceded by the failure of negotiations (or other process steps) designed to address grievances nonviolently.

The same can be said of the relationship between transactions and attitudes. An enemy image does not, on its own, cause group violence to occur. However, those enemy images can make it easier for key leaders to persuade others to take up arms in response to perceived injustice or to protect against the perceived hostile intent of a rival group. Again, this process of mobilizing groups to take violent action because of their negative perceptions of another group can be thought of as a transaction consisting of communication, persuasion, and negotiation.

Similarly, group attitudes can constrain the choices of key leaders. For example, if group attitudes are strongly against political accommodation with rivals, leaders have little ability to negotiate a settlement. The converse is also true; popular attitudes in favor of a political settlement can empower leaders to engage in negotiations (e.g., Woodrow's "grassroots mobilization theory").

The basic point is that transactions among key people make the difference between whether underlying structural and attitudinal factors trigger violence or peace. In 2004 and 2005, I was involved in a study, sponsored by Conciliation Resources as part of its Accord series, on whether to engage, and if so, how, with armed groups in the context of a peace process. One of the clear messages from consultations with former or current members of armed groups, academics, and practitioners was that violence is a choice taken by the leadership of an armed group.[29] Armed groups constantly face the choice between armed struggle and nonviolent political action. Whether the group opts for one path or the other is the product of negotiation among key leaders in the context of the overall structural and attitudinal environment.

PEACEBUILDING IN THE TRANSACTIONAL DOMAIN

Transactional factors differ from structural and attitudinal factors in two key ways. First, transactional factors are process related, while structures and (perhaps to a lesser extent) attitudes are substance related. For example, whether or not there is a functioning court system or the rule of law is more or less an objective fact. Similarly, a group either does or does not have widespread negative stereotypes of another group, or a certain level of social capital does or does not exist. However, transactions (e.g., negotiation, persuasion) are processes and can be applied to various substance issues (e.g., poverty, injustice, feelings of threat, etc.).

A second difference is that structures and attitudes operate at the mass level, while transactions operate at the level of key people. For example, bad governance, a structural factor, affects whole groups or an entire society. Similarly, enemy images also affect entire groups. Transactional peacebuilding takes key people as its unit of analysis, at either the national, regional, or local level. Take another example: In addition to structural and attitudinal factors, the conflict in Sri Lanka was influenced by the negotiations (transactions) between the president of Sri Lanka and the leader of the Liberation Tigers of Tamil Eelam (LTTE). Conflict in a village in rural Afghanistan will be affected by the relations of key people in that context, that is, negotiations between the local *malik*, mullah, district governor, and local "commander" (e.g., militia leader, Talib, etc.).

Transactional approaches to peacebuilding have long been seen as central to the whole peacebuilding endeavor. For example, for many years, bringing peace to the Middle East or Northern Ireland was thought of just in terms of negotiating a peace deal as opposed to creating structural and attitudinal change. There are volumes dedicated to defining best practices in the field of negotiating peace agreements or managing peace processes.[30] Two of Woodrow's peacebuilding theories are transactional in nature, including the "political elites theory." If anything, the importance of transactional approaches, such as national-level peace talks among key leaders, has been overemphasized.[31] After looking across studies of transactional processes, Michael Lund concludes, "Muscular diplomacy and peace enforcement alone could not consolidate peace."[32] This insight is perhaps the main inspiration for the field of conflict transformation. While conflict transformation theory rightly points out the limitations of solely transactional approaches to peace, transactional approaches themselves, when properly combined with structural and attitudinal approaches, are essential.

COMPARING THE SAT MODEL WITH OTHER SYSTEMIC MODELS

While structural, attitudinal, and transactional peacebuilding, on their own, are each important parts of achieving Peace Writ Large (PWL), the real innovation of the SAT model is to consider these three types of peacebuilding in concert with each other. So, an assessment of the SAT model must look at the degree to which it adequately captures this dynamic interplay. To assess the systemic validity of the model, it is helpful to look at the degree of convergence (and divergence) with other peacebuilding models that are, to some degree, systemic and also to look at field evidence indicating whether the SAT model might work in practice.

The SAT framework is similar to, yet distinct from, other attempts to build a more systemic theory of peacebuilding. Peacebuilding approaches developed by Johan Galtung and Christopher Mitchell have correspondences with the SAT model. Galtung began writing in 1969 about the ideas he would later develop into the ABC Conflict Triangle.[33] His model sees conflict as the product of the interplay between three elements[34]:

- *Attitudes:* "cognitive and emotive; ranging from glowing hatred of self or other to denial, from inner boiling to inner freezing"
- *Behaviors:* "physical and verbal; ranging from deliberate efforts to hurt and harm self or other to withdrawal, ranging from outer boiling to outer freezing, via wait-and-see, and constructive attempts to overcome the bloc"
- *Contradictions:* "the root incompatibility of goals"

In 1981, Mitchell adapted Galtung's model as follows[35]:

- *Conflict situation:* "Any situation in which two or more social entities or 'parties' ... perceive they possess mutually incompatible goals."
- *Conflict attitudes:* "(i) Emotional orientations, such as feelings of anger, distrust, resentment, scorn, fear, envy, or suspicion of the intentions of others. (ii) Cognitive processes, such as stereotyping, or a refusal to accept nonconforming information in an endeavor to maintain a consistent structure of beliefs about the outside world."

- *Conflict behavior:* "Actions undertaken by one party in any situation of conflict aimed at the opposing party with the intention of making that opponent abandon or modify its goals."

Although they differ, there is a good degree of resonance between the models of Mitchell and Galtung, and aspects of both validate elements of the SAT model. For example, the importance of attitudes appears in all three models, as does that of behaviors, with the acknowledgment that, in the SAT model, transactions are a key subset of a general category of behaviors. Both models also look at the impact of structures on conflict. In fact, Galtung introduced the idea of structural violence.[36] Contradictions, or conflict situations in Mitchell's model, come about as a result of structural imbalances in the society, which result in groups pursuing incompatible goals.

David Bloomfield and Norbert Ropers modify Galtung's ABC model in their conception of systemic conflict transformation, which takes a systemic view of how attitudes, behaviors, and contradictions drive violence similar to that of the SAT model: "Systemic conflict transformation envisions the triangle as a multi-directional circle where structures, attitudes and behaviors interact over time and reinforce each other to produce the dynamic spiral of destructive change."[37] In addition, Mitchell talks about dynamic "conflict cycles between linked parties" and "conflict spirals" where the behavior of any one party can be explained by the "previous conflict behavior received from an adversary."[38]

There are also important differences between the models, especially when one looks at what each defines as key focal points within the categories of attitudes, behaviors or transactions, and contradictions or structures. Both Galtung's initial formulation of the conflict triangle and the Bloomfield-Ropers revision construe "behaviors" much more broadly than the SAT model construes transactions. Bloomfield and Ropers define behaviors as "aggression, oppression, discrimination, reaction and escalation."[39] Mitchell is more concerned with behavior that is focused on modifying the goals of another party. In the SAT model, there is much more precision around a particular set of key behaviors (negotiation, communication, and joint problem solving) by a much smaller group of key people (leaders at the national, regional, or local level).

The Galtung and systemic conflict transformation models see dialogue (Galtung) or conflict transformation (Bloomfield-Ropers) as keys to intervening in the conflict system and building peace. The SAT model does as well, but it includes this form of intervention in the model itself. For example, dialogue and elements of conflict transformation are included under the transactional category in the SAT model (while changes in group stereotypes and intergroup relationships are included in its attitudinal category).

In terms of structures, the differences are more pronounced. The Galtung and Bloomfield-Ropers models focus on the creation of incompatible goals between groups in society and the impact that dynamic then has on relationships between these groups. Unlike the SAT model, they do not focus on the functionality of basic structures (institutions and systems) in the society and access to them as units of analysis in and of themselves. The SAT model does not deny that structures have an important impact on intergroup relationships and stereotypes. For purposes of analytic clarity, relationships and enemy images are included under attitudes in the SAT model. The point here is that a broken economic system may lead to strained intergroup relationships, but both phenomena are worthy of consideration and redress in their own right (e.g., the economy needs repair, as does the relationship between groups).[40] In Part II, the importance of this distinction will become clearer as the SAT model is applied to conflict analysis and intervention design.

On a more basic level, Galtung's definition of relevant structures in society differs greatly from that of the SAT model. Galtung defines "deep structures" creating "social earthquakes" by producing contradictions between races, genders, generations, and classes.[41] To a lesser extent, the systemic conflict transformation model focuses on transforming structural violence through reforms that promote "justice and empowerment."[42] As noted above, the SAT model defines structures in a much broader sense and in a manner much closer to how they would be defined in the humanitarian and development fields.

The models overlap most in the area of attitudes. All look at group norms, beliefs, and perceptions, although the SAT model puts intergroup relationships squarely in this category. The SAT model assumes that intergroup relations are much closer to psychological dynamics like enemy images than to governance or security institutions. Moreover, the SAT model's definition of attitudes is meant to capture the rich contribution of those working on the concept of social capital.

So, while the labels of the different categories are similar, a deeper look into each category reveals important differences between the models. These differences may seem smaller at the conceptual level, but they are much more pronounced when the models are put into practice (see Parts II and III).

CDA/Collaborative Learning Projects (CDA), through its Reflecting on Peace Practice (RPP) initiative, developed another model. CDA responds to the strategic peacebuilding deficit, or the micro-macro gap, by creating a matrix that assesses the degree to which a program affects "more people" or "key people," on one axis, or works on the "individual/personal level" or the "socio/political level."[43] "Individual/personal" change is defined as affecting the "attitudes, values, or perceptions of individuals," while "Socio/political" change is defined as affecting "politics, economics, justice systems, and other institutions."[44]

The RPP model was produced as a descriptive tool to capture the range of peacebuilding programs studied in the RPP project. However, it also has a prescriptive side in that it posits the hypothesis that peacebuilding programs will be stronger if their impacts address all four quadrants of the model's matrix as opposed to centering on only one. For example, Mary Anderson and Lara Olson argue that

> when programs focus only on change at the Individual/Personal level without regard to how these may be translated to the Socio/Political level, actions inevitably fall short of having an impact on larger goals.
>
> Evidence shows that even in activities at the Socio/Political level, work with More People is not enough if it does not reach Key People, and work with Key People is not enough if it does not reach More People.[45]

Both the SAT and RPP models talk about the importance of affecting institutions and systems in the society (e.g., "structural change" in the SAT model and "socio/political change" at the level of "more people" in the RPP model). Both models discuss changing basic values and norms (e.g., "attitudinal change" in the SAT model and "individual/personal change" at the level of "more people" in the RPP model). Additionally, both recognize the importance of "transactions" and relationships among key people (e.g., "transactional change" in the SAT model and "individual/personal change" among "key people" in the RPP model).

However, the RPP model predominately looks at attitudes (values, perceptions, etc.) on the individual level, as opposed to the group level, while the SAT model puts greater emphasis on the importance of large group perceptions, values, and relationships. The SAT model also looks at attitudes between key individuals as they affect their ability to conduct transactions (e.g., negotiate and communicate with each other). Perhaps the most important difference between the models is that the RPP model calls for movement across the quadrants in its matrix but does not take a position on how to move from affecting "more people" to affecting "key people" or how to move from the individual to the sociopolitical levels. The SAT model puts "transactional peacebuilding" in the role of a catalyst for structural and attitudinal change.

The RPP project has also launched a cumulative impacts study, which commissioned a series of case studies designed to identify the cumulative impacts in various countries affected by violence and how those impacts came about. The research effort entails looking across the case studies to find any patterns in what produces the cumulative impacts identified in the cases. Although based on different data, this exercise is similar to the inquiry used to develop the SAT model: "stepping back" to look across different complex systems to find any patterns for how change happens. While the results of the new RPP effort are tentative, it has begun to identify "key domains" in which progress needs to be made in order to create sustainable peacebuilding impacts. Significantly, these domains, as currently defined, do resonate with the SAT domains.[46]

A third model for systemic change that is relevant to the SAT model is the Reflective Peacebuilding (RP) approach of John Paul Lederach et al. (2007). The RP approach identifies four key dimensions of conflict transformation: personal, relational, structural, and cultural. The model posits that peacebuilders can organize their interventions around how they affect each of these dimensions.[47] It is similar to the SAT model in the implication that interventions affecting all four dimensions will be more effective than those that do not, just as the SAT model interventions that have impact at the structural, attitudinal, and transactional levels will be more effective.

The dimensions identified in the RP model are also similar to those in the SAT model. For example, structural dimensions in the RP model focus on issues of access to public goods and institutions.[48] Unlike structural factors in the SAT model, however, the RP approach looks at "patterns of relationships" created by social structures as opposed to assessing the functionality of the institutions and systems themselves.

Relational dimensions in the RP approach bear resemblance to transactional factors in the SAT model because they look at how people cooperate, make decisions, and communicate in interpersonal relationships.[49] However, transactional factors in the SAT model are more focused on key people and their transactional abilities, whereas the RP model looks at any "people who meet, interact, and are interdependent in everyday settings such as family, school, work, neighborhood, and local communities."[50] Again, for purposes of clearer analysis and intervention design, the SAT model breaks out these everyday transactions into the concept of social capital (the aggregate ability of groups of people to cooperate), which is included with attitudinal factors because these factors affect large numbers of people in the society and are more closely related to other group norms and perceptions. Also, both models talk about the importance of other "cultural" dimensions and the belief systems that shape how members of groups view the world.[51]

These other models that take a more systemic view of conflict and peacebuilding validate common key elements in the SAT model; for instance, the organizational change models reviewed earlier consistently hit on similar levers of change. All look at the impact of widely held group norms and beliefs. They all focus attention on structural aspects. They all focus on both individuals (key people) and broader social groups (more people). There are differences in definitions of these categories across the models. The SAT model makes the case that how it defines structures and attitudes is more conducive to getting a truly systemic picture of the conflict, divorced from any future decision about how to intervene in it. This point is a main focus of Part II.

A major difference between the existing models and the SAT model, however, is the specific focus on transactional factors in the SAT model. The ability to negotiate and work collaboratively to solve problems is referenced in other models, but not with the emphasis on how key people are able to achieve positive transactions or the ability of these transactions (and the people involved in them) to catalyze positive structural and attitudinal change. This is a key component of the SAT model and the interventions it suggests. This will be addressed in Part II but elaborated on at much greater length in Part III.

EFFECTIVENESS OF THE SAT MODEL IN THE FIELD

The validity of individual components of the SAT model and its resonance with (and potential improvement on) existing systemic change models give assurance that the SAT model holds promise for improving peacebuilding practice. As noted earlier, there is not a comparable amount of field application of the SAT model on which to base a comprehensive evaluation. Short of that, it is helpful to look at the evaluations of other, more holistic or interdisciplinary interventions, such as community-driven development, that combine elements of the SAT model.[52]

Evidence from Community-Driven Development

Participatory or community-driven development (CDD) is defined as an approach that "empowers local community groups ... by giving direct control to the community over planning decisions and investment resources through a process that emphasizes participatory planning and accountability."[53] In the terms of the SAT model, CDD combines transactional activity, such as the formation and operation of local development councils that negotiate and decide development priorities and manage projects, with structural activity, such as the implementation of various development projects that affect systems designed to meet basic human needs. In divided or conflict-affected communities, CDD is seen as a way both to create positive structural impact and to build transactional skills. For example, the outcome of a CDD project might be to rebuild a health clinic, road, or food-production system and to improve the ability of key local people to negotiate with each other. It also has the potential to create positive social attitudes, such as increasing the level of trust between groups as a result of working together to better their community.

There have been numerous studies of the effectiveness of CDD. Earlier studies looked at several CDD projects and found mixed results.[54] Often this was attributable to an inability to deal with entrenched community dynamics, such as the impact of powerful elites inequitably targeting resources to benefit themselves or their associates (family, clan members, etc.).[55] Other problems were attributable to the lack of a connection between CDD programs and a broad assessment of the conflict context or difficulties in "scaling up" or linking the results of localized programs to larger national peace processes.[56]

A 2006 study by the International Bank for Reconstruction and Development/The World Bank found much more positive impacts in its review of CDD programs. Overall, the study found a significant positive impact of integrating transactional activity into local development projects: "Formal training in conflict-related skills such as dispute resolution, basic human rights, cross-cultural communication, consensus building, and power monitoring can be highly valuable" in conflict-affected environments.[57] In terms of outcomes, the study found significant overall improvements in program effectiveness due to specific structural, attitudinal, and transactional impacts of CDD programs:

- *Transactional:* CDD programs "have a positive impact on people's capacity to manage local disputes," "buttress local stability in volatile contexts by enhancing interpersonal trust," and "serve as a model for cooperation and negotiation."[58]
- *Structural:* CDD programs can "lower unit costs, even in conflict settings," deliver "a peace dividend ... the visible reconstruction achieved through community cooperation," and "improve sustainability as communities recover from conflict."[59]
- *Attitudinal:* CDD programs "can improve trust.... Engaging community members in interaction with each other and with local institutions begins the process of reestablishing social and institutional relationships, networks and interpersonal trust—collectively known as social capital."[60] In addition, "the evidence seems to show that CDD can be a factor in creating new forms of community cohesion."[61]

Taken together, these structural, transactional, and attitudinal impacts strengthen the durability of individual projects (e.g., rebuilding a health clinic) because they build assets that will assist in future program implementation, such as better governance, increased levels of intergroup trust and social capital, and improved problem-solving skills by key people.

Although she qualifies her conclusions as tentative, Kim Maynard provides concrete examples of how combining transactional and structural activity has positively impacted the success of reconstruction projects in Afghanistan carried out by the International Rescue Committee (IRC) as part of the National Solidarity Program (NSP). The IRC program incorporated a number of consultative bodies that included participation of key local power holders, village members, religious leaders, elders, women, and former military commanders. These bodies helped guide and implement community-level development projects in a way consistent with local needs, cultural norms, and religious values. The projects incorporated a high degree of transactional processes into IRC's reconstruction (structural) projects.

At the time of the study, about four years into their work in Afghanistan, the results of the integration enhanced the effectiveness of IRC's programs. Again, there were structural, attitudinal, and transactional benefits and a synergy between them. In addition to the improvements created by the reconstruction projects themselves, there were two additional structural benefits. The project strengthened "institutions, principles and relationships necessary for good governance."[62] In addition, by engaging "erstwhile combatants" in the consultative process, IRC's programs improved security.[63] One Afghan participant in an IRC program explained that whereas "commanders used to fight and command people, now they advise and help people.... Instead of causing problems, now they communicate, consult, discuss, and solve problems."[64] This also speaks to a significant transactional impact of the program, which is to build the ability of key people to negotiate, in addition to improving the relationships among them, thus increasing the likelihood that they will handle conflicts nonviolently. The IRC approach also occasioned important attitudinal shifts. Early on, the programs had been seen as "government traps," but later, in the consultative process, they came to be seen as "supporting our society," a major shift in attitudes toward generally mistrusted Afghan government projects and international NGOs.[65]

In addition to the support for hypotheses generated by the SAT model from the reviews of CDD programs, the model is also consistent with other experience from the field. As noted in Chapter 1, there is general support by governments, NGOs, and academics for more coherence across various peacebuilding programs, more integrated missions, and more holistic approaches. There is also specific support for making programs more holistic as a means to increase program success. Participants in a dialogue between private voluntary organizations (PVOs) and USAID reported that "when structural or sectoral boundaries were crossed within their organizations, USAID and PVOs experienced increased effectiveness in their conflict efforts."[66]

The evidence is strong for the connection between peacebuilding success and the structural, attitudinal, and transactional domains when taken both individually and collectively. However, despite the validation of the SAT model, there are significant obstacles to its implementation because it entails significant changes to the conventional way that peacebuilding is currently practiced. Chapter 4 details the extent of the task that lies ahead for putting the SAT model into practice.

CHAPTER 3 SUMMARY

- Taken separately, the three SAT domains (structural, attitudinal, and transactional) have an established impact, from the perspectives of both theory and practice, on the ability to build peace.
- Taken together, the three SAT domains have a synergistic effect; interventions that combine impacts across the three domains appear to increase program effectiveness.

CHAPTER 4

THE SAT MODEL MEANS (RADICAL?) CHANGE

⤳

It doesn't work to leap a twenty-foot chasm in two ten-foot jumps.
—American proverb

In the mid-1990s, as part of a team from the Harvard Negotiation Project, I did a small bit of consulting for Vice President Al Gore's Task Force on Reinventing Government. The mission of the task force was to change the relationship between government regulators and the regulated communities from one that was overly adversarial to one that included more collaborative problem solving. The task force was developing a set of "commandments" for regulators that would help promote that change. These included advice such as "Get out of Washington" so that regulators would get to know the people they were regulating. One key guideline for government regulators was "Don't dictate, negotiate." While I liked the intent behind this commandment, it had a fatal flaw: It is very difficult to get people to be less dictatorial by dictating to them!

The means used to promote a certain goal must be consistent with the goal itself. The same is true for trying to use the structural, attitudinal, and transactional (SAT) model to make current peacebuilding practice more systemic. A systemic theory of peacebuilding has to be implemented with regard to the systemic context in which it will be used. It would be easier to simply use a reductionist, linear strategy: Convince some donors or NGOs to use the SAT model, and the world will be a better place. Using the SAT model may make a marginal improvement in the programming of any one NGO or donor. But, as discussed earlier, linear approaches, even those for implementing a systemic model like SAT, are not well suited to complex and dynamic issues like making peace last. As with trying to jump the twenty-foot chasm in two ten-foot jumps, trying to change only part of the system without regard to how it affects, and is affected by, the entire system is unlikely to work.

The SAT model has a lot going for it in terms of its roots in systemic change work, its resonance with previous theoretical approaches, and its validation by on-the-ground experience in peacebuilding. However, from a systems perspective, the chief obstacles to implementing the SAT model are twofold:

1. *The impact of the "system context" within a particular country.* For instance, the dynamics operating within Afghanistan that explain why Afghanistan is the way it is affect the ability of any one peacebuilding program to contribute to lasting peace.
2. *The impact of the "peacebuilding system."* The peacebuilding "industry" can be thought of as a system, with donors, NGOs, local governments, aid beneficiaries, international organizations, civil society organizations, and so forth, as parts that interact in a dynamic fashion. It contains a series of structures, attitudes, and behaviors that govern or constrain the ability of any participant in the system to act in a nonlinear way.

The two obstacles are related; how any one practitioner acts in a particular social context is constrained by the overall peacebuilding system, such as donors who insist on certain priorities (e.g., work on the agricultural sector versus human rights) or require particular processes for monitoring and assessing program impacts. This chapter focuses first on how the SAT model should be implemented in order to account for the demands of working within a particular social context. It then considers how to deal with the constraints that come from the peacebuilding system itself.

USING THE SAT MODEL TO FOSTER SOCIETYWIDE SYSTEMIC CHANGE

The SAT model helps identify what peacebuilders should work on to create systemic change—that is, which structural, attitudinal, and transactional changes will influence and sustain systems change and how transactional peacebuilding can be used as a catalyst. The problem is that one cannot implement these changes in a linear way. Unfortunately, most traditional models for designing and implementing peacebuilding programs try to do just that. Traditional planning models identify a disliked symptom or problem to be fixed, design a solution, set up contracting procedures that specify the problem and the remedial action, and set out accountability mechanisms to ensure that the contractor implements the program as designed and achieves success as measured by predetermined benchmarks. Program grants are typically awarded through a competitive process to see who is best suited to implement the program. An implementing agency is selected, funds are released, and donors then hold the contractor accountable for results. From a linear perspective, this approach is logical.

However, it also has problems. For example, take the recent experience of an aid program on the island nation of Kiribati in the central Pacific. The economy of the island offered residents two main livelihoods: fishing or coconut farming. Over time, the fish stocks began to be depleted, which threatened one of the main ways islanders supported themselves. Aid organizations and the government of Kiribati decided to find a solution. The problem was identified as a declining fish population, and the cause was overfishing: More people fished than could be supported by the surrounding environment. Due to the structure of Kiribati's economy, the solution seemed obvious: Make coconut farming more attractive than fishing so that more people will choose to grow coconuts instead of catching fish.

So, with the help of aid organizations, the government decided on a plan that would subsidize coconut farming, making it more profitable than fishing. According to Sheila Walsh, who evaluated the program, the plan would achieve two goals: "One, they would reduce overfishing; and two, people would be better off. They would have higher incomes."[1] A program was designed and implemented to accomplish just that. The immediate result of the program was a success; the subsidies did get more people to grow coconuts, and the plan did increase incomes.

From a linear perspective this seems like a creative and sound plan. The problem is that it backfired: "The result of paying people more to do coconut agriculture was to increase fishing." In fact, fishing increased by 33 percent, and the fish population dropped by 17 percent.[2] It seems that people on Kiribati loved fishing, so they used the extra income and leisure time they gained from coconut farming to buy better fishing equipment and to fish more often.

Systems Shift 1: From Solutions Focused to Learning Focused

This seemingly easy fix to a relatively straightforward problem illustrates the dangers of linear planning and defines how a systems view is different. The basic but fundamental difference is that a linear view sees problems that must be fixed, while a systems view takes the position that "solutions are not the answer."[3] The Kiribati linear thought sequence went like this: If more people grow coconuts, then fewer people will fish, and if they fish less, then the fish stocks will increase. The strategy assumed that overfishing was the problem (e.g., what was broken) and the way to fix it (e.g., the solution) was to pay people more to farm coconuts. It is a natural tendency. For example, the corollary to the axiom "If it ain't broke don't fix it" is "If it is broke, fix it." According to Donella Meadows, this is how many of us are taught from a young age: "We have been taught to analyze, to use our rational ability, to trace direct paths from cause to effect, to look at things in small and understandable pieces, to solve problems by acting on or controlling the world around us."[4] Understandably, this is how many policy makers approach peacebuilding.

As with taking apart a car engine to find the piece that is broken, central planners in the peacebuilding world try to take apart a country to find the broken piece. A car engine, which is a mechanical, closed system, can actually be taken apart, adjusted, and reassembled. Societies, however, cannot.

A systems view does not see complex systems, like societies, as broken; hence, they do not need to be fixed. A system is what it is. People may not like the outcomes of the system, but that does not mean the system is broken. For example, I may prefer sunny days to rainy days, but a rainy day does not indicate that our climate system is broken. On Kiribati, the government and aid organizations may prefer to see sustainable fish stocks, but the declining fish population does not mean that the Kiribati social system is broken.

However, seeking solutions to fix problems serves a key purpose: It gives the appearance that situations can be controlled and that we can thus impose our will on them. While this belief may be more prevalent in Western culture, it has defined the approach of many in the peacebuilding world, especially donors. For example, William Easterly cites the 2005 Human Development Report that describes how centralized planning works with regard to achieving the Millennium Development Goals (MDGs): "The starting point is for donors and the aid recipients to agree on a financial needs assessment that identifies the aid requirements for achieving the MDGs. Donors then need to provide predictable, multiyear funding to cover these requirements, and developing countries need to implement the reforms that will optimize returns to aid."[5] This allows for donors and recipients to be clear on expectations, to feel empowered to address important problems, and to ensure accountability in using public funds.

The problem is that complex systems do not work this way. Meadows is clear that those seeking to change complex systems "can't impose [their] will on a system" because systems cannot be controlled.[6] From a systems view, control is illusory. The complex and dynamic interworking among the myriad of components that make up a society creates a kind of chaotic order. How these different interrelated components will respond to any particular change in the system, like paying people to grow coconuts on Kiribati, is very hard to predict. As a result, Peter Checkland, founder of the soft systems methodology (SSM), explains that seeking solutions is not the answer to complex, dynamic problems: "[SSM] does not seek 'solutions' which 'solve' real-world problems. Those ideas are a mirage when faced with real-life complexity, with its multiple perceptions and agendas. Instead SSM focuses on the process of engaging with that complexity. It offers an organized process of thinking which enables a group of people to learn their way to taking 'action to improve.'"[7]

The first step in promoting systemic change is to understand the system in question. Rather than seeking a quick fix to Kiribati's overfishing problem, a systems view would start by asking the question, Why do people currently prefer (over)fishing to coconut farming? Or, what is the system, or pattern of behavior, that produces the current level of fishing in Kiribati? Then, as Checkland explains, the next step is not to impose a "fix" to "solve" the problem but to nurture processes of learning and change from within the system itself. Instead of generating an externally imposed solution, the key is to let the system, or a mental picture of it, be the guide to locating opportunities to nurture change. Meadows refers to this as "listening" to the system in order to "discover how its properties and our values can work together to bring forth something much better than could ever be produced by our will alone."[8] Meadows offers a good example of what it means to listen to the system:

> A friend of mine, Nathan Gray, was once an aid worker in Guatemala. He told me of his frustration with agencies that would arrive with the intention of "creating jobs" and "increasing entrepreneurial abilities" and "attracting outside investors." They would walk right past the thriving local market, where small-scale business people of all kinds ... were displaying their entrepreneurial abilities in jobs they had created for themselves. Nathan spent his time talking to the people in the market.... He concluded that what was needed was not outside investors, but inside ones.[9]

The key is to work with, not against, the energy and motion in the system. In the Kiribati example, rather than trying to coerce people in the system into a different way of behaving (e.g., farming coconuts instead of fishing), listening to the system would mean identifying and nurturing forces for change that already exist in the system.[10] For example, perhaps the islanders' love of fishing could have been nurtured to change their relationship to the activity in order to preserve fish stocks. The task of listening to the system is complex, but it is possible to build this practice into planning approaches. Part II describes how to understand systems and do analysis and program planning in light of the systemic context.

The transition away from seeking solutions to understanding and working with a system may be hard for donors to make because it means acknowledging that the system is in control, not the donors, policy makers, and interveners or even the residents of the system. Development analysts Michael Woolcock and Lant Pritchett see the international community as being on an "incessant quest for *the* solution."[11] Giving up a sense of control will be difficult, but the alternative is not chaos or inaction. In an online discussion of complexity theory and development, one expert wrote, "We should be hopeful and accept that because 'we only have influence (and not control) over development processes, we must not lose our courage and ambition. The fact that the large-scale, long-term change that is required cannot be planned in advance, or achieved based on any one actor's goals and intentions, is not a reason to give up the drive for change.'"[12]

The key is to focus on learning rather than on solutions. Systems change in unexpected ways, but planners can learn to expect the unexpected. They can learn to embrace the feedback they get based on how their actions affect the behavior of the system. The goal of a development project should not be to meet predetermined benchmarks but to learn which elements of one's initial understanding of the system were right and which were wrong. Which elements of a project nurtured the system in positive ways and which did not? These lessons can bring a sense of humbleness, which will encourage planners to listen to what the system is telling them instead of assuming they know best.[13] Listening to the system means accepting the fact that *systems change best when systems change themselves,* and the job of those wanting to be of help is to learn about where change is already happening, or is ready to happen, in the system.

This learning-focused approach to fostering change from within the system is similar to what Easterly calls "searching." While searching and the trial and error it entails may seem like an anathema to a donor committed to centralized planning, Easterly points out that from a mathematical perspective, searching is an effective way to find out what really works on the ground. He uses an equation to show that even if the probability of success of any one program is as low as 0.5, then if one tries only seven different programs, the probability of one of them being a success rises to 0.99.[14] And even with the unpredictability of systems change, most programs would have a higher than 0.5 chance of being successful, so the number of trials would likely be lower than seven. In this light, a learning-focused approach to planning may also be more efficient!

SAT Response: The Planning, Acting, and Learning Project Cycle

A key feature of the SAT model is the pursuit of transactional change as a catalyst to structural and attitudinal change by using projects that follow an iterative cycle of planning, acting, and learning (PAL). Because overly deterministic, linear planning models will not work, planning must start with an assessment of the system that exists in the particular region, country, or village in question. Based on that holistic picture, planning needs to start from the assumption that because systems change best when they change themselves, *the best peacebuilders can do (both from within and outside a particular social context) is to nurture change from within the system that best serves the values of those in the system.*[15] Various people in a system (including donors and international NGOs) can work to change systems in line with a range of values, from preventing war profiteering to ending poverty, but to qualify as peacebuilding, systems would be encouraged to evolve toward more sustainable levels of human development and healthier processes of change. Chapter 5 elaborates on the Systemic Peacebuilding Assessment tool, which is designed to help peacebuilders listen to and understand the systemic context within which they are working.

In the PAL approach, initial project designs are more like hypotheses than ends in themselves. Their purpose is to foster both positive impacts on the system and learning about the system. In this sense, planning works as the springboard for learning. Instead of monitoring and evaluation processes that force agencies into pursuing predetermined outcomes and punishing "errors," learning requires peacebuilders to be "error embracing."[16]

Like many organizations, donors and other peacebuilders are far from "error embracing." "Most social systems have properties that inhibit coping effectively, calmly, and rationally with failure," according to business school professors Amy Edmondson and Mark Cannon.[17] As such, there is a tendency to suppress any talk of failure. To implement the PAL approach to peacebuilding, this needs to change, and it can. Failure is less affordable in some settings. On an assembly line, a high failure rate can cause a business to go bankrupt. But, as Edmondson points out, in certain contexts, failure is to be expected and even embraced.[18] In research laboratories, a high failure rate for experiments is a sign that the laboratory is doing its job. With challenging tasks that involve high levels of process complexity (such as peacebuilding), Edmondson points out, failure is not desirable but should be expected. In these cases, peacebuilders should "acknowledge that failures are inevitable and hence the best thing to do is to learn as much as possible—especially from small ones, so as to make larger ones less likely; beliefs about effective performance should reflect this."[19] Donors who pretend that failure is not an option are inhibiting learning and jeopardizing their own success.

Errors are not the goal of peacebuilding projects; nor are they unwelcome, however, if they are made pursuant to responsible planning and lead to learning. Responsible planning involves sound data gathering, anticipating both potential successes and failures, and setting up a strong process of learning. Learning, whether from success or failure, is critical to shaping the future of peacebuilding interventions. Learning allows peacebuilding projects to be flexible and adaptive, like the systems they are trying to affect. Peter Coleman, a leader in the field of dynamical systems theory, cites the work of Dietrich Dorner to make the case for why flexibility and adaptability are central to working with systems. Dorner's findings, based on research into decision making in complex environments, suggests that "well-intentioned decision makers who set an early course for improving communities and fail to adjust their decisions in response to critical feedback often fail and often do more harm than good. The most effective decision makers in [Dorner's] studies were those who were able to continually adapt."[20]

The need for flexibility and adaptability poses a challenge for monitoring and evaluating peacebuilding projects because it cautions against predetermined outcome measures that can impose a straitjacket on peacebuilders. There is still a need to ensure accountability for funds, but flexibility and accountability are not incompatible.

Systems Shift 2: Linear Change (Adding Up) Versus Nonlinear Change (Interacting Out)

A bedrock assumption behind most peacebuilding projects is that immediate, localized, and short-term program impacts will "add up" to long-term systemic change. As discussed in Chapter 1, the problem is that they do not. However, the problem with this notion has less to do with the programs or their impacts. Rather, the problem is the erroneous notion that change happens through a linear process. For example, positive economic impacts in villages in Kunduz Province, plus positive economic impacts in villages in neighboring Baghlan Province, plus similar changes in Takhar Province do not necessarily add up to peace, or even a positive economy, in Afghanistan.

Easterly explains, from a mathematical perspective, why adding up does not work.[21] He poses the example of an organization trying to implement a comprehensive development plan that consists of ten complementary programs, which, if implemented successfully, would have a large-scale impact. Further, he assumes that each of the ten programs has a high probability of success (85 percent). However, taken together, the chances of the ten programs adding up to a comprehensive change is only 20 percent using Easterly's formula.[22] If the number of programs that must be implemented for comprehensive change is twenty, and even though each has an 85 percent chance of success, then the odds of the programs adding up to larger-scale success shrinks to 4 percent. In reality, the odds of multiple programs adding up are much lower. For example, the number of various programs that would have to be successfully administered across a diverse country like Afghanistan is much higher than twenty, and the odds for even micro-level success for each of these programs is likely to be lower than 85 percent. Using Easterly's formula, the odds of these programs adding up to macro-level peace in a country like Afghanistan quickly shrink to a fraction of a percent.

More importantly, systems do not change through a linear process of adding up. Alan Fowler, in an article addressing the implications of complexity theory for development work, explains why adding up does not make sense from a systems perspective: "What [complexity theory] cautions, among other things, is that social changes driven by planned, incremental efforts cannot be simply added up to larger scales, because the efforts themselves alter the initial conditions. Nor can intended outcomes be guaranteed."[23]

Consider a simple example to better understand the concept of "altering initial conditions" and why it makes linear adding up impossible. In a linear world, I can predict that adding two apples to a basket that already has two apples in it will result in a basket holding four apples. The initial condition, a basket holding two apples, remains the same when I add two additional apples. But suppose that the act of adding two apples to the basket alters the initial number of apples in the basket. If adding two apples causes the initial two apples to become seven apples, then the result will be a basket holding nine apples. Further, assume that the impact of adding two apples to the basket causes a different impact each time. So, the second time I add two apples, the bottom of the basket becomes a black hole, and all the apples disappear. This phenomenon of altering initial conditions makes predictability very difficult.

In real life, systems do not act like the magic basket in the apple example, but interventions into systems do alter initial conditions. So, in the arms race example from Chapter 2, A builds more arms in response to the threat it feels due to B's arms stockpile. This should reduce A's feeling of threat, but it does not, because when A builds arms, this results in B's increasing its arms stockpile (an initial condition), which increases, rather than decreases, A's feeling of threat.

In systems, change to an element in the system or to a relationship between two elements causes a chain reaction that spirals out from the initial intervention in the system. In Kiribati, paying some people to grow coconuts increases their disposable income and allows them to fish more and buy better fishing equipment. Others see this example and follow suit. The increasing amount and quality of fishing might make Kiribati more attractive to sport fishing enthusiasts, causing an increase in the island's tourist trade and an expansion of businesses associated with it (e.g., travel agents, hotels, restaurants). Greater demand for sports fishing might then increase the amount and profitability of fishing, leading to even greater overfishing and a much lower fish population. Eventually, lower fish stocks might cause intensified competition in the fishing industry, followed by a precipitous collapse, which could cause a deep recession on the island.

This is not a description of what actually happened on Kiribati but an illustration of how the impact of changes made in a social system is mediated by the relationship of each change to other elements and dynamics that exist in the society. This makes systems change nonlinear: Change does not happen in one, intended direction. Think of a ball thrown into not one but several strong, swirling winds. Where the ball lands, if it lands, is a function of the dynamics and changing directions of the winds. In addition, the ball itself will have an impact on each wind it comes into contact with, changing its direction and speed. Similarly, a change in a social system is carried away, in multiple directions, by the social dynamics that make up that society. Further complicating the nature of change in complex systems is the fact that the change that results from a specific input is not proportionate. In other words, small changes in a social system can have a big impact on it, whereas large inputs can result in very little overall change.[24]

The nonlinearity and unpredictability of systems change means that linear adding up does not work. So, rather than adding up, changes in a system "interact out," meaning that they cause multiple and often unpredictable ripple effects throughout the system. Does the lack of adding up and the unpredictability of change mean that interveners should not even consider making systemic societal change? Actually, no. Donella Meadows developed a list of "systems wisdoms" collected over her years of experience working with systems. One of these wisdoms encourages those who would intervene in a system to aim high, to try to "enhance total systems properties, such as growth, stability, diversity, resilience, and sustainability—whether they are easily measured or not."[25] In peacebuilding, "total system properties" are sustainable levels of human development and healthy processes of change.

The need to focus on "enhancing total system properties" has three important implications for programming. First, it means peacebuilders should consider both long-term and short-term impacts. Many systems thinkers see fundamental changes to systems as taking a long time.[26] Sometimes systemic change can seem to happen fast. For example, the bloody civil war in Angola seemed to come to an abrupt end following the death in 2002 of Jonas Savimbi, the leader of the UNITA rebel movement. However, the conditions that allowed a quick settlement of the war after Savimbi's death had been building for over a decade. For example, the political cohesion of UNITA began to fray significantly starting in 1992.[27] This contributed to the lack of a decisive UNITA leader to step in and take Savimbi's place. In addition, although the war was raging, important changes affected UNITA's war-fighting ability, such as the withdrawal of US support, sanctions imposed against UNITA, and growing popular resentment over the destructiveness of the war. Savimbi's death was a short-term tipping point, but the process of change in the system of Angola took at least a decade.[28]

The second implication of enhancing total system properties is the need to focus across the depth of a social system, from the grassroots, to the "grasstops," to the elite. John Paul Lederach developed the notion of the Conflict Pyramid, which describes three distinct levels of a society that are affected by conflict and play a role in transforming it.[29] He divides the society into "top leadership," "middle-range leadership," and "grassroots leadership." In the SAT model, each level contains key people who can be transactional catalysts for systemic change. Potential drivers for total system change can come from any, and most likely all, of these levels. The Reflecting on Peace Practice case studies find that programs that spread from "key people" to "more people" were more successful than those that did not. Lederach argues for the need to integrate peace strategies that work from the "top down," the "middle out," and the "bottom up." This integration across the levels of a societal system, called vertical integration, is a key aspect of the SAT model for systemic change.

In addition to vertical integration, enhancing total system properties also requires horizontal integration. As discussed in Chapters 2 and 3, the SAT model argues for horizontal integration across the structural, attitudinal, and transactional domains. On a more operational level, there is also a need for integration across traditional professional disciplines, such as economics, engineering, health, anthropology, geography, computer science, and so forth. Another of Meadows's systems wisdoms is to "defy the disciplines" because following the pathways of systems change is "sure to lead across traditional disciplinary lines."[30]

SAT Response: Networks of Effective Action[31]

No one organization can affect an entire system on its own. No one organization can provide vertical and horizontal integration across a social system or capture the learning that can come from multiple perspectives on how a system works and the feedback from different projects aimed at nurturing change in the system. In order to promote systemic change, a network needs to meet certain basic parameters in terms of who is part of it:

- *Horizontal integration:* Networks need to include members who cross the three domains (e.g., can do structural, attitudinal, and transactional peacebuilding) and can cross disciplines (e.g., economics, health, engineering, social psychology, etc.).
- *Vertical integration:* Networks need to include members from the international community as well as from Lederach's three levels within a society (elite, midlevel, and grassroots).

A diverse membership is critical to achieving the goals of the network:

- *Fostering systemic change or PWL:* The overarching goal of the network is to promote sustainable levels of human development and healthy processes of societal change.
- *Promoting learning:* It is essential to achieving the overarching goal that networks promote learning among their members. In addition to mapping which organizations are active in a social system, networks can promote joint analysis (e.g., a shared systems map of a conflict), joint planning, and sharing of best and worst practices.
- *Facilitating joint action (when appropriate):* Rather than compelling co-operation, networks need to help their members learn where there are opportunities for joint action and determine the benefits and costs of working together or not. Joint action includes things like collaborative analysis and planning, program coordination, collaboration, and joint advocacy.

Lastly, the structure of the network needs to support its goals. Top-down, command-and-control structures are neither feasible nor appropriate. In the peacebuilding world, where ideological, political, and financial issues drive organizations apart, it is difficult to have structures that rely on command and control. In order to allow flexibility and autonomy on one hand and to foster collective action on the other, networks must be self-organizing and "chaordic," that is, a mixture of both chaos and order. Chaotic aspects of a network come from the lack of a centralized controlling authority. Collaboration is not mandated but relies on network members' self-organizing to accomplish specific tasks. Order comes from laying out "rules of the road," such as confidentiality in managing information and a protocol for dealing with donors and handling funds. The network can also provide structure by setting up technical means for interaction, such as a communication infrastructure or a knowledge-management system for information sharing, planning, and learning.

Certain elements of the current peacebuilding system work against the formation of networks of effective action (NEAs). The competitive bidding process that donors use for most projects leads to competition between organizations. For example, two development organizations might have each established extensive vertical networks in different parts of Nepal. Combining these networks might be essential to forming an NEA in Nepal, but the competitive bidding process prevents this as international NGOs often compete to get local civil society organizations to "join their proposal." Similarly, the same command-and-control structures demanded by donors often work against setting up networks that are chaordic, adaptive, and self-organizing.

Table 4.1 summarizes the ways the SAT model differs from current linear change models.

Table 4.1 Implications of the SAT Model for Current Peacebuilding Practice

Current Linear Assumptions About Change	Systems Thinking Assumptions About Change	Why?	Implications for the SAT Model
Goal • Find solutions to problems. **Means** • Control and predict change. • Create preset, static benchmarks. • Believe that small projects add up to large-scale change.	**Goal** • Nurture change from within the system. **Means** • Listen to the system. • Foster learning through flexible, adaptable interventions. • Create vertical and horizontal integration.	• Systems are not problems to be fixed. • Control over complex systems is illusory. • Systems change in unpredictable ways. • Smaller changes "interact out" in a dynamic relationship with other parts of the system.	• SPA as a means to listen to the system • PAL project cycle to foster learning • Networks to create vertical and horizontal integration

USING THE SAT MODEL TO FOSTER CHANGE IN THE CURRENT PEACEBUILDING SYSTEM

Using the SAT model within the context of a particular social system, be it the Democratic Republic of Congo, Colombia, or Cambodia, means departing from many established practices in the peacebuilding world. Unfortunately, those practices exist for a reason and will not be easily altered. In any one context, using the SAT model effectively requires an understanding of why the peacebuilding field currently insists on finding fixes, controlling and imposing change, and assuming that micro-level changes will add up.

The first step toward making the peacebuilding industry more systemic is to understand and listen to the peacebuilding system itself. Following the advice of the SAT model, altering the peacebuilding system means creating a dynamic interaction between changes in the structural, attitudinal, and transactional domains. To better understand what those changes might be, it is necessary to get a picture of what the traditional peacebuilding system looks like. The key questions to answer are (1) what patterns of behavior make the use of linear thinking and planning tools commonplace in current peacebuilding practice, and (2) are there places within the current peacebuilding system where change is already happening, or is ready to happen, that could be nurtured to make the peacebuilding industry as a whole more systemic?

THE PEACEBUILDING SYSTEM

Peacebuilding can be looked at as a system: a series of interconnected parts that achieves some impacts on the world.[32] This is not to say that only one peacebuilding system exists in reality and is waiting to be discovered. In the SAT approach, developing a systems map is not like mapping the human genome. A systems map is a way to view reality—*but it is not reality.* While there exists one sequence of DNA that is the human genome, there are infinite ways to represent the current peacebuilding industry as a system. Figure 4.1 provides one view. Judge it in terms of the story one can tell based on the map and whether that story resonates with one's view of reality.

Start reading the map by looking at the middle of the right side at the term *ineffective peacebuilding programs.* Reading backwards (down and to the left), the mixed peacebuilding track record is fueled by the rate of peace agreements relapsing into violence and the paradox of micro-level (localized) success versus the lack of long-term, macro-level change. Moving up from ineffective peacebuilding programs, note that the lack of effectiveness in peacebuilding programs has actually led to calls for more funds to be dedicated to foreign assistance. William Easterly, in *Reinventing Foreign Aid,* captures this counterintuitive dynamic:

Figure 4.1 The Peacebuilding System

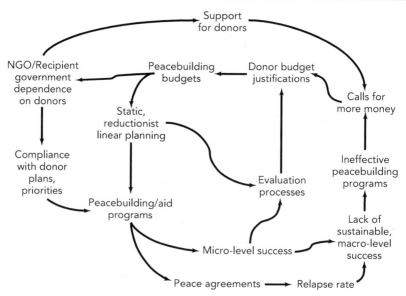

*This map is based on one drawn by Peter Woodrow of the Reflecting on Peace Practices project of CDA/Collaborative Learning Projects.

One view that seems to command almost universal assent from observers of the aid system (including from the aid agencies themselves about their own operations) is that the current aid system is not working very well.

Despite this dissatisfaction with the current system, all the main political actors in the rich countries seem to agree on increasing the volume of aid.[33]

Following the arrow out of *calls for more money*, the many voices calling for increased levels of aid serve as a basis for donor organizations to justify increased foreign aid budgets. Following the arrow down from *donor budget justifications,* these justifications are bolstered by evaluations of peacebuilding programs that are largely positive because they are based on shorter-term indicators of micro-level success, which are limited to a government's annual budget cycle, and a lack of attention to longer-term indicators of macro-level failure. At the same time, evaluation processes tend to discourage discussion of errors because they might jeopardize new funding requests, both from donor agencies to their legislatures and by recipient governments and NGOs to the donor agencies. Further bolstering the case for increased foreign aid budgets is support from NGOs and governments that are recipients of foreign aid.

When donors successfully argue for peacebuilding budgets, new funding allows them to continue running peacebuilding programs and making grants to NGOs and recipient governments. This builds a form of dependency on the part of aid recipients (upper left of the diagram). For example, studies of the long-term impact of aid on recipient countries indicate that those governments tend to become more responsive to international donors than to their own citizens: "If donors are providing the majority of public finance and governments are primarily accountable to those external agencies, then it may simply not be possible to expect a credible social contract to develop between the state and its citizens."[34]

Similarly, NGOs that get a large amount of funds from various donor agencies may become more responsive to the needs of those agencies than to the beneficiary populations they are trying to serve. For example, deforestation is a growing problem in Afghanistan, and to address the issue, a donor set up a program to replant forests in and around rural villages. An aid worker, who was working on a program funded as part of this initiative, went into a village to involve its inhabitants in the process of replanting trees, such as mulberry trees, that would restore a vital resource for the families there.

However, the villagers said that instead of a forest, they really needed a bridge across the river that separated the settlement from their animals' grazing fields and from a nearby health clinic. The aid workers appreciated the villagers' need for a bridge but said they only had funds to replant a forest. The villagers appreciated the aid workers' need to rebuild a forest but stressed that if the aid organization really wanted to help them, it would first build a bridge. The conversation ended at a respectful disagreement. The aid agency went ahead and planted a variety of young trees with the feeling that, even without a bridge, the village would still be better off with a new grove of fruit-producing trees. After the saplings were planted, and without a bridge for their animals to cross safely onto better grazing land, the villagers sent their animals into the newly planted forest, where they promptly ate the new saplings.[35]

The net impact of the program was extremely short-lived: one satisfying meal for the village's livestock. But was the aid agency necessarily wrong for planting the trees instead of building the bridge? The constraints of the donor's reforestation programs would not allow the aid organization to use those funds to build bridges instead, and doing so might jeopardize the agency's relationship with the donor. And if the workers redirected the funds, the donor would have a hard time justifying to its funders (e.g., a parliament) why instead of building forests, parliament's expectation in approving the funds, the public monies were used for bridge construction. Regardless of who was right or wrong, the story does show how aid agencies are often more responsive to the demands of their donors than to the needs of the people they are trying to serve.

One of the main reasons programs like the reforestation program described above miss their mark is that donor organizations tend to use static, reductionist, linear planning models to shape their peacebuilding priorities and programs—despite the lack of effectiveness of these approaches. The problem is both known and pervasive. For example, a group of development experts responded to an article on the problems with foreign aid written by Alan Fowler in the journal *The Broker*.[36] A July 28, 2008, posting by Willemijn Verkoren reads, "Interestingly, all of the experts who have responded so far to Fowler's article agreed on what is wrong with the current methods: planning models that assume linear cause-and-effect relationships and predictable outcomes, such as the logical framework, are ineffective when applied to a reality that is messy, unpredictable and impacted by multiple agencies and processes beyond the development intervention that is being carried out."[37] Despite the fact that many in the peacebuilding system know that their planning tools are not well suited to "messy" and "unpredictable" realities on the ground, the recipients of foreign aid tend to comply with the donor's priorities and plans because of their dependence on these donors.

One driving factor behind using linear planning models is that they feed donors' need to demonstrate tangible gains through short-term evaluation processes that focus on micro-level successes. Because government budget cycles tend to be annual, there is no incentive to track long-term, macro-level success or failure. Rather there is an ethos that "only what can be counted counts."

In fact, it is much easier to count short-term impacts, such as schools built, people trained, and resources distributed. The members of the system seem to be aware of but resigned to the micro-macro gap (e.g., between short-term countables and long-term success). Easterly points to a Millennium Development Project report acknowledging that "'it is often difficult to precisely quantify the link between coverage of interventions and MDG outcomes.' Rather than change the planning and evaluation process, the same sentence concludes that 'national MDG planning involves mapping interventions to MDG outcomes.'"[38] As a result, the peacebuilding system tends to replicate, not correct, ongoing inefficiencies in the system. So, a turn through the existing peacebuilding system, one cycle through the map, results in keeping the aid flowing but not necessarily improving outcomes. This is not to say that organizations and practitioners have not learned anything about how to improve performance or that all aid is wasted. Chapter 1 explores this point. It does say that, on balance, peacebuilding outcomes are mixed; yet, there is pressure to keep aid flowing and at increasing levels.

Can We Make the Current Peacebuilding System More Systemic?

The tendency of the peacebuilding system to perpetuate the lack of long-term sustainable change raises the question, What is the purpose of the current peacebuilding system? The espoused purpose of those in the system is to build peace, end poverty, enhance security, promote justice, and so forth. However, as Meadows notes, the purpose of a system is "deduced from behavior, not from rhetoric or stated goals."[39] If the actual impact of the system is more to keep aid flowing than to deliver long-term outcomes through cost-effective programs, then keeping aid flowing is the system's dominant purpose. This may be interpreted as a harsh criticism of the current system; it is not meant that way. Systems mapping is meant to be a value-neutral exercise to help us understand why something is the way that it is—not a judgment on it. Donors and peacebuilders in general are not scam artists trying to make a quick buck. Nothing could be further from the truth. However, the purpose of the system is deduced from its impact, not from the collective motivations of people in the system.

Understanding the purpose of the current system is critical. Changing the overall purpose of the system is difficult, and asking actors within it to behave in a way that seems inconsistent with the system's purpose will meet with resistance. For example, asking peacebuilders to look to the long term, or to abandon preset program benchmarks, or to embrace errors, and so forth, will meet with resistance from within the system—such as grants being terminated for a failure to meet those preset, static benchmarks regardless of how much was learned in the process. Attempts to build networks and share learning will meet with a culture that works against freely sharing information. So, even though it may be justifiable to demand that the system change its purpose and produce more systemic and sustainable outcomes, elements within the system will work against this goal because the system is putting more pressure on people to keep aid flowing, even at the expense of investing in making peace last.

The alternative is to listen to the system—to look for areas within it where change is already happening. The strategy is to find areas where a transactional intervention can nurture structural and attitudinal change that will move the system toward producing more sustainable outcomes. One such area may be in the use of static, reductionist, linear planning tools. There is a recognition that planning processes need to be broader in scope, and this has prompted a series of innovations in analysis and planning tools in general and conflict analysis in particular. There has been a move toward more horizontal integration in that these tools have begun to blend considerations of the root causes of conflict with traditional development-focused frameworks. The Do No Harm movement, spurred by Mary Anderson and CDA/Collaborative Learning Projects, has been a leader in this regard. Anderson's thesis that humanitarian and development aid can foster both war and peace has led to a general acceptance that aid planning has to incorporate a "conflict lens."

Analytical tools have also been embracing more vertical integration as analysts stress the importance of including local voices in the planning and execution of aid programs. Various tools for conflict assessment used by donor governments and international organizations like the World Bank have begun to stress the need to be sensitive to local voices and to include local participants in gathering and analyzing data. The Global Partnership for the Prevention of Armed Conflict (GPPAC) represents a movement to integrate local civil society organizations working for peace and justice into governmental peace and development efforts. GPPAC is dedicated to strengthening "civil society networks for peace and security by linking local, national, regional, and global levels of action; to establish effective engagement with governments, the UN system and regional organizations."[40]

One of the most important developments in the area of reforming how agencies do conflict analysis and planning for intervention is the Interagency Conflict Assessment Framework (ICAF). The creation of ICAF was spurred by National Security Presidential Directive (NSPD) 44, the December 2005 Bush administration order that set up the office of the Coordinator for Reconstruction and Stabilization (S/CRS) at the Department of State. The mandate of S/CRS is to strengthen coordination across US government agencies that are active in conflict-affected countries. The impetus for NSPD 44 was the severe criticism of the United States for its failed efforts at reconstruction in Iraq and Afghanistan. As part of this effort, S/CRS was tasked with generating an agreed-on conflict analysis framework that was endorsed by the Department of State, the Department of Defense, and the US Agency for International Development (USAID). In November 2007, the ICAF tool came out of intensive conversations among representatives of the three bureaucracies. The document that emerged from these meetings is affectionately called the Treaty of Carlisle, after the place where the meeting was held and as a nod to the fact that getting these three large agencies to agree on a common set of concepts and language was like negotiating a peace treaty.

Tjip Walker, then with USAID's Office of Conflict Management and Mitigation, led the USAID participation in the development of ICAF. Walker said that "no one went into the ICAF process with the intention of making the system more systemic."[41] But the development of ICAF began to do just that. In 2008, ICAF was applied to several countries in "desktop" exercises in Washington, DC, involving the three agencies. Cynthia Irmer, who led the participation of S/CRS in the ICAF negotiations and participated in these planning exercises, noticed that the analyses that emerged had a bureaucratic advantage over those produced within any one of the agencies. Policy recommendations forwarded to decision makers within State, Defense, or USAID with a mutually agreed ICAF assessment attached as support carried more weight because those decision makers did not have to worry about whether the other agencies would object to the background analysis. According to Irmer, "Participation in ICAF removed a potential roadblock" in the bureaucratic process.[42] Irmer added that ICAF served as a fair procedure for resolving differing views held by the three agencies of a country or conflict zone.

ICAF is still a relatively new process, and its first field application was conducted in Cambodia in March 2009. I participated in that exercise, along with personnel from Defense, State, and USAID. This was also the first time that systems mapping was added as a part of ICAF. The analysis was well received at the US Embassy in Phnom Penh, and discussions began at the embassy between representatives of the three agencies on how to better coordinate and implement their defense, diplomatic, and development initiatives in the country. Both in Cambodia and Washington, DC, as people began to see that having an analysis that emerged from an interagency process like ICAF was an advantage, the interagency process was strengthened. While ICAF may not be a fully "systemic" instrument, its use has built an appreciation for the value of getting a view of a context from a vantage point outside of one's own bureaucracy. This is an important step toward building a structural commitment to getting a "systems view" of a situation before intervening. It also promotes an attitudinal shift away from a belief that agencies can pursue peacebuilding initiatives in isolation and expect that they will add up to larger-scale change.

ICAF and other efforts to make analytical tools more systemic is evidence that there is energy and receptivity in the system to using systemic approaches like the SAT model. Chapter 5 describes these efforts in more detail, but suffice it to say that in general, these developments speak to an area where change is already happening, and this may be an entry point to introduce the SAT model in order to make the peacebuilding system more systemic. If peacebuilding agencies and NGOs can redefine their view of the social systems within which they work, then there is a stronger case for altering the interventions produced based on those analyses. If planning frameworks can integrate systems insights and the SAT model as a systemic theory of change, this may lead to more experiments with systemic models of intervention (e.g., PAL, the use of transactional peacebuilding as a catalyst, and building networks of effective action). If the use of these tools and methods can produce more effective, longer-term outcomes, then the positive feedback from within the system may strengthen support for the use of the SAT model or approaches like it.

Table 4.2 summarizes the structural and attitudinal changes needed to make the peacebuilding system more systemic and the transactional changes that might be used as a catalyst for nurturing changes in the other two domains. In order to nurture the current change in the peacebuilding system toward better analysis and more effective collaboration in the field, Chapters 5, 6, and 7 describe how peacebuilders can do systemic analysis and planning. Further, Chapters 8, 9, and 10 provide specific guidance on how to turn this systemic analysis and planning into more sustainable peacebuilding programs by using transactional peacebuilding as a catalyst for structural and attitudinal change.

Table 4.2 Using the SAT Model to Change the Peacebuilding System

Structural Change	Attitudinal Change	Transactional Catalyst

• Less use of reductionist, linear planning models.
• Less use of preset, static benchmarks.
• Balance flexibility with accountability.
• Require the SPA and hold people accountable for what they learn.
• Modify bidding and contracting procedures to encourage the use of NEAs.
• Expand time horizons and invest beyond annual budget cycles.
	• "Adding up" doesn't add up.
	• Control is illusory.
	• Change cannot be predicted, only nurtured.
	• Solutions are not the answer.
	• Learning is key.
	• What can be counted is not all that counts.
	• Success is judged based on enhancing total system properties not tinkering with parts.
		• Build on evolution of analytical tools by nurturing more systemic analysis (SPA).
		• Based on this analysis, which contains system maps, foster program planning that incorporates
		  ◦ the PAL cycle;
		  ◦ networks that foster vertical and horizontal integration.

CHAPTER 4 SUMMARY

- In order to cope with the complexity of a social system, the SAT model requires the use of a PAL project cycle, horizontal and vertical integration, and networks of effective action.
- Implementing a more systemic practice also requires changes in how the current peacebuilding system works. Currently evolving practices for assessment planning in governmental and nongovernmental agencies may be an entry point for implementing more systemic practices, such as the SAT model.
- See Tables 4.1 and 4.2.

PART II

SYSTEMIC PEACEBUILDING ASSESSMENT AND PLANNING

CHAPTER 5

SYSTEMIC ASSESSMENT

◦

"Come to think of it ... ya cahn't get they-yah from hee-yah."
—Punch line from the story "Which Way to Millinocket"

Part II takes up the challenge of how to listen to a system in order to plan interventions meant to nurture systemic change, or Peace Writ Large (PWL), and offers the Systemic Peacebuilding Assessment (SPA) as a means to that end. Chapter 4 ends on the optimistic note that the key to making peacebuilding practice more systemic is to build on changes already happening within the system to improve how peacebuilders do assessment and planning. There is a growing recognition of the limits of linear models, such as the "log frame" (or logical framework), that treat a social system, which is complex and chaotic, as though it were predictable and controllable. However, in order to build on these good intentions, peacebuilders need to overcome four challenges that will thwart any effort to make peace last by working in a more systemic fashion:

1. *We get seduced by marginal change.* Innovations like "conflict sensitivity" are improvements over "conflict-insensitive" practice. It would be convenient if adopting systemic methods for doing analysis and planning, such as the SPA, involved just marginal changes to existing conflict-sensitive frameworks. However, using a tool like the SPA means making

a fundamental shift, not a marginal change, in how peacebuilders do analysis and planning.

2. *We ask the wrong question.* The question we ask at the start of any assessment is critical. Current analytical tools tend to ask questions that limit the effectiveness of the analysis produced. The SPA asks a question that is subtly, yet profoundly different.

3. *We fall into bad analytical habits.* Regardless of the specific analytical instrument used, analysts tend to fall into habits that compromise their ability to do assessment that will support systemic change. The SPA has safeguards built in to protect against these bad habits.

4. *We have difficulty dealing with complexity without oversimplifying.* Listening to a system all at once would be like trying to listen to ten symphonies, every heavy metal rock band, and the tantrums of 1,000 two-year-olds all at the same time. To avoid information overload, analysts need to make strategic decisions about where to focus their limited attention. On the other hand, oversimplifying means cutting out essential data. The SPA uses the structural, attitudinal, and transactional (SAT) domains to focus attention on the most critical aspects of a social system without compromising the usefulness of the analysis.

CHALLENGE 1: MOVING BEYOND CONFLICT SENSITIVITY (MARGINAL CHANGE IS NOT AN OPTION)

Dublin, Ireland, is a beautiful city. I was there on business for a week working with a colleague. He was staying in a hotel that was an easy fifteen-minute walk from mine. The best part of the day was that beautiful fifteen-minute walk past Trinity College, down the cobblestones, and through a park. I took that path, exactly retracing my steps, on each of the first four days of the week. I became proud of my ability to get around Dublin without using a map. On my last day, I decided I liked Dublin so much that I wanted to see more of it. I decided to test my navigational skills and started out, with just my instincts, on a different path that went south then west, as opposed to my usual west then south route.

I walked for fifteen minutes but found myself in unfamiliar environs. No matter, I might be a bit off, but persisting would get me there soon. Still no luck. Perhaps I had gone too far south and needed to go north (or what I thought was north)? No good. Perhaps a bit east? No. Maybe further south or west? When I came to a canal that had not appeared on any maps of Dublin I had seen, I decided it was time to get help.

I finally made it to my meeting about an hour after it had started. Later, when I tried to uncover my navigational error using a map of greater Dublin, I realized that I had been completely turned around. What I had thought was north was south. When I thought I was going west, I was heading east. I had gotten off to a bad start, and every move I made to correct my error only compounded the problem. I had a general idea of where I was going, but I had no map that showed me the whole of Dublin and how each street was interconnected. Instead, I used a linear form of navigation: "I believe I started here, then went south, then west, so perhaps north will work?" When that did not produce the desired results, I tried another direction, and so on. I felt like the tourist in the old yarn "Which Way to Millinocket," who when he stopped to ask directions was told, "Ya cahn't get they-yah from hee-yah." Not only was I lost, but it was impossible to find my way to where I was going—not because it was physically impossible to get there but because my way of navigation, a loose form of dead reckoning, was so flawed and disoriented that I was incapable of finding the right way.

Albert Einstein is credited with the insight that the same way of thinking that produced a problem is incapable of also solving the problem. In the same way, peacebuilding agencies, governments, donors, and NGOs will find it impossible to work toward systemic change using linear models of analysis, just as I was unable to find my way through Dublin using a flawed method of navigation. The change from my unhelpful mode of dead reckoning to using the Global Positioning System (GPS) is similar to what peacebuilders need to do in shifting from using conflict-sensitive analysis and planning tools to the SPA.

It may be unfair to compare smart, hardworking peacebuilding practitioners to my inept self in Dublin, but there is a common theme: Neither of us can be effective without a systemic view of the context within which we are working and a systemic theory for how we will achieve our objectives. In peacebuilding, we need to take our planning cues from listening to the system. But without a systems map, a mental model of how the parts of a system are interrelated, it is impossible to listen to the system. Good peacebuilding work has undoubtedly been performed without those involved taking (at least consciously) a systemic perspective. However, the lack of a systemic approach puts peacebuilding programs and the human, financial, and material resources that go into them at risk of being misdirected, misexecuted, or counterproductive.

As a GPS could have helped me find my way through Dublin, an SPA can be a guide for agencies like the European Union, UN Development Programme, US Agency for International Development (USAID), or World Bank when they design their country strategies or for implementing agencies like Médicins Sans Frontières, CARE, Mercy Corps, or World Vision as they implement individual programs. An SPA is designed to be their navigation tool as they ask, How can we be sure that our programs have lasting impacts, are cost-effective, and maximize their contribution to achieving Peace Writ Large?

Do we really need another approach to assessment as a guide to effective programming? After all, there has been significant progress in making analysis more holistic, such as the development of conflict sensitivity, which integrates conflict analysis into development practice. Conflict-sensitive approaches to development in general, and the Peace and Conflict Impact Analysis (PCIA) in particular, are the prime movers in this shift.[1] PCIA is intended to help peacebuilders understand the potential impact of a conflict on their programming as well as the potential impact of their programming on the conflict.

For years, many in the humanitarian and development communities resisted looking at the interconnection between their programs and issues of peace and conflict. Involvement in ameliorating a conflict was seen as compromising the apolitical humanitarian ethos that allowed such agencies to operate in the midst of warring factions. The "humanitarian neutralist" school of thought says that aid must be given "on the basis of need alone and should be above and beyond any political, military, strategic, or sectarian agenda."[2] Agency involvement in trying to manage or transform a conflict was seen as directly violating this neutralist position. Conflicts are inherently political, and the perception was that any interventions into them would taint the humanitarian intervener in the eyes of one or more parties to the conflict.

Mary Anderson's seminal work *Do No Harm* (1999) represented the pin that burst the illusory bubble that aid in the midst of conflict could be apolitical.[3] While aid may be given with a neutral intent, Anderson and others pointed out the ways that it often has unintended negative and political impacts. This collective recognition set the stage for dozens of efforts that began to look at how to better understand the relationship between aid and conflict and to make good programming decisions in light of that awareness.

Since the mid-1990s, many different models for conflict assessment have been developed. Anderson's own organization, CDA/Collaborative Learning Projects, helped pioneer a methodology that looks at assessing local capacities for peace as a way of understanding a development program's impact on a conflict. The World Bank, Department for International Development (DFID) (UK), USAID (US), Deutsche Gesellschaft für Internationale Zusammenarbeit (GIZ) (Germany), World Vision, CARE, Swisspeace, and many others have also developed tools. A very helpful summary of fifteen different models was compiled as part of a resource pack of conflict-sensitive approaches put together by an international consortium of peacebuilding organizations.[4] These models are all in line with conflict-sensitive development and the principles of PCIA.[5] Some go further than helping to insure that programs "do no harm" by trying to help them "do some good" relative to a conflict.[6]

These frameworks capture many important insights about how to understand and address conflict dynamics and build peace. For example, they are based on the common insight, consistent with systems theory, that individual programs take place in a conflict context, and to better manage the relationship between those programs and the conflict, one first has to understand the root drivers and dynamics of the surrounding conflict. A lack of awareness about or misdiagnosis of the conflict could result in wasted efforts or compromise the sustainability of a program and its intended impacts. There is also a recognition that understanding the roots of a conflict helps maximize "aid's potential to 'do good.'"[7] These are significant shifts in traditional humanitarian and development mind-sets.

However, conflict sensitivity and PCIA are also flawed in that they are, for all their merit, basically a half measure. They suffer from the erroneous assumption that conflict or peacebuilding, on one hand, and development, on the other, are different things and that the goal is to manage the relationship between them. They assume that development and humanitarian organizations that work in conflict zones could choose not to work on the conflict itself.

The SAT model takes a holistic approach and views conflict and development as inseparable. As such, under the SAT model, it is a fiction to believe that you can work in conflict zones without working on the conflict. To return to the medical analogy, doing conflict-sensitive development is like doing health-sensitive heart surgery. Health and surgery, or any kind of medical intervention, cannot be separated. It would be potentially disastrous for a heart surgeon to start by trying to understand how heart surgery would affect the lungs, brain, or circulatory system, without first starting with (or working from) a general diagnosis of a patient's overall health (or illness). The doctor would want first to understand the causes of a patient's ill health and the potential drivers for a return to health and then to see whether heart surgery would be part of the patient's treatment, and if so, how.

Similarly, peacebuilders, whether rule-of-law specialists, environmental engineers, or trauma healers, should not start by looking at the potential impacts (positive or negative) of their programs on the overall level of peace or conflict. Rather, they need to start with a systemic analysis of the causes of a conflict and the drivers of peace before settling on what, if any, programming to pursue. It is wrong to start by thinking about the impact of a potential intervention on peace and conflict as opposed to first understanding the social system in its own right, separate from any programming consideration. In this sense, PCIA misses the mark because it does not look at the social context as a whole (within a holistic frame) or try to understand it as a complex system (using a systemic frame). Systemic thinking in peacebuilding is a remedial response to our tendency to think in a linear fashion, which can have unanticipated negative consequences (see Part I).[8]

The word "holistic" goes to the content of that (systemic) thinking (e.g., does it address the range of factors that contribute to violence or peace?). The reason to talk about being both systemic and holistic is that it is possible to think systemically without thinking holistically. For example, a development NGO in Afghanistan that specializes in agricultural programs can analyze the agricultural sector there in a systemic way: The lack of quality seeds, bad farming practices, an eroded environment, and the lack of infrastructure all contribute to a depressed agricultural sector. And the agricultural sector is one component of a peaceful Afghanistan. While this analysis incorporates the dynamic causality of systems thinking, this analysis is not holistic in that it does not consider the role of nonagricultural or noneconomic factors such as armed groups, divisive community leaders, or social divisions. Basically, one can think systemically but still be too narrowly focused on a particular sector, which in turn will compromise one's ability to build PWL successfully.

The SPA marks a fundamental change from conflict sensitivity because it aims at producing analysis of a social context that is both systemic and holistic. Conflict sensitivity is a way of listening to two important parts of a system, development issues and conflict issues, and assuming that doing so will provide a view of the whole of a social system. It is like driving down the highway and instead of looking in just your lane (development issues), looking in the lane next to you (conflict issues). This is better than only watching your lane, but it will not give you the systemic picture you would get by looking at a map or using a GPS. An SPA is a way of getting a GPS-like view of a social system so that you might more effectively navigate your way around it.

CHALLENGE 2: ASKING THE RIGHT QUESTION

In order to take a holistic and systemic view, the SPA starts with a different question than simply asking what impact a development project will have on a conflict or a conflict on a development project. To return to a medical analogy, when a patient visits a general practitioner, the doctor asks questions and does an examination to diagnose that person's overall health. Unlike the medical field, the peacebuilding arena has few equivalents of a "general practitioner" (e.g., an organization that is responsible for systemic macro-level peace in a country). So, few organizations ask the equivalent of the general practitioner's question: What is a society's overall health? Most peacebuilding organizations, like medical specialists who ask about specific subsystems in the body, ask about parts of the social system, like its economy, intergroup relations, or security. For example, the World Bank's assessment instrument asks mainly about structural or institutional aspects of a society that reflect the types of interventions the Bank makes.

Few peacebuilding organizations start by asking, What is the overall health, or level of peace, in a country? The level of peace is the degree to which the society has sustainable levels of human development and healthy processes of societal change. It is a subtle but critical point because the basic question one asks determines the usefulness (or lack thereof) of the analysis generated. Asking about a society's level of peace has several advantages as a starting point for analysis. First, looking at the factors that affect the level of conflict or violence can be too limiting because peace is more than just the absence of violence. By looking at the level of peace, an SPA is a "context" analysis, not a conflict analysis. Looking at the context is a broader inquiry than looking just at the causes of a conflict or of violence. An SPA is defined in terms of the desired end state (peace) and not in terms of the undesired status quo (violent conflict). While this may seem like a semantic difference, it reflects the fact that building peace is much more complex than merely ending violence. In addition, an SPA is relevant to contexts such as addressing persistent poverty and underdevelopment in a country like Tanzania, where violent conflict is not the primary concern.

Interestingly, we do not have a good word for the opposite of peace when peace is defined in more complex terms than simply the absence of violence. Perhaps we can use the term *unpeace* to denote societies that do not have sustainable levels of human development and/or have unhealthy processes of change.

A second advantage to asking about a society's level of peace is that violence is too limiting as a convening question; it predisposes us to looking for negatives in the society (e.g., those things that lead to violence) versus finding both factors that contribute to violence (or unpeace) and assets in the society that build peace or counter provocations to violence.[9] Lastly, the goal of the analysis is to produce a picture of a system so that peacebuilders can "listen" to it as a guide for planning. If peacebuilders ask about what contributes to the level of violence or levels of poverty, then the systems map they produce will give them guidance on dealing with those issues. If the central question they are asking has to do with the factors and patterns of behavior that affect a country's level of peace, then the guidance they get will be more useful in achieving PWL.

This issue goes to the fundamental question of the purpose of conflict-sensitive models of analysis versus the SAT model of context analysis. Is the goal to do development well (however defined), or is it to achieve PWL? Or does it lie somewhere in between, such as to do development well and have some positive impact on the conflict (e.g., "to do some good")?

For traditional conflict-sensitive models, the goal is to do development well by countering the potential negative impacts of violent conflict on a particular project, to avoid inadvertently making the conflict worse, and, when possible, to contribute to reducing the level of violence. For example, the UK DFID states that its conflict assessment instrument can be used to assess

- risks of negative impacts of conflict on programs;
- risks of programs or policies exacerbating conflict;
- opportunities to improve the effectiveness of development interventions in contributing to conflict prevention and reduction.[10]

Similarly, the resource pack for conflict-sensitive approaches says that "making development assistance sensitive to conflict should improve its overall impact on development goals and objectives as well as on decreasing violence."[11]

Both these examples put achieving development objectives as the central purpose of doing assessment with a secondary value given to reducing levels of violence. And reducing violence is a far less ambitious goal than achieving sustainable peace. Both examples stop short of contributing to a society's level of peace, or PWL, the goal of the intervention. Further, doing "good development that does good," while a laudable goal, has two potentially negative impacts. First, there is the risk of reduced cost-effectiveness. Because these approaches lack a theory for how a local-level development project will contribute to PWL, they will feed into the micro-macro peacebuilding gap (as described in Part I) and, in turn, lessen the potential for lasting program impacts. Second, the lack of a systemic theory (and analysis based on it) allows practitioners to proceed on the basis of vague assumptions about how their programs will "do some good."[12] Mary Anderson and Lara Olson expand on this phenomenon: "Agencies rarely articulate the theory of change that guides their work. Rather, these remain implicit and undiscussed.... The result is that agencies develop programs assuming they are the 'building blocks of peace' without tracing actual impacts to different approaches to [PWL]."[13]

Without this clarity of thinking about how achieving certain development goals contributes to PWL, there is the danger that this contribution may have little or no impact; worse, it may have unintended negative impacts. The potential for such a negative impact on peace is precisely what these conflict assessment methodologies are intended to avoid. The heart of the problem is that they tend to have a linear versus a systemic approach to change. As argued in Part I, it is dangerously simplistic to assume that doing good work at the local level must add up to positive change in the broader context.

In addition to starting with the more systemic question of what factors in a social context affect the level of peace, an SPA is linked to a systemic theory of change that does not rely on "adding up" or on unarticulated theories of change to make the bridge between analysis and action.

CHALLENGE 3: AVOIDING BAD ANALYTICAL HABITS

In addition to risking the dangers of sloppy thinking, analysts who use methodologies that prioritize good development as their goal instead of PWL can fall victim to two other analytical traps: the phenomena of wearing disciplinary blinders and confusing list making with analysis. The concept of disciplinary blinders is a more sophisticated version of "If you have a hammer, all the world looks like a nail." One's analysis becomes limited to the range of possible remedial responses one might make in regard to a situation. Again, to quote Anderson and Olson, peacebuilding agencies

> do "partial" analysis, shaped, on the one hand, by their expertise as an agency (or individual) and, on the other, by their beliefs about how to bring positive change in conflict settings. That is, peace practitioners in general focus their analysis on where, in a given context, the things they know how to do can be useful and on whether their approach to change fits that particular context.... They rarely examine in detail the broader and developing context or consider concerns that lie beyond their immediate programmatic reach.[14]

Basically, this means that if a development agency that specializes in building rural health clinics looks at a conflict situation, it will tend to focus its analysis for how health clinics would have a positive effect on the conflict and how they might best implement a program of health clinic construction in rural communities. The same dynamic affects other disciplines as well; dialogue facilitators focus their analysis on issues related to doing a dialogue project well, social capital builders look to how to build social capital well, and so forth.

The phenomenon of disciplinary blinders is understandable. For example, if one is going to do a development project, why look at non-development-related aspects of the conflict? The answer should be obvious. These "unrelated" aspects of the conflict or context may have the power to undermine the work one is doing in a specific development sphere. Despite the dangers of disciplinary blinders, there is one strong factor in favor of limiting one's view to a predetermined strategy as opposed to listening and responding to the system. Agencies receive funds from donor organizations to implement specific projects or programs. In this context, an agency might ask, Why should I listen to the system if it might tell me not to do a project that I have already been funded to implement? The question is valid, though a bit distressing, because it points to a structural barrier to implementing an SPA-type assessment. However, it is difficult to argue that "ignorance is bliss" when it comes to avoiding a systems view of a context. Even if one cannot make wholesale changes to one's programming, seeing both a program's effect on the larger social context and the impact of the context on one's program will help avoid obvious pitfalls or perhaps generate alterations to the program that might increase its sustainability.

In response to the dangers of disciplinary blinders, many analytic tools use a checklist approach to force analysts to expand their field of vision. The end product of many of these analyses is a "list of lists," to borrow a phrase coined by the Reflecting on Peace Practice Project (RPP). They try to break a context down into its component parts in order to provide a picture of the whole: "These tools and frameworks outline a range of political, economic and social indicators which, when combined, serve to present a comprehensive picture of the overall conflict risks in a given context."[15] The problem is that such reductionist analyses do not succeed in presenting a picture of the whole. These lists may contain insights into different aspects of a context, but they often do not provide a way of prioritizing factors or shaping action. After filling out checklists that contain dozens of indicators, peacebuilders are left with scores of factors with no way to sort through them and make decisions. "Making lists is not analysis," according to RPP's Diana Chigas.[16]

The first part of the SPA includes tools for doing separate structural, attitudinal, and transactional assessments. However, in order to avoid the problem of getting lost in lists, the SPA helps analysts understand how factors identified on the three lists relate to each other and can be used to make a causal loop diagram (systems map). A systems map can then be used to plan and prioritize action.

CHALLENGE 4: LISTENING EFFECTIVELY TO THE SYSTEM

In sum, the trend in peacebuilding analysis has been either to oversimplify the situation by allowing our disciplinary blinders to block out needed information or, in the name of comprehensiveness, to include unhelpful "everything but the kitchen sink" checklists. To avoid either oversimplifying or drowning in data, the SPA has three critical aspects:

1. To be holistic and avoid the dangers of disciplinary blinders, the SPA breaks the country context down into the structural, attitudinal, and transactional drivers of a society's level of peace.
2. To be systemic and move beyond conflict sensitivity and to avoid the dangers of linear and/or sloppy thinking and confusing list making with analysis, the SPA uses systems diagramming to reconstitute the structural, attitudinal, and transactional factors into a dynamic whole.
3. To assist being both holistic and systemic, the SPA needs to be a living, ongoing, and inclusive process—that is, a planning, acting, and learning (PAL) cycle. The SPA is as much about process as substance. Its value is not in replicating reality but in deepening understanding of a context, sharpening thinking, and testing assumptions and hypotheses about how to be effective. An SPA benefits from inclusion of diverse voices with differing expertise and experiences, from across both disciplines (horizontal integration) and levels of society (vertical integration), which interact with and learn from their environment over time.

Because social systems are so complex, all analytic tools try to make this complexity more comprehensible by focusing the analyst's attention on the most important aspects of a situation. Like a doctor who relies on a limited set of diagnostic tests to understand a patient's general health, a tool for understanding how to make systemic change in a social context needs to rely on a few basic units of analysis. The SPA uses the structural, attitudinal, and transactional domains as those basic analytical units. The SAT model holds that systemic change is driven by changes in these three domains. If this is correct, then these domains can help define why a system is the way it is and thereby hold the key to understanding how it may evolve and change in the future. Breaking a system down into these component parts is intended to force peacebuilders, in a gentle but effective way, to get outside of their comfort zone and assist them in understanding an area that may not be their forte.

Structural Assessment

Structural factors, that is, social systems and institutions meant to meet people's basic human needs, have perhaps the most obvious connection to a society's level of peace. Poor structures almost always affect levels of human development, such as poverty rates, or the health of a society's change mechanisms, such as its courts or other dispute-resolution structures, governance, and so forth. In order to get a better picture of a country's "physical" or structural health, it is necessary to ask how well the basic systems and institutions in the society are meeting people's basic human needs. This is the fundamental question behind the structural assessment. To help answer this basic question, it may be necessary to "step into" the country context further to examine specific structures, such as governance, security, or the economy. To do this, the structural assessment poses a series of more specific diagnostic questions. The SAT model defines seven basic "structures" in a society, and two questions help us better understand each: (1) how well does that structure work to address people's basic human needs (functionality), and (2) do people and groups in the society have access to that structure? Table 5.1 lists some illustrative access and functionality issues (both problems and assets) associated with each of the seven systems.

For example, if looking at the economy, a basic structure intended to meet people's basic human needs for vitality and community, we might notice as fairly common access problems a maldistribution of wealth or a denial of economic opportunity to certain groups. Recurrent functionality problems include high levels of unemployment, deep recessions, or falling commodity prices. On the other hand, societies may also benefit from equal access to economic opportunities for all groups, steady levels of increasing economic

Table 5.1 Illustrative Structural Analysis

Structure	Governance	Security	Economy
Description	Institutions designed to manage issues of common concern *Basic needs addressed: vitality, security, identity*	Institutions that provide safety for people and groups *Basic needs addressed: security, identity*	Markets, capital, means of production needed to allow people to subsist and prosper *Basic needs addressed: vitality, community*
Illustrative access issues	*Problems?* • Ethnic groups denied voting rights *Assets?* • Government is present throughout the country	*Problems?* • Security forces dominated by an ethnic group *Assets?* • Security forces provide equal protection to ethnic groups	*Problems?* • Groups denied access to economic opportunity *Assets?* • Groups enjoy equal economic opportunity
Illustrative functionality issues	*Problems?* • Government inability to deliver basic services • Predatory or discriminatory government practices • Public "bads" • Voter intimidation *Assets?* • Public goods • Strong local governance • High rates of voter participation	*Problems?* • Predatory, inadequate, or oppressive security forces • Criminal violence • Undisciplined armed forces • Former fighters not laying down their arms, ineffective demobilization, disarmament, and reintegration (DDR) *Assets?* • Local citizen watch groups • Professionalized armed forces • Civilian/military cooperation	*Problems?* • Underdevelopment • Grey, illegal markets • Unemployment, recession, inflation • Lack of infrastructure • Falling commodity prices *Assets?* • Strong entrepreneurial spirit • High levels of economic adaptability • Sustained economic growth

Table 5.1 (continued)

Structure	Rule of Law/Human Rights	Social Services	Environment/Natural Resources	Media/Civil Society
Description	Laws, law enforcement, and judicial institutions designed to protect basic rights *Basic needs addressed: community, identity, security*	Institutions such as health care and education that meet primarily noneconomic needs *Basic needs addressed: vitality, community*	Institutions, policies, and practices that affect the physical environment *Basic needs addressed: vitality, security*	Institutions that allow access to information and the formation of interest groups (religious organizations, unions, etc.) *Basic needs addressed: community, identity*
Illustrative access issues	*Problems?* • Groups denied access to courts *Assets?* • Legal system is seen as legitimate	*Problems?* • Unequal distribution of social services *Assets?* • Effective health infrastructure	*Problems?* • Groups excluded from owning land, productive resources *Assets?* • There is shared access to productive resources	*Problems?* • Media controlled by an ethnic group *Assets?* • Groups are able to self-organize
Illustrative functionality issues	*Problems?* • Lawlessness • Human rights abuses • Institutionalized racism • Corruption • Restrictions on social/cultural rights *Assets?* • Vibrant community justice structures • Widespread human rights education • Independent court system	*Problems?* • Lack of a peace dividend • Epidemics, lack of basic health care • Displaced people • Illiteracy, poor educational opportunities *Assets?* • Community self-sufficiency • Strong social safety net • Professional, effective health system • Strong educational system	*Problems?* • Blood diamonds (use of natural resources to fund armed groups) • Land disputes • Elites profiteering off public resources *Assets?* • Use of national resources for public good • Sustainable local land use practices • Effective environmental laws and enforcement	*Problems?* • Hate radio • Limited press freedom • Repression of unions, religious groups • Civil society co-opted by the government *Assets?* • Information–, rumor–management structures • Active, independent press • Freedom of unions, civil society from government interference

growth, highly adaptive local economies, or a social safety net to guard against extreme poverty.

The tool is not an exhaustive list of all potential structural liabilities and assets but, rather, provides prompts to stimulate thinking and help analysts identify important structural factors, especially for those who are not from a development background or who do other structural peacebuilding work. A key question at this point is how one knows if something is a key factor or not? Chapters 2 and 3 made the connection between structural factors and peace and conflict in general, but this does not mean that all structural factors are key factors worthy of inclusion in an SPA. An SPA helps answer the question of relevance in two ways. First, as described below, the process used to do an assessment is a critical safeguard. The more inclusive of diverse participants the process is, especially of indigenous voices, and the more the analysis is updated in light of experience, the better.

As a second relevance check, the SPA asks analysts to give a general assessment of the impact of a particular factor. Since the data gathering part of the SPA is meant to serve as the basis for producing a systems map of a social system, the SPA asks analysts to characterize the nature of the impact that a factor has on other factors and dynamics in the system. In general, a factor can have three potential impacts on its environment[17]:

- *Escalatory:* A factor tends to make things worse or to lower the level of peace. For example, the factor "large populations of displaced people" might be escalatory in that when these populations move to urban areas, they create competition for scare resources and overtax the government's ability to deliver basic services, which in turn lowers the level of peace.
- *Ameliorating:* A factor tends to make things better or to increase the level of peace. For example, a strong local economy might be ameliorating in that the better the local economy becomes, the greater the incentive for cooperation across groups, the lower the potential for violence, and the higher the household income.
- *Stabilizing or stagnating:* A factor tends to counteract escalatory or ameliorating factors. For example, take the factor of "community self-sufficiency." In the Cambodian Interagency Conflict Assessment Framework (ICAF) analysis, community self-sufficiency tended to counteract a potentially escalatory factor: the large number of unemployed garment workers moving from factories in urban areas back to their rural villages. High levels of community self-sufficiency allowed villages to absorb the influx of workers without undo stress. Similarly, poor local governance structures might counteract the potentially ameliorating influence of another factor: government aid flowing to villages. Local conflicts might keep the aid from being spent or lead to aid being siphoned off. In either

case, stabilizing factors work to maintain the status quo, whether in a "positive" way (e.g., by countering the negative influence of an escalatory factor) or in a "negative" way (e.g., by countering the positive influence of an ameliorating factor). Stabilizing or stagnating factors help explain why societies remain stuck or why the status quo persists.

Attitudinal Assessment

An analyst can also step in to better understand a social system by asking, What attitudinal factors affect the society's level of peace? As discussed in Chapters 2 and 3, attitudinal factors go to the shared norms, beliefs, social capital, and intergroup relationships that affect the level of cooperation between groups or people.

In general, attitudinal factors affect the sustainability of the levels of human development in a society. For example, a high poverty rate is more sustainable if it does not give rise to core grievances, such as popular anger or feelings of deprivation. In addition, a society's level of social capital and the types of intergroup dynamics, which affect the ability of people and groups to cooperate, affect healthy processes of change.

Understanding key attitudinal factors is crucial because changing behaviors without changing underlying attitudes will be difficult or impossible, and new structures will be ineffective or even resisted if attitudes remain unchanged. For example, if there is an extreme distrust of government (attitudinal factor), then the creation of a new government or the holding of new elections may not be well received. Similarly, attitudes can also serve as the basis on which to build new structures or encourage new behaviors. For example, a general sense of war weariness among a population can lead to an opportunity for peace talks or support the creation of new structures, like integrated schools or interethnic business cooperatives.

As with the structural analysis, the complexity of social attitudes can be organized in various ways. In order to help focus the attitudinal analysis on important social attitudes, the SAT model looks at three different types of attitudinal factors: core grievances (or how a group sees itself in relation to the larger society), social capital (or attitudes that specifically affect how well groups will cooperate with others outside their group), and intergroup relations (a subset of social capital that comprises intergroup perceptions and dynamics that affect levels of trust between groups).

Identifying key attitudinal factors requires that an analyst first identify significant identity groups in a society. An identity group is any collectivity of people drawn together by a common interest or trait. Although traditionally thought of as ethnic or religious groups (e.g., Kurds or Sunnis in Iraq), identity groups are also defined by gender, age (e.g., Generation X), social standing, or geographic location (e.g., "mountain peoples" or rural versus urban populations). The members of a society determine what counts as an identity group, so it is important not to be constrained by a preset, exclusive list of traits that do or do not qualify.

Core grievances. Perhaps the easiest attitudinal factors to spot are core grievances, which tend to show up as group anger or frustration. Drawing on the definition used in the ICAF, core grievances can be defined as a "deep sense of frustration and injustice that emerges out of [chronically] unmet needs and persistent social patterns."[18] They are distinctive in the attitudinal analysis in that they speak to how a group feels it is being treated by the rest of society. Core grievances alone do not cause violence. However, as stated in the ICAF, key people can mobilize core grievances to exacerbate conflict or incite violence or other action motivated by popular anger. Core grievances are not necessarily directed toward another ethnic group but can be aimed at the government or toward their condition in general. Some common core grievances include the following:

- *Exclusion:* a feeling that the group has been excluded from core social institutions—for example, that members have been denied access to economic or political power.
- *Marginalization:* a feeling that the group's concerns are undervalued or unrecognized by the rest of society. Often, when minority populations live in rural areas far from large cities or the national capital, they feel their concerns are invisible to dominant social groups.
- *Deprivation:* a feeling that resources or other necessities are being affirmatively withheld or taken away from a group. For example, inhabitants of the Niger Delta in Nigeria feel deprived of the region's oil resources without fair compensation by the Nigerian government or foreign oil interests, and this feeling of deprivation has fueled repeated violence.
- *Discrimination:* a feeling that a group is being treated unfairly. For example, the "Troubles" in Northern Ireland were in part born out of a feeling among Catholics of being discriminated against in public housing and by other government policies promulgated by the Protestant majority.
- *Emotional wounds:* traumas or memories of distressing events that are passed down through generations. For example, the fall of Serbian forces to the Ottoman Empire in the 1389 Battle of Kosovo forms a key element in Serbian identity. In more recent times, Serbian leaders used the events of 1389 to assert their claim to what is now an independent Kosovo.

Social capital. The flip side of core grievances are attitudes that work against mobilization of grievances by key people.[19] In the SPA framework, these attitudes are included in the social capital category, which refers to "group norms and beliefs that affect the ability of group members to participate in social structures and cooperate with other groups."[20]

The SPA's use of social capital is both narrower and broader than is commonly associated with the term. In the SPA, social capital does not include structural elements, such as social networks or laws that promote or incentivize cooperation, as these are included in the structural analysis. Core group beliefs that enable or inhibit cooperation or participation in social structures include the following:

- *History of violence versus a tradition of dispute resolution:* If groups perceive their history as glorifying violence or accept its inevitability, then they are more likely to see future violence as acceptable. Conversely, a community with a strong norm of dispute resolution (e.g., through meetings of elders or village courts) is more resilient when faced with provocations. In many communities, years of warfare or outside interference (sometimes in the name of development) can shut down traditional processes of governance and dispute resolution.
- *Rigid group identities versus porous social boundaries:* This refers to the degree to which individuals keep to themselves versus moving freely between their identity group and other groups or institutions in society. For example, is there intermixing in the market, social organizations, schools, marriages, and businesses, or are group members discouraged from associating with people outside their identity group?
- *Value of participation/engagement versus isolation:* This refers to the degree to which groups feel that their individual and collective interests are best served by participating in government or engaging in other forms of social activism versus boycotting those structures.
- *Group adaptivity or openness to change versus resignation:* This refers to a belief that a group, such as a village or family, can adapt and adjust to any circumstance. The feeling of community self-sufficiency that our ICAF team found in Cambodia is a type of community adaptivity. Groups can also have an openness to change fostered by a sense of confidence in their ability to survive or even flourish in hard times. At the other extreme, a sense of war weariness can lead to a feeling that there has to be a better way. A spirit of group self-reliance, coupled with neglect from the broader society, can lead to a feeling of resignation, that a group should accept its fate, however dire, or that there is little hope for improvement in its condition. In the Democratic Republic of the Congo,

Mt. Nyiragongo erupted in 2002, and lava from the volcano destroyed major parts of Goma, the capital of North Kivu Province. After living through years of war, atrocities, epidemics, and other natural disasters, residents of Goma felt as though the 2002 eruption was "just our fate."

• *Mistrust versus trust:* Perhaps the most important group norm or belief is whether one group feels that it can trust other groups or social institutions. Trust exists on a continuum from minimal levels, where a group trusts that other groups are not out to harm them, to more maximal levels, where a group believes that other groups or social institutions will actually work to protect and fulfill their core interests and needs.

Intergroup relations. Because the level of trust or mistrust between groups has such an important impact on group cooperation and participation in society, the category of intergroup relations is meant to expand on how to assess drivers of this factor. How members of one group perceive members of a different group is a core determinant of trust. For example, if members of one group see those of another in a complex and nuanced fashion, they are less likely to interpret actions by that group as necessarily hostile, even when a hostile intention is a possibility.

An example from the former Soviet Union in the early 1990s can help illustrate the point. In the northern Caucasus, where a number of ethnic groups have fought with each other over the centuries, a motorist from one ethnic group hit and killed a child from a different ethnic group in a traffic accident. This happened during a period when overall relations between the groups were tense. The incident could have been viewed as an unfortunate accident, in which the driver did not mean to kill the child. Even if evidence indicated that this particular driver meant to hit the child, he could have been viewed as a lone nutcase. Both these interpretations would reflect a more nuanced view of the driver and the group to which he belonged—a belief that neither this person nor any one person represented the intentions or actions of all the other members of his ethnic group. Better still, there could have been a belief that the overall intentions of the one group toward the other were positive, and the accident could have been viewed as a tragedy for both groups. However, because tensions between the groups had been escalating and the level of trust was low, the incident was viewed as an attack on the child's ethnic group by the ethnic group of the driver. The driver was hauled out of his car and severely beaten by a mob from the rival ethnic group.

In addition to some common "perceptual biases" that affect the level of trust among groups, there are also identifiable patterns of behavior, or intergroup dynamics, that shape, almost predetermine, how one group will react to the actions of another group. As a guide for people doing an attitudinal analysis of a context, the SPA breaks out a few different intergroup perceptual biases and dynamics that greatly affect the ability of groups to trust each other. Often these perceptual biases or dynamics serve as a justification for extreme actions, even violence, by group members against a rival group. Some common intergroup perceptual biases include the following:

- *Reactive devaluation:* This refers to the tendency of a group to discount actions or statements by a rival group, especially when they run counter to the perceiving group's dominant perceptions of the rival. For example, at the height of the US-Soviet arms race, the United States made a radical proposal to eliminate all intermediate-range nuclear weapons from Europe (known as the Zero Option). The Soviets initially rejected the proposal, but after Mikhail Gorbachev came to power, they reversed their position. However, hawks in the US administration dismissed the Soviet acceptance of the Zero Option as a trick and further sign of their evil intentions. Reactive devaluation can cause a group to dismiss or even punish conciliatory behavior from a rival group, such as an invitation to negotiate or other confidence-building measures.

- *Dehumanization:* A group perceives members of a rival group as less than human; thus, actions against them are excluded from norms of justice, fairness, or morality. Chapter 3 offers an example of how militant Hutus used dehumanization of Tutsis in Rwanda (e.g., calling them cockroaches) to convince others that killing them was not morally wrong.

- *Mythmaking and stereotyping:* In a less dramatic fashion than dehumanization, racism, mythmaking, and stereotyping by members of one group can excuse them from taking a complex, nuanced view of members of other groups in society. For example, in the United States, the stereotype of Muslim men in the Middle East as violent leads some Americans to see Muslim men in their communities as hostile or dangerous.

- *Fundamental attribution error:* Similar to reactive devaluation, this dynamic involves a group's misinterpreting the intent behind the actions of a rival group. There is a tendency for one group to interpret the behavior of a rival group as evidence of bad intentions. For example, in 2006, I was cofacilitating a negotiation-training session in Iraq for secular, Sunni, and Shia politicians. In one exercise, the large group was voting on ideas generated by several smaller groups. The ideas were posted on flip charts, and each person voted for the five ideas he or she liked the best. Because the training was being conducted in the Green Zone, which made commuting to and from the workshop precarious, the group was down to only one Shia politician on the second day of the training. When this lone Shia politician announced that she wanted to put all five of her votes on the list of ideas her group had developed, there was a loud response. One Sunni politician said, "This is why Iraq is in crisis—Shia think they know best, and only they have good ideas!" Others followed suit. The Sunni politicians made an assumption, consistent with their stereotype of Shia politicians, that the Shia lawmaker's intention was to prove Shia were smarter than Sunni. My cofacilitator, David Seibel, intervened to ask the group to reflect on the different possible intentions behind the politician's votes. The group members came around to realizing that they had jumped to a conclusion based on a stereotype that did not necessarily reflect reality. In fact, many agreed that the ideas on the Shia politician's list were better formulated than similar ideas on other lists.

The following are common intergroup dynamics:

- *Victim-oppressor relations:* A group consistently sees itself as a victim and a rival ethnic group as the oppressor. For example, in Rwanda, minority ethnic Tutsis tend to see themselves as the victims of oppression by the Hutu majority. Interestingly, a group does not need to be in the minority to feel victimized. Hutus in Rwanda saw themselves as victims of Tutsi dominance during Rwanda's colonial period. Similarly, Greek Cypriots, a majority on Cyprus, see themselves as a minority as compared to the Turks on Cyprus plus the Turks living in neighboring Turkey.
- *Action-reaction escalation cycle:* Chapter 2 describes the action-reaction cycle that was the US-Soviet arms race. Groups in general can get caught in an increasing cycle of attack and retaliation. I remember listening to the story of a former member of a Protestant paramilitary in Northern Ireland in the summer of 2004. He explained that he had joined because some of his relatives had died in a bombing conducted by Catholic paramilitaries. He in turn carried out several attacks on Catholic populations before he was caught, tried, and incarcerated. In prison he realized that his struggle had been for naught: His use of violence against Catholics to avenge their killing of Protestants only served to create more Catholic paramilitaries who killed Protestants.
- *Competition for scarce resources:* A group sees itself locked into a life-or-death competition for needed resources, such as land and water, and views the actions of other groups as a continuation of this struggle. In Rwanda, intense land usage and scarcity of arable land for subsistence farming heightened conflict between Hutus and Tutsis. The conflict in Darfur, Sudan, also involves competition between farming and grazing groups for control of land.
- *Relative negation:* In an even more intense version of the competition for scarce resources, a group sees the existence of a rival group as incompatible with its own survival. This zero-sum mentality says both groups

cannot live in the same space. Some experts claim that many Israelis and Palestinians see their struggle in this way: The land they each claim cannot support both groups, and for one to exist, the other must cease to exist, or its continued existence poses a necessary threat to the first group's survival.[21]

- *Generational and gender gaps.* Most, if not all, societies have some form of generation gap, where the views of a younger segment of the population are seen as markedly different from those of an older segment. The same can be said of gender groups where the statuses of men and women differ markedly. Sometimes the differences are so extreme as to seem irreconcilable, and a person's age or gender plays a dominant role in shaping his or her thinking and behavior.

As with the structural assessment, I have used a tool to help analysts identify potentially important attitudinal factors, organized according to the categories described above, that affect the level of peace in the social system in which they are working. Like that for structural assessment, the attitudinal assessment tool asks users to characterize the impact of a given attitudinal factor as either escalatory, ameliorating, or stabilizing/stagnating.

Transactional Assessment

Transactional peacebuilding refers to the processes and skills used by key people to peacefully manage conflict, build interpersonal relationships, solve problems, and turn ideas into action. The SPA's analysis of the transactional domain is probably its biggest departure from traditional assessment instruments. Some assessment tools simply overlook transactional factors in favor of more conventional structural issues. Others, however, deliberately deprioritize transactional factors. Many conflict assessment instruments distinguish between "root causes" and "triggers" of violence. The distinction is valid in that some drivers of violence are more proximate. The chain of events between a factor and violence is much shorter for triggers than for root causes. For example, in Rwanda in 1994, extremist Hutu leaders rallied their supporters to kill Tutsis and moderate Hutus (a transactional factor). The actions of these ethnic-conflict entrepreneurs can be classified as triggers of the genocide, while the history of Hutu-Tutsi tensions (an attitudinal factor) and several years of a deteriorating economy (a structural factor) can be classified as root causes.

However, some approaches take the distinction between triggers and root causes too far by arguing that peacebuilders should focus on root causes and not triggers. Most triggering factors would rightly be classified as transactional factors, while most root causes would usually be considered structural or attitudinal factors. If the SAT theory is correct, and violence (or peace) is driven by a dynamic interplay between or among transactional, attitudinal, and structural factors, then discounting the importance of transactional factors is likely be counterproductive.

Therefore, no attempt at a comprehensive but useful context analysis is complete without a transactional assessment. A transactional analysis differs, however, from both structural and attitudinal analyses. Structural and attitudinal assessments are substantive and are conducted relative to the context as a whole. More of a process analysis, the transactional assessment is done relative to the results of the structural and attitudinal analyses. The transactional analysis asks, How are key people dealing with key structural and attitudinal issues in a particular context? To help answer this fundamental question, the analysis has three steps:

1. Make a list of key structural and attitudinal factors based on those assessments (as described above).
2. Identify key people, as defined below, relative to those key issues.
3. Understand how those key people are dealing with those key issues.

Step 1: Key factors. Based on the factors identified in the structural and attitudinal analyses, make a list of the factors that seem most important (e.g., that seem to have the most significant impacts on the level of peace). There is no hard-and-fast guideline for how many factors to include in this list. It is more important that the process of selecting them be participatory and include the "gut" assessments of a diverse group of analysts as well as hard data. It is helpful to include factors, though certainly not in equal numbers, that are categorized as escalatory, ameliorating, and stabilizing in the structural and attitudinal analyses.

Step 2: Key people. There are many ways to define who is a key person in a given context. The following criteria, based on USAID assessment tools and Anderson and Olson's *Confronting War: Critical Lessons for Peace Practitioners* (2003), are helpful for assessing who the key people are in a particular situation:

- *People who have influence over the behavior, opinions, or attitudes of others.* They can make decisions or take actions that will affect the behavior of larger groups of people. This may be because of their position in a hierarchy (e.g., as prime minister, sheik, bishop, etc.) or because of more intangible assets (e.g., their perceived legitimacy, intelligence, experience, etc.) regardless of their formal position.
- *People who are necessary in order to take some important action (e.g., reach a cease-fire) or without whom it is impossible, or much more difficult, to take action (e.g., the person is a potential spoiler).*

- *People who have access to needed or critical resources.*
- *People who other people think are key people.* One independently valid criterion is who others in the social context think are key people, for whatever reason.

Key people also change over time. As circumstances change in a conflict, a person previously not seen as key, as measured by these or other factors, may become so as circumstances change. It is also possible to see key people across John Paul Lederach's Pyramid of Leadership. Key people can be found in villages, regions, and provinces or at the national level. They can also be international players, such as a special representative of the UN secretary-general, the head of a multinational corporation, or an NGO's country director.

An important check on your lists of key people and important structural and attitudinal factors is to ask generally who strikes you as a key person in the given context. If you select someone who is not key to dealing with one of the important structural or attitudinal factors, then ask, Is this person important or essential for dealing with a certain issue? Based on the answer to that question, an analyst may need to expand the list of important structural and attitudinal factors.

Step 3: Key interactions between key people and key issues. In the SAT model, the interaction over time between transactional factors (the behavior of key people) and structural and attitudinal factors drives systems change. To help identify those key interactions, it is useful to look for three different types of transactional factors:

- *Disabling or enabling dynamics:* These either prevent key people from, or assist them in, dealing with key structural and attitudinal factors. They may include internal dynamics (e.g., group divisions that impede decision making, strong consensus-building processes that enable decision making, levels of organizational cohesion), skills (e.g., weak or strong negotiation and communication skills), relationships (e.g., strong, collaborative, trust-based relationships between key people can increase their ability to deal with difficult issues just as bad relationships impede that ability), and processes (e.g., the presence or absence of negotiation processes, poorly versus well-structured or well-facilitated negotiation processes).
- *Exacerbating dynamics:* These are things that key people do to exacerbate structural or attitudinal issues, such as exploiting group tensions for personal gain, profiteering (e.g., elites who perpetuate a conflict so that they can continue illegally trafficking in drugs or natural resources), or engaging in corruption. Actions that key people take to prevent a situation from improving can also be included here.

- *Ameliorating dynamics:* These are things that key people do to help address or ameliorate structural and attitudinal factors, such as mobilizing resilience (e.g., encouraging groups to resist provocations to violence or organizing to peacefully address group needs) or promoting cooperation or reconciliation between groups. Stabilizing impacts, such as preventing a situation from getting worse, can also be included here.

Identifying the key ways that transactional factors interact with structural and attitudinal factors helps those conducting an SPA to pull all the various parts of a social system together by showing the dynamic interrelationships among them.

THE PROCESS OF LISTENING TO A SYSTEM

At a smaller meeting on the applicability of systems thinking and peace-building hosted by the Institute for Conflict Analysis and Resolution at George Mason University, an expert who specializes in more mathematically precise uses of systems modeling compared the kind of systems mapping used in the SPA to performance art. He made a subtle but fundamental point: The value of systems mapping as part of the SPA is not the map itself but the process of interaction that the analysis and systems-mapping exercise provokes.

An SPA process (or performance art) is better to the degree that it involves a diversity of perspectives. As the story about the meeting on Guinea-Bissau in Chapter 2 illustrates, each person brings to a meeting his or her own perspectives, priorities, and experiences. All participants have their own theory of change, which filters how they collect and interpret information. For example, a fireman may see smoke coming out of a building as a sign of fire danger, while an electrician might see faulty wiring as an early warning sign of fire danger. In terms of the SAT model, a structural peacebuilder is more likely to see ways that particular structural variables affect the level of peace in a society, while a transactional peacebuilder will see a different set of disliked symptoms. The analysis is better for involving these and other diverse perspectives. This is the idea of horizontal integration in the analysis process. Ideally, an SPA will bring together people with expertise or experience in the structural, attitudinal, and transactional domains, in addition to practitioners from diverse disciplines (e.g., economics, anthropology, engineering, health sciences, communication, social psychology, etc.).

Different people also have their own networks of relationships and experiences with regard to a conflict; in turn, this means they will have access to different information. Again, increasing the amount and diversity of available information will improve the process. It is especially important to be sure that local voices have a central role. This may seem obvious, but too often they are left out of analyses done by international actors. Including actors from each of Lederach's three levels (national, regional, and local), as well as international experts, provides a necessary degree of vertical integration to the analytical process.

Further, an SPA needs to be treated as an ongoing process. Like any assessment, it is a snapshot of a moving train: As soon as it has been taken, the situation on the ground changes. So, an SPA needs to be undated in light of new information and changing circumstances. Similarly, an SPA is a hypothesis, not an exact replica of the society in question. It is meant to simplify reality in a way that captures key dynamics. An SPA should reduce the complexity of a given situation in a way that produces actionable knowledge (e.g., informed and well-crafted policy and programmatic responses). And as part of the PAL program cycle, the SPA needs to be a living document.

In a way, an SPA is like a subway map. A good subway map does not replicate reality (it does not show every change in grade, tunnel, or wall tile); rather, it highlights the relevant information that will help riders achieve their ends (or get them where they want to go). Like a subway map, a systems map of a situation (part of an SPA) represents an educated guess that the "blue-line train" will lead from station X (e.g., a particular driver of a conflict) to one's final destination (e.g., Peace Writ Large). Each experience applying the SPA provides useful feedback—for instance, that the blue line is a dead end (e.g., our program did not get us the result we wanted). Experience from peacebuilding projects will then provide confirming or disconfirming information about initial assumptions, and that information needs to be fed back into the planning process.

Lastly, just as it is important to disaggregate a context into its transactional, attitudinal, and structural parts, it is equally important to put them back together into a dynamic system that shows how these factors affect each other and ultimately the level of peace (or other problem variable). Systems diagramming or mapping is an essential tool for this. This exercise can be very difficult, even overwhelming, for those new to systems work, but the SPA tool includes processes for building up systems maps. Chapter 6 provides guidance on how to create a causal loop diagram, or systems map, from the structural, attitudinal, and transactional analyses.

CHAPTER 5 SUMMARY

- The SPA is a major change from conflict-sensitive analysis.
- The goal of an SPA is to support the building of Peace Writ Large (as opposed to good development), and it starts with a holistic question: What factors drive a social system's level of peace?

- In order to avoid bad analytical habits and capture complexity without oversimplifying, an SPA focuses attention on the key structural, attitudinal, and transactional factors that affect the level of peace in a society.
- The process of conducting an SPA is as important as the outcome and requires the inclusion of voices that ensure both vertical (across levels of society) and horizontal (across domains and disciplines) integration.
- An SPA is a living process that must be updated in light of experience.
- An SPA is not complete without a systems map based on an analysis of the key structural, attitudinal, and transactional factors.

CHAPTER **6**

SYSTEMS MAPPING
PUTTING IT ALL TOGETHER

↤

The notion that all these fragments are separately existent is evidently an
illusion, and this illusion cannot do other than lead to endless conflict
and confusion.

—David Bohm

In March 2009, I was part of a US government interagency team composed
of participants from the US Department of Defense, US State Department,
and US Agency for International Development, which traveled to Cambodia to do the first field application of the Interagency Conflict Assessment
Framework (ICAF). The ICAF team's "client" was the US Embassy in
Phnom Penh and, specifically, Ambassador Carol Rodley, a career Foreign
Service officer and an expert on Cambodia. When our ICAF team arrived in
Cambodia, Ambassador Rodley served notice that she would be a skeptical
audience. She had found previous ICAF reports to be a bit dense and not
overly helpful. Over the next three weeks, the core ICAF team of eleven people fanned out across Cambodia, interviewed hundreds of people, attended
conferences, and collected dozens of reports. All of this information, plus
weeks of pretrip desk research and interviews with specialists in the United
States, was processed into a report for the ambassador. The presentation to
her revolved around several systems maps. After the presentation, she noted
that when we first put up the systems maps, her eyes had started to glaze

over a bit, but in the end she found the maps and the report in general to be very helpful.

I like this story because it captures both the potential downside and the potential upside of systems mapping. On the one hand, many people find systems maps to be an incomprehensible mess of words and squiggly lines. In fact, a report on systems thinking prepared for the Organization for Economic Cooperation and Development noted, "One slightly depressing stream of thought in systems thinking puts forward the view that many systems are now so huge and so complex, e.g. the US health care system, the global economy, the European Union—that mere mortals can no longer understand them."[1] If even looking at systems maps can cause people's eyes to glaze over, just imagine the resistance of some to drawing them. To paraphrase the old saying, If systems diagramming were so easy, everyone would be doing it.

However, as the chapter epigraph by David Bohm suggests (not to mention Part I of this book), getting a systems view is unavoidable if one hopes to be effective in dealing with complex and messy realities. The Cambodian ICAF experience illustrates how systems mapping can distill mounds of diverse data and perceptions into a rich picture (to use Peter Checkland's term) that tells a compelling story about a complex social system, like Cambodia. My guess is that, had our ICAF team presented the ambassador with lists of all the data that went into the creation of our systems maps, her eyes would have glazed over completely.

This chapter addresses the critical question of how to draw a systems map based on an analysis of a social context, like the structural, attitudinal, and transactional (SAT) analyses of the Systemic Peacebuilding Assessment (SPA) described in Chapter 5. It should be noted that while the SAT tools are specifically designed to support the drawing of a holistic systems map, systems mapping can be used to integrate findings arrived at using other analytical tools. For example, in Cambodia we used systems mapping to integrate findings from the ICAF tool. In either case, a systems map is only as good as the assessment on which it is based. Analytical frameworks that are not holistic and systemic, as described in Chapter 5, will not produce a useful systems map. Said another way, just because an analysis takes the form of a systems map does not necessarily mean that one is going to get a systemic view of the context. The underlying analysis has to avoid bad habits, especially disciplinary blinders, in order to produce a good map.

Further, it is important not to overemphasize the importance of the map itself. Although creating a systems map is critical in that it allows one to "listen to the system," the physical map is less important than the process and quality of analysis that precedes it, the quality of the interaction that produces it, and the ongoing nature of the planning, acting, and learning that goes on after the initial map is produced (e.g., the process of redrawing the map over time). So, while it is critical to develop the skill of drawing a systems map, it is also critical to appreciate and nurture the process that produces it. Recall the image from Chapter 5 of systems mapping as performance art: The process is not about re-creating reality or even about the map itself; it is about the process of dialogue and learning that goes into producing a map. The group act of drawing a systems map requires participants to discuss their perceptions, assumptions, and beliefs about the social context they are studying. The discussion makes them set priorities (e.g., what is important and why) and requires them to make their implicit assumptions about cause and effect explicit. It is a check on each person's unconscious filters and theories of change; it makes participants decide what to include in the map and what not (e.g., what gets represented in the map and what goes into the narrative they tell based on it).

SYSTEMS MAPPING PART I: STEPPING BACK

While the process of mapping is more important than the map itself, the single most challenging part of an SPA is physically drawing a systems map. To give an example, I will refer to an abbreviated SPA and systems-mapping exercise that I participated in with a senior country team from Mercy Corps, an international NGO that had been working in Afghanistan for over two decades.[2] Although the purpose of the workshop was to introduce the idea of systemic peacebuilding, as opposed to producing an effective systems map of Afghanistan, it does provide a useful, concrete example of how to do causal loop diagramming. Compared to an ideal SPA, the two-day workshop had many shortcomings: too little time devoted to systems mapping and the lack of a more scientific research and data-gathering effort. The group consisted of senior Afghan and expatriate staff from a variety of nationalities but did not have sufficient vertical integration (e.g., the group consisted of regional directors but did not include enough local voices); nor did it have sufficient horizontal integration (e.g., the group consisted primarily of structural peacebuilders).

After a "miniteach" on systemic peacebuilding and the SAT model, the group did an abbreviated version of a structural, attitudinal, and transactional assessment of Afghanistan. Part I of this volume introduced the definition, by George Richardson, of a systems view as "stepping back" just far enough to blur discrete events into patterns of behavior. In the Mercy Corps session, this meant bringing together people who had decades', if not lifetimes', worth of experience in Afghanistan and asking them to step back from it. Looking at Afghanistan through the lens of the three SPA analytic categories was the first exercise in "stepping back" from the complexity that was each person's view of that country.

The fifteen participants split into subgroups, and each did a structural, attitudinal, and transactional analysis. After reporting their groups' findings, the participants had identified 101 factors (47 structural, 21 attitudinal, and 33 transactional) that they felt affected the level of peace in Afghanistan. The factors were recorded on flip charts, which ended up covering a large wall in the meeting room. This process fills another key role, which is to facilitate information sharing among the participants in an assessment process. This is especially important for teams that split up to do interviews with people in the society they are studying. Each data collector has developed a unique view of the situation and needs to share this perspective with others on his or her assessment team.

The next exercise in stepping back is for analysts to sort or process the information they gather. This process is critical because it helps analysts move from generating particular data (e.g., through field interviews, quantitative studies, and expert input) to defining a group of key factors that may ultimately end up in their systems map of the context they are studying. Essentially, participants can use two criteria to identify key factors out of a larger pool of data: *prevalence,* or the degree to which a factor or data point appears over and over again, and *salience,* or the power or importance of a factor in the eyes of interviewees or experts.

There are various processes for doing this information sharing and information processing. In Cambodia, we did a "headlines" exercise in which each member of the study team, after returning from two weeks of data gathering, wrote out headlines for the most important things they thought they had learned. A headline might be something like "high degree of community self-sufficiency" or "patron-client politics." Participants could write out as many headlines as they wanted on a large Post-it note, including a few bullet points elaborating on the data on which the headline was based and discussing significance. The Post-its were put up on a wall and grouped by theme. Affinity diagramming is another common process by which a large number of ideas can be grouped around a few themes and then consolidated (see Chapter 9).

In the Mercy Corps case, the participants voted on which of the 101 factors they identified as the most important. Voting on factors or developing headlines may seem like a terribly unscientific way to do analysis. Certainly, a quantitative analysis that coded then analyzed each group's (or each person's) findings would provide a more exact interpretation of the data collected. However, with limited time and resources, this kind of analysis is often not possible at present, though there is the potential to create specialized software tools. Moreover, even a user-friendly, field-use-ready quantitative analytical tool cannot substitute completely for a more subjective and interactive analysis like the headlines exercise. A quantitative analysis may seem determinative, but it does not necessarily cause participants to surface their implicit assumptions and unconscious biases. Good information as the basis for decision making is critical, but it may be as important to have good intergroup dynamics and effective dialogue among the people who will act on and live with the analysis. Moreover, good data and hard analysis cannot overcome poor intergroup relationships, bad communication, and flawed decision-making processes.

The importance of the dialogue process created by these subjective, qualitative analyses means that the diversity of voices created by horizontal and vertical integration among the participants in the analysis is critical. In order to capture the benefit of a diversity of perspectives, there is a need to invest in managing group dynamics, such as avoiding groupthink or domination of the discussion by a few voices (e.g., the views of expatriate staff or those higher in a hierarchy silencing local voices or those of field staff) (see Chapter 9).

Affinity diagramming, headlining, voting, and other processes (or some combination) help groups step back even further from the minutia of their particularized analysis. The Mercy Corps Afghanistan country team reduced its list of 101 factors down to 15:

- *Structural:*
  - Lawlessness
  - Drug (illicit) economy
  - Educational opportunities
  - Economy
- *Structural/attitudinal:*
  - Insecurity
  - Lack of voice for communities
- *Attitudinal:*
  - Unmet expectations
  - Rural versus urban divide
- *Attitudinal/transactional:*
  - Ethnic tensions/politics
- *Transactional:*
  - Conflict in communities
  - Active armed groups
  - Divided government
- *Transactional/structural:*
  - Corrupt/ineffective government
  - International interference
  - Lack of infrastructure, resources, and skills

Some of these factors fall squarely into one of the three domains. For example, "lawlessness" is a structural factor, "unmet expectations" is an attitudinal factor, and "divided government" is a transactional factor. Others represent crossover factors, such as "international interference," which is both structural in that it represents an illegal arms trade and transactional in that key external actors (e.g., the United States or Pakistan) use their influence to affect the conflict in Afghanistan. "Insecurity" represents both physical insecurity (structural) and psychological feelings of insecurity (attitudinal). The factor "ethnic tensions/politics" represents both difficult intergroup relations (attitudinal) and the manipulation of ethnicity to further the agendas of some key people (transactional).

The categorization of the factors matters less than the group's having a clear idea of why each factor is significant. More importantly, it is useful to do a holism check to ensure that structural, attitudinal, and transactional factors are represented in the map to help avoid the danger of disciplinary blinders. In the Mercy Corps case, where participants were drawn entirely from a structural peacebuilding background, the danger was that the group would only see or prioritize structural factors in its analysis.

SYSTEMS MAPPING PART II: CREATING A MAP

Winnowing a long list down to a dozen or so key factors still leaves an analyst with a static, unconnected list of parts, the equivalent of the pieces of a disassembled car engine spread out on the floor of a garage. Creating a map is like reassembling the engine to see how it runs. A systems map helps to explore the interconnections between the factors and to provide one image that captures several component parts. The map begins to express how that whole is more than just the sum of its parts. This is the opposite of a reductionist approach, which breaks a whole up into smaller pieces so that one can more closely examine each.

The Basics

It is difficult to convey the idea of a dynamic systems map using a linear delivery vehicle (e.g., words on a page), especially to someone who has never seen or worked with one before. Chapter 4 contains a fairly simple example of a systems map. These maps are also known as causal loop diagrams because they capture two important features that make up a system: causal relationships and dynamic feedback. The map uses a simple convention—an arrow connecting two factors—to denote a causal relationship. For example, Figure 6.1 depicts an arrow connecting *Active armed groups* and *Insecurity.* This diagram is meant to show that active armed groups affect the level of insecurity in Afghanistan. This simple convention is the basic building block of a systems map. In this case, the arrow is meant to show that the more the activity of armed groups increases, the higher the level of insecurity becomes. Arrows connecting two factors can also mean that more of one factor means less of another. In Figure 6.1, the arrow connecting *Insecurity* and *Economy* is meant to indicate that the higher the level of insecurity, the worse the state of the economy.

There are various ways to distinguish whether an arrow indicates a parallel cause-and-effect relationship (e.g., the more of one factor, the more of another factor or the less of one factor, the less of another factor) or an opposite cause-and-effect relationship (e.g., the more of one factor, the less of another or the less of one factor, the more of another). As shown in Figure 6.1, the symbols "+/+" or "–/–" can be added next to an arrow to denote a parallel relationship, and "+/–" or "–/+" can be used to denote an opposite cause-and-effect relationship.[3]

Another way to represent the nature of the cause-and-effect relationships is to describe the nature of the dynamic feedback loop(s) of which a factor is a part. As described in Chapter 2, a central premise of systems thinking is dynamic causality, or the notion that any part of a system acts as both a cause and an effect. The impact of any one factor reverberates around the system until it comes back, in one form or another, to affect the factor that made

Figure 6.1 Basic System Mapping Tools

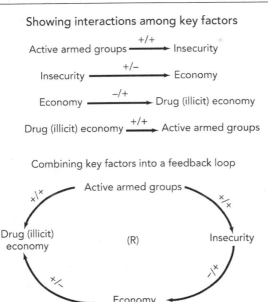

Showing interactions among key factors

Active armed groups —— +/+ ——▶ Insecurity

Insecurity —— +/– ——▶ Economy

Economy —— –/+ ——▶ Drug (illicit) economy

Drug (illicit) economy —— +/+ ——▶ Active armed groups

Combining key factors into a feedback loop

SPA: Afghanistan Systems Map 2007.

the initial impact. Dynamic feedback is represented as a loop. For example, a basic causal loop in Afghanistan involves the connection between four factors: *Insecurity, Active armed groups*, the *Economy*, and the *Drug (illicit) economy*. As Figure 6.1 shows, the loop comprises four causal relationships between pairs of these factors.

In addition to the connection between active armed groups and insecurity, the higher the level of insecurity, the worse the economy; the worse the economy, the greater the economy for drugs and other illicit trade (a "−/+" relationship); and the greater the illicit or drug economy, the stronger the active armed groups (a "+/+" relationship). As shown in Figure 6.1, connecting these four causal dynamics creates a feedback loop.

Feedback loops are of two different fundamental natures: reinforcing and balancing. In a reinforcing feedback loop, if one traces an initial causal impact around the loop, then that initial causal impact gets reinforced or amplified. For example, if the activity of armed groups increases, the level of insecurity increases, which worsens the economy. A worsening economy increases the level of the drug (illicit) economy, which in turn increases, or amplifies, the activity of armed groups, and this kicks off another reinforcing cycle around the feedback loop. The feedback from the initial increase in activity of armed groups further increases the activity of armed groups. The feedback loop acts as a kind of amplifier for the initial condition. This is the definition of a reinforcing loop. Reinforcing loops are denoted by placing an (R) in the loop, as in Figure 6.1.

This lets the reader of the map know that, in total, the nature of the feedback loop is a parallel relationship. Reinforcing loops can be escalatory, like the armed groups–insecurity loop, or ameliorating, meaning that with each circuit around the feedback loop, a positive change is amplified or reinforced. For example, if the activity of armed groups decreases, then presumably this will lead to decreasing levels of insecurity, an improving economy, and so on.

It is also worth noting that a reinforcing loop does not mean that each individual causal relationship in the loop is parallel (e.g., that more of one factor means more of the second factor), even though the loop as a whole functions that way. The armed groups–insecurity loop contains both parallel and opposite causal relationships. However, it is a reinforcing loop because the number of opposite causal relationships is even (two). If there were an odd number, the loop would be a balancing feedback loop, meaning that whatever the initial causal impact, the feedback loop would serve to counteract that impact. For example, a classic balancing feedback loop is a thermostat for a heating system. If the thermostat is set at a desired temperature of sixty-eight degrees Fahrenheit, and the actual temperature of the room drops to sixty-two degrees (the initial causal impact), then the thermostat detects a gap between the desired room temperature and the actual room temperature.

This is an opposite ("−/+") causal relationship because the lower the room temperature, the bigger the gap between the actual and desired temperatures. If a gap is detected (the room is colder than desired), then the thermostat triggers the production of hot air (a "+/+" relationship because the bigger the gap, the more production of hot air). The more hot air is produced, the warmer the room gets ("+/+"). This is represented in Figure 6.2.

This is a balancing loop because the initial causal impact, the room getting colder, is counteracted by the system. If the room gets colder, the system works to warm the room until the desired temperature is attained. And, as is consistent with the definition of a causal loop, there is an odd number of opposite causal relationships: there are two parallel causal relationships ("+/+") and one opposite causal relationship ("−/+").

In the context of a social system, a more common balancing loop explains why powerful regimes maintain their hold on power despite potential challenges from political opposition groups (see Figure 6.2). The more effective political opposition groups become, the weaker the political elite's hold on power ("+/−" causal relationship). But the weaker the elite's hold on power, then the more they use repressive state means (politically motivated arrests, control of the media and courts) to undermine the opposition ("−/+"). And the greater the elite's control by means of state repression, the weaker the political opposition ("+/−"). One circuit around the loop counters the initial causal impact; that is, if the political opposition becomes more effective, the system responds by undermining its effectiveness.

How one represents the nature of the cause-and-effect relationships is an issue of clarity for the person(s) reading the map and/or the ease of the

Figure 6.2 Balancing Loops in Power Relations

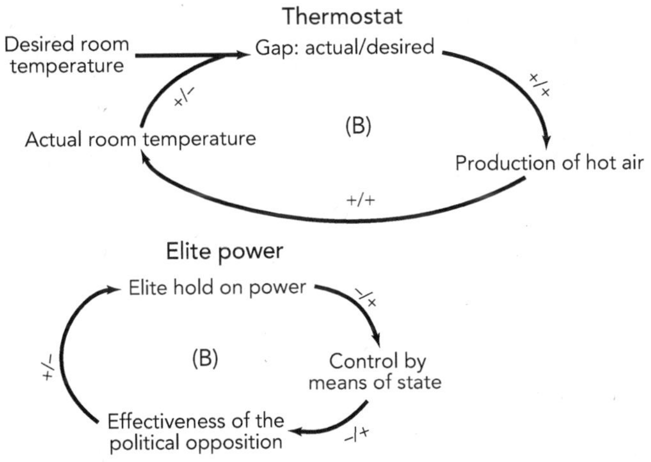

person(s) drawing it. When a systems map becomes more elaborate and more cluttered, there is a need to reduce the number of symbols and words, so it is usually not feasible to mark each arrow with a "+/+" symbol (or the like). But while it may not be possible to use the "+/+" symbols for each arrow in the map, using them at the early stages of drawing a map is usually helpful to keep track of the feedback dynamics as they are developed.

Getting Started

Perhaps the hardest part of drawing a system map is deciding where to start. One advantage of a linear model is that it presents a clear place to start and stop. When working with systems, there is no one clear place to begin. The purpose of systems mapping in the SPA is to produce a mental image of the factors and patterns of behavior that contribute to the level of peace in a society. One place to start is to ask, What factor seems to have the most salient impact on the level of peace? While this question might start a heated discussion, it is critical that group members make explicit and discuss their assumptions about why certain factors are important and then pick a factor with which to begin.

Also, while it is essential to work as a group to discuss what factors, interconnections, and dynamics are reflected in a systems map, there is often a need to jump back and forth between holding a larger group discussion and having one person or a small subgroup actually produce a draft of a map. Drafting a map is like the "one-text" mediation process where, after an initial consultation with a larger group, a drafting team produces a draft of an agreement (e.g., a "one text").[4] The draft is then shown to the stakeholders, who comment on how it could be improved. After consulting broadly, the drafting team produces a second draft, which serves as the basis for another round of consultations, and so on, until a consensus emerges or time runs out. In Cambodia, the ICAF team went through seven formal drafts of our main systems map (and many more informal drafts) after three days of intense work as a large group to define the main factors we would include in the map and the interconnections between them.

In the Afghanistan workshop, we did not have enough time to work as a team on producing a systems map using the fifteen key factors the group identified. Instead, the group split into three subgroups, and each produced an initial draft of a system. Comparing and contrasting the three maps helped surface and test assumptions within the group about how these factors interrelated to produce the current status quo in Afghanistan. The Afghanistan systems maps that I use as examples here are a compilation of the three different maps.

"Loopify" Causal Factors

However the group is organized, the easiest way to start drafting a systems map is to pick a key factor and draw an initial causal relationship. This is an inductive approach to building up a causal loop diagram. A systems map consists of multiple dynamic feedback loops. Because it is impossible to draw multiple, fully formed, and interconnected feedback loops, this approach starts by picking a causal relationship and then trying to uncover the feedback loop(s) of which it is a part. For example, the Mercy Corps group identified three factors that they felt had a significant impact on the level of peace in Afghanistan: corrupt, ineffective government; insecurity; and the economy. Assume that the group picked corrupt, ineffective government as the key factor to start with. One can ask two questions to define an initial causal relationship:

- What impact does that factor have? (Or what other factor on the list of key factors does the chosen factor most strongly affect?)
- What affects that factor? (Or what other factor on the list of key factors most strongly affects the factor chosen?)

Both questions involve picking out a factor and following the causal pathway that connects it to the rest of the system, like pulling a strand from a spiderweb and following where it leads. The first question asks the analysts to push forward from an initial variable to uncover a causal loop (dynamic feedback loop). Conversely, the second question asks the analyst to push backward from the initial variable to uncover a causal loop.

In the Afghanistan case, a good starting question is, What factor does corrupt, ineffective government strongly affect? The group saw a strong connection between the corrupt, ineffective government and the general state of lawlessness or respect for the rule of law in Afghanistan. The more corrupt and ineffective the government (at all levels), the lower the rule of law (see Figure 6.3). Continuing the process, the next step is to take the second factor, rule of law, and ask what factor it affects. The group felt there was a strong connection between rule of law and insecurity: The lower the rule of law, the higher the level of insecurity. At some point, the series of linear causal relationships needs to become a feedback loop. The purpose of pushing forward or backwards from the initial causal factor is to end up back where one started. If one is pushing forward, following a string of causal relationships starting with the factor "corrupt, ineffective government," then the feedback loop is complete when one finds a causal relationship that ends with "corrupt, ineffective government." Taken together this string of causal relationships forms a reinforcing feedback loop as shown in Figure 6.3.

Figure 6.3 Afghanistan Governance/Insecurity Subsystem

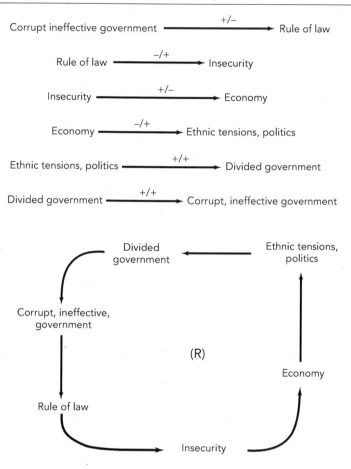

A common question that people wrestle with at this point in the process of creating dynamic feedback loops out of a linear list of causal factors is, How does one know when one has a loop? Should it include three factors, five factors, ten? How does one know if one has too many factors? There is no hard-and-fast rule, but two considerations may help. First, consider what seems most representative of the situation that the analysts are trying to understand. Remember that systems maps are mental images of a situation. They are representations of reality, but they are not reality itself. This gives the person drawing a systems map some creative leeway, though there needs to be a basis in fact for the factors identified and the dynamics created by the interplay of these factors. A key question is whether or not a map helps explain why a society is the way that it is. If a causal link is not supported by credible evidence, do not include it. As a check, each of the key factors identified through the SAT analysis should find its way into at least one feedback loop. If some do not, the map may be missing something, or a factor identified as key may not actually be that important.

A second consideration is how much detail it is helpful to include. A systems map is designed to help tell a coherent and meaningful story about a social system. It tries to capture complexity in a way that furthers comprehension. If a factor is necessary to make your story more comprehensible, then include it. One may find that there is a causal relationship between two factors, but the leap between them is too big to move directly from one factor to the other. This is a sign that one may need to add in a factor, as long as it is supported by credible evidence, to help a feedback loop tell a coherent story.

For example, in Cambodia, when our ICAF team did its data gathering, we found recurrent evidence of a strong and deeply rooted cultural norm of patron-client relationships that helped to explain why there was a tendency toward stability in Cambodia as a whole. This tendency existed despite the presence of factors, such as widespread land grabbing, that would seem to destabilize a system. This was especially so at the national level. The challenge was to better understand how this dynamic worked. It was clear that there was a culturally rooted acceptance of a patron-client relationship. The strength of this attitude contributed to the effectiveness of the Cambodian People's Party (CPP), which had been in power since the late 1980s. In fact, over a series of elections, the CPP had been strengthening its hold on power, winning more and more seats in the parliament, and dominating more locally elected commune councils. The stronger the patron-client mind-set, the more effectively the CPP doled out rent-seeking opportunities to elites, and the more these elites were able to capitalize on the opportunities, the more elite support the CPP enjoyed. This elite buy-in served to reinforce or strengthen the fundamental patron-client mind-set, which closed the feedback loop, as illustrated in Figure 6.4.

However, the jump in the causal loop from *Effectiveness of the CPP* to *Rent-seeking opportunities* seemed too big and did not adequately explain how the CPP was able to strengthen its hold on power. For example, the team felt there was a difference between the CPP's ability to dole out rent-seeking opportunities and the elites actually being able to collect rents. The growth in the global economy and the support from the international community (which most years accounted for up to half of Cambodia's federal budget) facilitated the ability of elites to actually make profits off of gambling, fishing, or forest concessions. This was an important distinction because the CPP's reliance on rent seeking might be vulnerable to challenges by internal political opponents (who might contest the party's ability to dole out rents), but external forces, such as the global economic recession, might also compromise it.

Figure 6.4 Developing Causal Loops

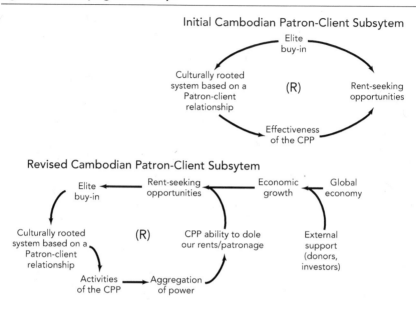

The effectiveness of the CPP really comprised two factors. One was its willingness to act as a patron, which allowed it to behave autocratically when it needed to, despite the constraints of a nominally democratic system. This gave the CPP freedom of movement, which in turn allowed it to aggregate power. And the more the CPP aggregated power, the more it was able to dole out rent-seeking opportunities. This distinction was important because the activities of the CPP included practices that had the potential to weaken popular support, such as selective land grabbing and spotty provision in rural areas of basic services like electricity and education. However, the ability of the CPP to aggregate power was a main driver of stability in national politics, which, in turn, helped strengthen popular support for the CPP. So the initial feedback loop that consisted of four factors ended up as a six-factor feedback loop with three "input" factors (as shown in Figure 6.4).

Recap: Systems-Mapping Conventions

Before we move on to the last major step in creating a systems map, aggregating multiple causal loops into one diagram, it may be helpful to review some basic systems-mapping conventions touched on so far in this chapter that will help make drawing a map easier. These conventions are summarized in Table 6.1.

Table 6.1 Systems-Mapping Conventions

Convention	Description
Factors	Factors are short, pithy descriptions of variables that affect the level of peace in the society. They are best framed as unqualified nouns that can be scaled up or down (e.g., "economy" versus "poor economy"). Factors form part of a feedback loop and thus have arrows, denoting causal relationships with other factors, coming into and out of them.
• Inputs	Inputs are factors that only show arrows pointing out, connecting the input with one or more factors. Inputs feed into, but are not part of, feedback loops.
• Outputs	Outputs are factors that only show arrows pointing into the factor. Outputs represent the outcome of a system or feedback loop. In the SPA analysis, the output factor is the level of peace in the society.
• Color coding	Factors can be written in different colored letters to distinguish their relative importance. For example, factors that have the most direct or proximate impact on the level of peace can be written in blue, the next most important factors can be written in green, and third-tier factors can be written in brown.
• Bubbles	Factors can be grouped together in a colored shape, but not connected with arrows or put in a feedback loop, to show that these factors interact with and contribute to affecting factors outside the bubble.
Causal relationships	Arrows (→) connect factors to show that one factor affects another factor. Factors can have parallel or opposite causal relationships.
• Parallel	A parallel causal relationship means that a change in one factor will cause a parallel change in another factor (e.g., more of factor A will lead to more of factor B, or less of factor 1 will lead to less of factor 2). This can be represented with a ("+/+") symbol or a ("–/–") symbol above an arrow.
• Opposite	An opposite causal relationship means that a change in one factor will cause an opposite change in another factor (e.g., more of factor A will lead to less of factor B, or less of factor 1 will lead to more of factor 2). This can be represented with a ("+/–") or ("–/+") symbol above an arrow.
• Line coding	The thickness of an arrow can be used to show the strength of the causal impact of one factor on another (e.g., the thicker the line, the stronger the causal impact).
• Time delays	Sometimes the impact of one factor on another is not immediate and takes time to be fully realized. This relationship can be noted by putting a "?" in the middle of an arrow connecting two factors.
• Feedback loops	Feedback loops are made up of multiple interconnected factors that are part of the same causal chain reaction. Because the reaction ends where it started, it forms a loop (e.g., A affects B affects C affects A). These loops represent the notions of dynamic causality and interconnectedness. A feedback loop is either reinforcing or balancing.
• Reinforcing	When the initial causal impact of a factor is amplified by the other factors in the feedback loop, it is a reinforcing feedback loop (e.g., a feeling of threat might cause a country to build up its army, which may cause a rival to also build up its army, which results in increasing the initial country's feeling of threat). A reinforcing loop is noted by putting a symbol (R) inside the loop.
• Balancing	When the initial causal impact of a factor is counteracted by the other factors in the feedback loop, it is a balancing feedback loop (e.g., an increase in an ethnic group's feeling of grievance against its government might result in a dialogue and programs that actually lower the group's initial feeling of grievance). A balancing loop is noted by putting a symbol (B) inside the loop.

Key factors. It is very important to summarize causal factors in short, pithy descriptions for inclusion in a systems map. Often, these factors are stated as descriptions that are longer than the few words that can be included in a systems map. For example, in the transactional analysis the Mercy Corps team did in Afghanistan, a key factor was framed as "international actors support different groups making them unwilling to negotiate." Eventually, this was combined with similar factors and summarized as "international interference," which is more manageable given the limited space in a systems diagram and more useful because it was used to capture both the transactional impact of international actors on negotiations between key people and the structural impact of outside arms shipments to armed groups in Afghanistan. The detail behind this factor was captured in the longer SPA analysis and in the analytical narrative that accompanied the systems map.

It is also important to frame or reframe factors as nouns that can be scaled up or down. For example, the group identified Afghanistan's "poor economy" as a key factor that affected the level of peace. However, "poor economy" assumes a low level of economic performance at a particular point in time. The problem is that if the factors contributing to the state of the economy, such as the level of insecurity, were to change, then the economy would theoretically improve, and the label "poor economy" would no longer be accurate. A better way to frame this factor is as "economy," which can be poor, improving, or strong, depending on the performance of the rest of the system. The same is true with a factor like "lawlessness," which the group also identified as a key factor in Afghanistan. Lawlessness, however, assumes a low level of respect for the rule of law, and a better label is just "rule of law," which can be high or low. It is not essential that factors be framed as scalable nouns, and sometimes qualifying a factor with "lack of . . . " or "poor" may simplify the process of drawing a map (as is the case in the Afghanistan maps included here). But such exceptions should be made sparingly.

In addition to factors that are part of a feedback loop (e.g., have arrows both coming into and out of them), there can also be factors that only have arrows either coming in or going out of them. In the patron-client loop from Cambodia, the impact of the global economy is represented as an input factor (see Figure 6.4). The use of input factors allows one to include a significant factor in the map without also having to draw a whole feedback loop that includes that factor. There is a preference in systems thinking to include factors as part of a system to underscore the idea that no factor or phenomenon exists in a vacuum. In the Cambodia example, the global economy is influenced by what happens in Cambodia, but this feedback is relatively small, so drawing the links between the Cambodian economy and the global economy would do more to complicate an already crowded map than it would to provide useful information.

Outputs are the inverse of input factors, as they are meant to show the outcomes of a system. Outputs are factors that only have arrows coming into them. In the case of the SPA, the output of the causal map is level of peace (Figure 6.6 provides an example). This output factor is meant to represent the purpose of drawing the causal loop diagram in the first place: to better understand the factors and patterns of behavior that affect the level of peace in the society. A system can have all kinds of outputs, from environmental degradation to violence to increasing population. The SPA, however, is intended help peacebuilders improve sustainable levels of human development and healthy processes of change. Therefore, the output they are most focused on is the level of peace, and the systems map is intended to highlight the dynamics most critical to this task. In the Afghanistan map, three factors were seen as having the biggest impact on the level of peace: corrupt, ineffective government; insecurity; and the economy. Certainly, there could be arrows connecting level of peace back to these three factors or other factors in the map, but again, for readability and to reduce clutter, the lines are omitted.

Two other conventions help integrate factors into a systems map: color coding and bubbles. Color coding is simply a way of providing some visual order to a map by using different colors to signify the importance of a factor. For example, first-tier, or key, factors could be represented in blue, second-tier factors in green, and so forth. Designation as a first-, second-, or third-tier factor is the result of an initial group consensus (e.g., based on a voting or affinity-diagramming exercise) but is revised based on how prominently different factors appear in the feedback loops and subsequent systems map (e.g., if a factor appears over and over again in several feedback loops, it is probably a first-tier factor). Bubbles are another way to simplify and unclutter a map. They can be used to represent several important factors without a feedback loop. In the Cambodia map, we used bubbles to represent the mind-sets of the older and the younger generations and to show that those mind-sets affect other factors in the system (see Figure 6.5). Placing four factors in the bubble, without all the connecting arrows, conveys the notion that all these factors shape the mind-set of the older generation without the clutter and formality of a full feedback loop.

Causal relationships. As described earlier, arrows denote causal relationships, and symbols can be used to indicate the nature of that relationship—for instance, a parallel relationship is noted as ("+/+") or ("–/–"), and an opposite relationship as ("+/–") or ("–/+"). Line coding is a way of expressing the strength of a causal relationship by using thicker or thinner lines: The stronger the impact of one factor on another, the thicker the connecting arrow (see Figure 6.6 for an example of line coding).

Figure 6.5 System Mapping Conventions: Cambodia Example

Combining factors into a bubble

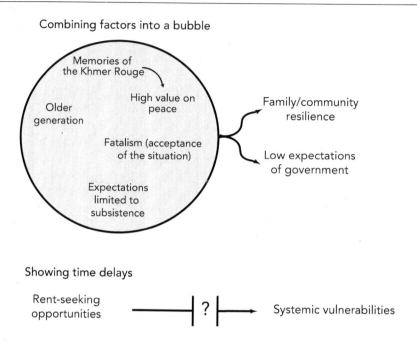

Showing time delays

Rent-seeking opportunities ——|?|——▶ Systemic vulnerabilities

Another convention uses a question mark ("?") to show a time delay between a change in the first factor and its impact on another factor. For example, in Cambodia, the extensive use of rent seeking to dole out patronage jobs or resource concessions posed a long-term threat to key systems and institutions, for instance by weakening state ability to respond to crises caused by environmental degradation or a pandemic. This threat was latent (e.g., not apparent without a crisis requiring a response), and because the risks were increasing over time (e.g., the system might be able to cope with a crisis today but not in six months), we represented the causal link between rent seeking and systemic vulnerabilities using this symbol (see Figure 6.5).

Feedback loops. When the impact of a causal factor sets off a chain reaction of causal impacts that ultimately affect the factor that set off the chain reaction in the first place, this forms a feedback loop. The principles of interconnectedness and dynamic causality (factors are both causes and effects) mean that any action (causal impact) of a factor will receive feedback from the rest of the system. This feedback can be one of two kinds: reinforcing (promotes more of the same initial action) or balancing (counteracts the initial action).

SYSTEMS MAPPING PART III:
AGGREGATING FEEDBACK LOOPS

As challenging as it may be to develop elegant feedback loops, it is even more difficult to put multiple loops together on a single page legibly. A systems map comprises multiple feedback loops. The Afghanistan case included several loops, such as the armed groups–insecurity and corrupt, ineffective government–rule of law loops described earlier in this chapter. To create a full systems map, these various feedback loops must be combined into one diagram that is true to the complexity of the situation but also user-friendly. In addition to combining feedback loops, the map also needs to show the relation between key factors and the level of peace (the output factor), plus any input factors. Before we get into the mechanics of the process of aggregating feedback loops into a map, see Figure 6.6, which provides an example of how to combine the two Afghanistan feedback loops already discussed, plus the output factor (*Level of peace*) and one input factor (*International interference*).

It is fairly easy to see the two distinct feedback loops in this combined map: The armed groups–insecurity loop is in the lower left, and the corrupt, ineffective government–rule of law loop is the taller loop on the right side of the diagram. Combining these two loops illustrates the two

Figure 6.6 Afghanistan Combined Feedback Loops

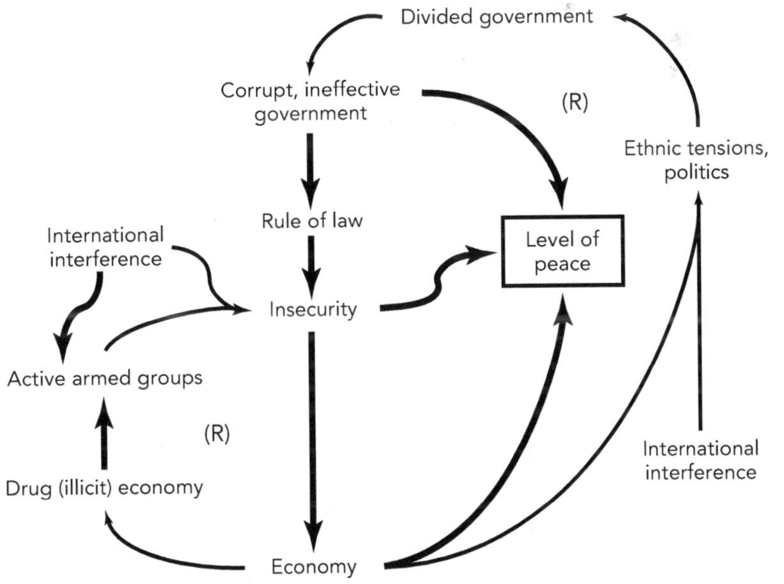

main challenges to creating more elaborate loops: the more mechanical task of managing spatial relations and the difficulty of managing detail versus dynamic complexity.

Managing Spatial Relations

While there is no one right systems map that represents a given situation, there tend to be better or worse ways to efficiently and effectively arrange a map within the confines of a single page. The guiding principle is to be as economical as possible in ordering factors, arrows, and feedback loops. For example, the two feedback loops represented in Figure 6.6 share two factors in common: *Insecurity* and *Economy.* These two factors should be near the midpoint of the combined diagram so that there is room to draw the two loops, one on each side of these two factors. Some space in the diagram is saved (or clutter eliminated) because the two loops share the connecting arrow between *Insecurity* and *Economy.*

The map also needs to show the factors with the most proximate causal impact on *Level of Peace.* In order to draw in that relationship effectively, the three drivers must be arranged so that they are close to each other but not so near as to cause all the arrows coming in and out of them to get jumbled and tangled. In this case, the three factors are stacked in the middle of the diagram so as to maximize the ability to draw arrows in and out. *Level of Peace* is drawn within the corrupt, ineffective government–rule of law loop so as to avoid having the arrows in that loop cross those that connect the three main factors and *Level of Peace.*

As more factors and feedback loops are integrated into the map, it becomes more and more important to experiment with how the map is laid out. It is best to use a medium that allows one to rearrange the diagram easily. Software programs like Vizio or PowerPoint are useful if one is fluent with them. Often, lower-tech is better. I commonly give groups Post-it notes and flip chart paper. The sticky notes allow analysts to arrange and rearrange factors and feedback loops as they test different ways to use the space and position factors in relation to each other. Flip chart paper is useful as the background for the diagram because one can draw connecting arrows on it (using pencil at first so it can be erased). Once the diagram is set, moving and storing it is easier.[5]

In sum, there are a few basic guidelines to help manage spatial relations while one develops a systems map:

- Put key factors, or those that appear recurrently in various feedback loops, in a central location in the map to make drawing arrows in and out easier.

- Avoid drawing arrows that cross each other in order to reduce clutter.
- Avoid repeating a factor (e.g., writing the same factor into the map more than one time) unless doing so is necessary to avoid clutter.
- Give analysts room and the ability to experiment with many different configurations of their systems map, and have user-friendly supplies on hand.

Managing Detail Versus Dynamic Complexity

Unfortunately, no helpful hints can avoid the hard reality that systems maps cannot show all relevant or important causal relationships or feedback loops. Everyone who draws a systems map faces the choice of what detail to include and what to cut out. Diana Chigas, of CDA/Collaborative Learning Projects and the Fletcher School of Law and Diplomacy, distinguishes between different kinds of complexity illustrated by a systems map:

- *Detail complexity* shows the extent of the interconnections between factors in a systems map.
- *Dynamic complexity* shows how factors are part of one or more feedback loops.[6]

Detail complexity is useful to show how changes to any one factor in a system will affect a wide range of other factors. Dynamic complexity is useful for highlighting the most important feedback loops in a system, which is key for understanding how systems behave and change over time. A map with lots of detail complexity is like a map of Manhattan with every street, alley, sidewalk, building, and pedestrian included. A map that features more dynamic complexity is like a subway map of Manhattan. Both types of complexity are useful, though maps that feature more dynamic complexity tend to be easier to read and more helpful when you are trying to listen to a system to decide where change can be usefully nurtured. Similarly, if a person is trying to get around Manhattan, a subway map is more useful than a map that includes every feature of the city.

The best way to see the difference between a detail complexity map and a dynamic complexity map is to view them side by side. Unfortunately, the limited space in this book makes reproducing such maps impossible. To help convey the obvious difference between the two types of maps, I compared the detail and dynamic complexity map that I produced of Afghanistan. Both maps contained the same fifteen causal factors. However, the detail complexity map contained more than twice as many connecting arrows (sixty-four) as the detail complexity map (thirty) in the same-sized diagram.

Doubling the number of arrows makes the detail complexity map very difficult to read, but it also provides more information about how each factor in the map connects to other factors. This is useful if an analyst is interested in tracing the ripple effects of affecting any one factor in the map (e.g., if one affects the level of conflict in communities, what other key factors in the system will be affected?). The detail complexity map, however, makes it difficult to see the "motion" in the system and to isolate key dynamics. Without seeing key dynamics, it is difficult to take action (see Chapter 7 for a discussion of planning based on a systems map).

The hard part is getting from a map showing detail complexity to one showing dynamic complexity. The biggest difference is that maps showing dynamic complexity have fewer connecting arrows in them, meaning that one has to decide which causal relationships are important enough to show and which feedback loops to prioritize. For example, in the detail complexity map of Afghanistan, *Corrupt, ineffective government* has nine arrows coming out and six arrows going in. In the dynamic complexity map, the same factor has only six arrows coming out and only three arrows going in. *Economy* in the dynamic complexity map has only five of seven arrows out and just two of six arrows in. The criteria for deciding which arrows to include are (1) whether an arrow is necessary to illustrate a key feedback loop in the map, and (2) whether, if a direct causal relationship is not shown, a particular causal relationship is captured as part of another feedback loop. For example, there is a direct and strong relationship between *Corrupt, ineffective government* and *Economy*, but this arrow is not included because that relationship is captured well enough in the feedback loop that links *Corrupt, ineffective government, Rule of law, Insecurity,* and *Economy.*

Another way to simplify is to avoid showing back-and-forth causal arrows. For example, a thick arrow shows the impact of *Insecurity* on the *Economy,* and an arrow leads back from *Economy* to *Insecurity* because a worsening economy contributes to higher levels of insecurity. However, most back-and-forth causal relationships are not worth showing. For example, even though *Unmet expectations* affects the *Rule of law* and vice versa, the return arrow is not illustrated because this is a less important relationship, and drawing in the arrow would be more confusing than clarifying.

So, when deciding what causal relationships to include in a map showing dynamic complexity, users should consider a few basic questions:

- Is the arrow needed to capture an important, direct causal relationship?
- Is it necessary to highlight an important feedback loop?
- Is the marginal gain worth the marginal cost? In other words, does including the arrow or feedback loop add more to readers' understanding of the situation than it lessens their ability to understand other (more important) feedback loops or causal relationships?

- Is the causal relationship captured indirectly? For instance, instead of an arrow directly connecting two factors, A and C, are they connected through their relationship with another factor; that is, A is connected to B, which is connected to C?

PRIMING THE PUMP: SYSTEM ARCHETYPES

While each specific situation, and its corresponding systems map, is unique, general patterns of behavior and feedback dynamics reoccur over time. For example, the simplified version of the arms race feedback loop introduced in Chapter 2 is a version of an action-reaction cycle that occurs over and over. And the cycles of violence and revenge between Protestant and Catholic paramilitaries in Northern Ireland or Sunni and Shia militias in Iraq are

Figure 6.7 System Archetypes: Vengeance-Retaliation and the Fix That Backfires

Vengeance-retaliation/action-reaction archetype

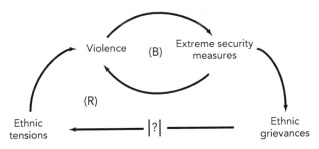

The fix that backfires archetype

versions of a vengeance-retaliation cycle (see Figure 6.7), which is a kind of action-reaction dynamic.

These recurring, basic dynamics, called system archetypes, can be helpful to spur thinking about how to form feedback loops in any particular situation. For example, one could ask, Is there a version of the action-reaction archetype in Afghanistan or Sri Lanka? If so, how is that general archetype manifested in this particular context? Archetypes are useful templates that can help analysts spot important dynamics in the contexts they are studying and provide examples of how the key factors they uncover can be arranged into a feedback loop. Peter Senge, Donella Meadows, Peter Woodrow, David Stroh, and others provide examples of general system archetypes.[7] This chapter concludes by illustrating six additional systems archetypes that are more common in the peacebuilding context.

The Fix That Backfires

An all too common archetype captures the dynamic in which efforts to address or suppress a problem actually exacerbate it (see Figure 6.7). In this dynamic, the initial disliked symptom is violence, and the state or another group attempts to reduce or eliminate violence using extreme security measures, such as massive arrests, intimidation, or violence against those it believes to be perpetrators of the violence or their sympathizers. The initial impact of the extreme security measures is to lower the level of violence; hence, the balancing loop in the middle of the diagram (e.g., the greater the security measures, the lower the level of violence). However, the extreme security measures also lead to increasing ethnic grievances among the group targeted by them. In time, those grievances increase the level of ethnic tensions (note the "?" in the arrow connecting these two factors), which in turn causes an increase in the levels of violence. This reinforcing loop serves to defeat any short-term gains in lowering violence achieved by the original fix (the extreme security measures)—hence, the label "the fix that backfires."

Victim-Oppressor Archetype

Another common dynamic that contributes to levels of violence is the victim-oppressor feedback loop (see Figure 6.8). In this scenario, a high level of grievances by a minority group leads to a widespread feeling of victimization, which is attributed to an oppressive dominant group in society. This feeling of victimization leads to two different responses from the minority group. One response is for the minority group to lash out at the oppressor, causing the dominant group to take reprisals, which in turn leads to increasing levels of grievances among the minority group (the reinforcing feedback loop on the right side of the diagram). The other response to the feeling of victimization is for the minority group to withdraw and isolate itself, which also leads to increasing levels of grievance (the reinforcing feedback loop on the left of the diagram). Both responses lead to increasing levels of grievance and victimization, which makes this a particularly vicious cycle.

Figure 6.8 System Archetypes: Victim-Oppressor and War Weariness

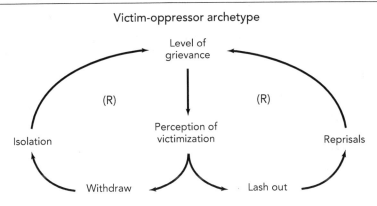

Victim-oppressor archetype

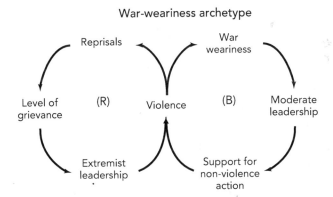

War-weariness archetype

War-Weariness Archetype

While many dynamics that involve violence are vicious, or continually escalating, cycles, not all are. Many contain both escalatory and stabilizing dynamics (see Figure 6.8). For example, levels of grievance can lead to the rise of extremist leaders, who in turn mobilize their supporters to respond to their grievances by using violence. This violence prompts violent reprisals, which increases the level of grievances, strengthens extremists, and so forth. This dynamic forms the reinforcing loop on the left side of the diagram in Figure 6.9, which is labeled "the war-weariness archetype." Over time, however, violence can also cause an increasing level of war weariness in a population, where people just want to return to a "normal life," regardless of the hardships they might face. These sentiments can lead to the rise of more moderate leadership that wants to address the grievances of their group through political or nonviolent means. If successful, this more conciliatory, nonviolent action might actually reduce levels of violence; hence, this forms the balancing loop on the right side of the diagram. The presence of both the balancing and reinforcing loops tends to make this dynamic more stable than, for example, an action-reaction cycle or the victim-oppressor dynamic.

Competition for Scarce Resources/Exclusion Archetype

Peter Woodrow detailed another archetype that contains elements of both stability and violence. The archetype is complex because it contains two balancing and two reinforcing loops. The dynamic starts with a situation in which multiple groups compete for scarce resources, such as land, power, markets, and the like. This dynamic assumes there are two groups, A and B. Group A sees the competition for scarce resources as a threat, and in order to protect itself, A takes measures to exclude B from access to these resources (e.g., by denying B the right to vote, run candidates for public office, own land, or access markets). Initially, this exclusion strategy lowers the competition for scarce resources and A's feeling of threat. This is the first balancing loop (B1) on the left of the diagram in Figure 6.9.

A's exclusion of B also leads to a second balancing loop (B2) at the bottom middle of the figure. In response to being excluded, B feels resentment, which leads to efforts to restore equity, or to undo the exclusion (e.g., campaigns to restore voting rights, proposals for land redistribution, etc.). Some of these efforts may succeed and actually lower the level of B's exclusion. Interestingly, the efforts to restore equity, if effective, will also increase the level of competition for scarce resources (e.g., if more members of B are allowed to own land, there will be more competition among A and B for limited tracts of land). This forms a reinforcing loop (R1) because the efforts to exclude B have led to more competition for scarce resources, which only leads to more efforts by A to exclude B. A second reinforcing loop (R2) is formed when feelings of resentment lead some members of B to use violence against

Figure 6.9 System Archetypes: Competition for Scarce Resources

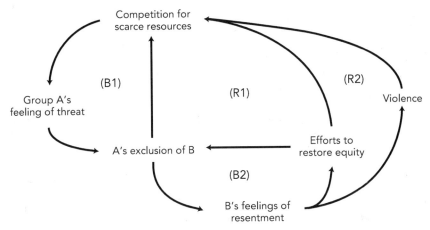

Competition for scarce resources/exclusion archetype

Based on the work of Peter Woodrow of CDA Collaborative Learning Projects.

A in order to compete for scarce resources. This archetype is an interesting example of how a dynamic can comprise multiple, smaller reinforcing and balancing feedback loops.

Patron-Client Archetype

One of the more common stabilizing archetypes is the patron-client dynamic. Forms of patron-client politics exist at the international, national, and local levels, and they often have deep cultural roots. Essentially, the dynamic entails one or more reinforcing loops that involve patrons who are defined by their ability to hold and wield power in the social context and use it to provide for the basic needs of their clients. The clients, in turn, provide their loyalty to the patrons, who use that support to keep the system stable. In this version of the patron-client dynamic (see Figure 6.10), the patrons use their power to dole out rents (e.g., land concessions, control of gambling, patronage jobs, etc.) to win the support of key elites, which in turn furthers the patrons' hold on power (R1). The patrons use this hold on power to exercise control over any potential opponents and the broader society through means of state, such as the use of the military and police, control of the courts and the media, and the like, to enforce stability. This stability meets another core interest of the elites (R2), which is to make sure that the R1 dynamic continues.

Figure 6.10 System Archetypes: Patron-Client and Community Resilience

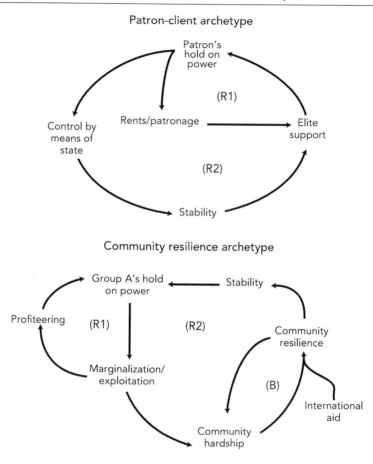

Patron-client archetype

Community resilience archetype

Community Resilience Archetype

An archetype that often accompanies an elite-level patron-client dynamic, like the one illustrated above, is the community resilience archetype (see Figure 6.10). Often, the practice of relying on rents to gain elite support or maintain dominance of one group over another results in exploitation of rural communities or groups. For example, the profits made from an elite receiving the fishing rights to a section of a river in Cambodia (a rent) means that the local community along that stretch of river loses a key source of income, let alone a major food source (R1). The hardship this exploitation imposes on the community is counteracted by a strong tradition of community self-reliance, adaptivity, and cohesiveness (B). This resilience is bolstered by programs run by international aid organizations that help these communities improve their access to water, improve their agricultural techniques, and develop alternate livelihoods.

These are all positive impacts for the people in the communities; however, they may also have a cost. Higher levels of community resilience lead to greater levels of stability. The more stability there is, the stronger the patrons' (or dominant groups') hold on power, and the better able they are to marginalize or exploit communities (R2). In an odd way, community resilience is critical to community survival, but it also contributes to the conditions that further strain the ability of the community to survive.

CHAPTER 6 SUMMARY

- Drawing a systems map starts with the process of stepping back from the data and using the power of a group discussion to surface assumptions and prioritize the factors with the most significant impact on the level of peace. While quantitative analytical processes can aid this process, more qualitative processes (like the headlines exercise, voting, and affinity diagramming) are useful ways to prioritize factors and facilitate group discussion.
- Creating feedback loops (or "loopifying" the data) starts with identifying a key factor and pushing forward or backward to create a causal loop. It is important to identify whether individual causal factors have a parallel or opposite causal relationship and to determine if a feedback loop is reinforcing or balancing.
- Several systems-mapping conventions can be used to draw feedback loops and to aggregate them into a larger systems map.
- Merging feedback loops means managing spatial relations and detail versus dynamic complexity. It may be useful to draw two maps, one showing detail complexity that serves as a resource in drawing a second map that shows dynamic complexity.
- There are recurrent patterns of behavior, or system archetypes, that occur over and over, and these can be useful templates for drawing feedback loops.

CHAPTER 7

MOVING FROM ANALYSIS TO ACTION

✑

Plans are useless, but planning is indispensible.
—Dwight D. Eisenhower

The movie *Field of Dreams* is one of my favorites. The film's main character, Ray Kinsella, is a novice farmer who finds his path to personal salvation in the middle of a cornfield when a ghostly voice advises, "If you build it, he will come." Ray does as the voice commands and triumphs in the end, despite incurring public scorn and near financial ruin. The film and this line have come to symbolize the virtue of doing what you believe is right and trusting that good things will follow, even if the process does not make sense or the ultimate end is not apparent. In peacebuilding, the equivalent phenomenon is when organizations implement projects at the local level and trust that somehow these good deeds will add up to Peace Writ Large (PWL) in a particular context.

Peacebuilding is not like the story in *Field of Dreams*. It would be great if doing a Systemic Peacebuilding Assessment (SPA) and generating a systems map of a social context were enough to ensure peacebuilders will act more systemically. Unfortunately, the adage "If you map it, peace will last" will not work for peacebuilders in the same way that "If you build it, he will come" worked for Ray Kinsella. Micro-level peacebuilding successes do not necessarily add up to sustainable macro-level change. Systems thinking and the structural, attitudinal, and transactional (or SAT) model are necessary steps in bridging the micro-macro gap and making peacebuilding more cost-effective. However, they are not sufficient.

Peacebuilders need to turn a systems map of a social context into programming that has a greater chance of making peace last. This link from assessment to planning to implementation and back to learning is known as feed-forward. The alternative to feed-forward is hoping that the lessons from good assessment will be obvious and persuasive to other actors, who are usually not involved in the assessment itself. A frustration that I regularly hear from analysts with agencies like the US Agency for International Development and at NGOs is that assessment has little impact on planning, and there is little learning over time because there is no feedback or updating of assessments. Feed-forward tries to remedy this by helping analysts identify and hand off the most useful insights from their systems maps to those who do planning, project design, and monitoring and evaluation. Ultimately, good feed-forward should increase the likelihood of analysts getting helpful feedback from experience in the field by ensuring that programs test out hypotheses formed in the assessment phase.

So, how can analysts effectively feed-forward the learning from their assessments? Peacebuilders have two planning tasks: (1) determining how to implement a program at the micro level, such as building a school for girls in a village in rural Afghanistan, and (2) maximizing the chance that this program (building a school) will make a contribution to macro-level peace. The first planning task is a more mechanical, linear process (i.e., it entails the steps necessary to physically erect a school). The second planning task requires peacebuilders to think and act differently. Specifically, systemic planning requires them to augment traditional planning processes by using a systems map to

1. *listen to the system* to identify what change(s) to nurture in order to increase a society's level of peace;
2. *work with the system* to maximize the productivity and sustainability of interventions by
   ◦ finding a leverage point and articulating a pathway to macro-level change;
   ◦ maximizing holism by ensuring that programs have impacts in each of the SAT domains;
   ◦ understanding interdependence in order to maximize positive interdependence and minimize negative interdependence;
   ◦ building networks to complement and augment the potential for a program to contribute to sustainable macro-level change;
3. *learn from the system* and feed-forward information effectively in order to get good feedback. Feedback from experiences on the ground with

programs designed based on a systems analysis will allow analysts to test and revise their understanding of a social system in order to improve effectiveness over time.

Systemic planning is not meant to be a wholesale replacement of conventional, more linear approaches to planning that are used widely by governments, international organizations, and NGOs. Most peacebuilders are not starting an intervention from scratch and have been using nonsystemic planning tools in a particular social context for some time. It would be naive and counterproductive to supplant these practices. Systems thinking, the SAT model, and the SPA are as much a mind-set as a specific set of analytical tools. Similarly, listening to, working with, and learning from the system are as much habits of mind as specific planning tools that can help improve any peacebuilding initiative.

And changing habits of mind is difficult. Before we explore the specifics of how to listen to, work with, and learn from a system in a practical sense, it is necessary to examine the conceptual contradictions and conundrums peacebuilders confront when they try to make their planning processes more systemic.

SYSTEMIC PLANNING: CONTRADICTIONS AND CONUNDRUMS

It can be difficult to mesh systemic with nonsystemic planning approaches. The starkest difference between systemic and current approaches to peacebuilding is in the area of planning: the difference between the dynamic, holistic, and nondeterministic systems thinking approach and the more linear, reductionist approaches to development that rely on centralized planning (see Tables 4.1 and 4.2). These differences are both practical and philosophical and present a series of difficult issues peacebuilders need to resolve in order to do systemic planning effectively:

1. *The systems thinking–planning paradox:* Is systems thinking, which is based on dynamic causality, in contradiction with a traditional approach to planning, which is based on a linear view of reality?
2. *The heightened ethical dimension:* To what degree does the idea of an intervener trying to affect the development of an entire society (e.g., PWL) raise serious ethical problems for peacebuilders?
3. *The danger of paralysis by analysis:* Does the complexity of systems analysis, plus these increased ethical issues, make systemic planning too difficult?
4. *Thinking macro in a micro world:* Peacebuilders espouse macro-level goals (e.g., PWL) but only operate at the micro level. Is it possible to

implement a macro-level approach to peacebuilding in countries like Somalia or Colombia when no one actor operates at the macro level?

The Systems Thinking–Planning Paradox

One reason that current planning approaches do not incorporate systems thinking is that the two disciplines seem to be antithetical. For example, planning is about how to better control one's environment to attain a desired goal, while systems thinking is founded on the beliefs that systems change in unpredictable ways and that control over a system is an illusion. Certainly systems thinking is inconsistent with planning akin to the heavy-handed five-year plans that for decades guided the centrally dictated development of the Soviet economy. These plans took the notion of planning as a means for "controlling reality" to an absurd extreme. For example, in the late 1980s, I was talking with a former Soviet diplomat about conditions in our respective countries. He expressed respect for the strength of the US economy and the prosperity Americans enjoyed. When I said that there was also extreme poverty in the United States, he said that this was one area in which the Soviet Union had an edge on the United States. "In fact," he assured me with a grin, "there is *no* poverty in the Soviet Union because it's not in the five-year plan."

The Soviet-era approach, like the centrally dictated development planning that William Easterly critiques, assumes that the goal of planning is to produce a plan, which in turn can be used to create orderly remedies to messy social problems. The epigraph by President Dwight D. Eisenhower at the start of this chapter represents a very different approach to planning. The whole quote reads, "In preparing for battle, I have always found that plans are useless, but planning is indispensible."[1] One might think that if ever plans would be useful, it would be when heading into battle. But Eisenhower is saying that plans only represent a hypothesis about what one thinks he knows at any one point, and real value derives from continuing to learn and adjust a plan in light of experience. In this sense, *planning is a structured process for learning.* The "indispensible" planning process precedes the development of a plan and continues as the plan is put into action. Battle planning, in Eisenhower's conception, is responsible for producing an initial battle plan and, more importantly, learning how strategy and tactics need to change based on what is and is not working on the battlefield.

This concept of planning as learning is consistent with the insights from systems thinking. Like a battle plan, a systems map is only a hypothesis about how a particular social system works. Analysis of the dynamic interplay between structural, attitudinal, and transactional factors is ongoing, just as the strategy and tactics based on that analysis must be constantly updated. The SPA and systems mapping are designed to help structure the process of learning about how a social system works and how best to nurture change toward a greater level of peace in the system. Planning is not just an event; an ongoing team must continually look at how key structural, attitudinal, and transactional drivers change over time and assess whether the feedback loops and causal relationships identified in the systems map are accurate. Systemic planning is more about how to structure that learning process than it is about how to define an initial plan of action.

The Heightened Ethical Dimension

Planning as learning is a way out of the systems thinking–planning paradox. However, planning as learning sounds a lot like trial and error. The potential costs of trial and error at the micro level, such as in regard to building a school in a village, are much less than if one is trying to effect change throughout an entire country. At the macro level, a peacebuilder's learning might come at the cost of many lives. What is the appropriate standard of care for a peacebuilder working at the macro level? Moreover, what right does any peacebuilder have to intervene in a social system at the macro level in the first place?[2]

Many peacebuilders seem to assume that because they have good intentions, there are no ethical issues. The good intentions trap, however, means that they often impose their values on a society: "Most peacebuilding interventions by Western (or Northern) actors can be accused of being ethnocentric and 'top-down' in the sense that they try to impose external values on the target society within which the peacebuilding initiative is being undertaken."[3] This is especially true when donors and NGOs build certain liberal values into their aid programming. These values include advancing democracy, religious freedom, women's rights, and the like. Personally, I generally find these values laudable, but the ethical question is, Who gets to decide which values do and do not get implemented? Increasing a society's level of peace may be less controversial than advancing democracy or human rights, but it does not eliminate the need for ongoing and explicit discussion of intervention ethics that includes a diversity of voices, especially from the society in question. In this respect, vertical integration, as called for in the SAT model, is especially important.

An inclusive and transparent discussion of the ethics of intervention must be included as part of the planning process. Kristoffer Liden provides an excellent explanation of why planning processes benefit from explicit dialogue about ethics: "Ethics does not produce moral certainty, but it raises the awareness of our already present morality. Like philosophy in general, it helps us asking the right questions and guides us in our pursuit of their answers. It is also a language for communicating these thoughts, hence making our doubts and beliefs public and allowing us to benefit from the reasoning of others."[4] Just as the process of drawing a systems map requires that participants air and discuss their assumptions about causality in a social system, the planning process requires participants to discuss their assumptions and beliefs about what is and is not ethical in terms of effecting change in a social system. Further, the SAT model emphasizes transactional peacebuilding, meaning that local stakeholders play a critical role in decision making. This ensures that local voices are central to discussions of the values underlying any program. Of course, involving local voices does not absolve or disqualify external actors from being transparent about their own values and ethics. External actors need to participate in this debate and ultimately decide, in accordance with their values, what projects they will participate in. They key is that these discussions make ethical considerations explicit, bring a diversity of voices (both local and external) to the table, and ensure that the dialogue is ongoing.

The Danger of Paralysis by Analysis

Making explicit discussion of ethics part of the planning process may help manage the potential moral pitfalls of systemic peacebuilding, but it does not lower the stakes of macro-level interventions. If anything, the addition of the ethical dimension to the already complex task of understanding a social system may augment the perceived risks and lessen the chances that a peacebuilder will take any action. Too much process and data can impede action. The term *paralysis by analysis* is meant to capture the hard truth that human brains can quickly become overwhelmed by data and decision making. Concern over making the best choice can inhibit one from making any choice.

To better understand the paralysis-by-analysis phenomenon, a group of researchers did a study where they gave two groups of doctors the same basic scenario: A patient is suffering from osteoarthritis and has undergone every available drug treatment with no effect. The only remaining treatment option is the difficult and painful process of hip-replacement surgery. One group of doctors, after being told that the pharmacy had discovered one last drug, was asked whether they wanted to try this drug before opting for surgery. Out of this first group, 47 percent of the doctors chose to try the drug therapy.

The second group of doctors was given the same fact scenario, except that they were told that the pharmacy had found two drug options. When given the choice of two nonsurgical options, only 28 percent of this group chose to use either drug.[5] It seems improbable, but when given a choice between two drug options as opposed to one as an alternative to surgery, 40 percent fewer physicians opted for any drug treatment. "More options, even good ones, can freeze us," observed Dan and Chip Heath, who wrote about the study in *Fast Company*.[6]

The remedy for this is to realize that it is impossible to make the "best" choice and that the most a planner can do is to make a responsible choice. The planning process must help peacebuilders do the due diligence necessary to be confident that they are maximizing their potential to contribute to Peace Writ Large. Further, instead of just presenting options, the planning process needs to help decision makers reason through the choices they face. Lastly, because no one can make all the right or even best choices, having a structured process for learning provides planners with confidence that they will learn from their mistakes when they happen. This is critical because, as Amy Edmondson of Harvard Business School argues, failure in complex endeavors (such as peacebuilding) is inevitable, and the real failure comes from the failure to learn from experience.[7]

Thinking Macro in a Micro World

Making responsible choices about how to act systemically requires peacebuilders to listen to the system and let it direct their efforts rather than imposing their will on the system. But is listening to the system realistic if few, or any, peacebuilders are in the position to act solely based on the cues they get from the system? Having a macro-level view inform macro-level operations to achieve a macro-level goal resembles what doctors often do in the medical field. Physicians who are general practitioners often take responsibility for a patient's overall health (a macro-level or systemic view) and coordinate an overall treatment regime (macro-level or systemic approach) that may involve working with various specialists, such as a cardiologist, physical therapist, or nutritionist. This seldom, if ever, happens in the peacebuilding field. For example, donors usually develop a country strategy, which, while not necessarily systemic in view, is a macro-level perspective in that it addresses the society as a whole. However, no one donor or agency takes responsibility for implementing a systemic approach and coordinating the work of all the diverse peacebuilders working in a country.

As a consequence, most donors, governments, and intergovernmental agencies, like the World Bank or United Nations, tend to take a macro-level view but operate through multiple micro-level (or even meso-level) programs. For example, the Department for International Development (DFID) of the British government has a country assistance plan for Tanzania that establishes a series of midterm goals for the country.[8] Pursuant to this macro-level assessment (in 2010), DFID mainly funds programs in four sectors: governance, health, education, and economic growth. DFID knows this "course of treatment" is not sufficient on its own to build long-term sustainable peace in Tanzania. Because of resource and other constraints, DFID is forced to work through bundles of micro-level programs (e.g., several local programs in the governance sector, another bundle in the health sector, etc.). Implementing these bundles of micro-level programs may be thought of as a "meso-level" approach.

However, DFID's planning process is not necessarily systemic or holistic. First, while DFID is taking a macro-level view of Tanzania, that view is not necessarily systemic. For example, is DFID sure that changes in the governance, health, education, and economic sectors will be the prime drivers of systemic change in Tanzania's level of peace? Second, even if these are the prime drivers of systemic change, what is DFID's theory about how the programs they are funding in these four sectors, if successful, will "interact out" (see Chapter 4) and bridge the gap between the micro/meso and macro levels?[9]

Implementing agencies, NGOs that run micro-level programs, tend to have slightly different planning problems. In regard to any one project, they have a micro-level perspective and are aiming for micro-level results in the short term. For example, an education program in a Tanzanian village aims to improve education outcomes in that village. However, these agencies also espouse macro-level goals; they identify attaining PWL as their motivation for doing peacebuilding work in the first place. Again, like the donors, implementing agencies need to bridge the gap between their micro-level programs and the macro-level goal of increasing a society's level of peace over the long term.

So, peacebuilders who have a predominately macro-level perspective, like donors, face a different planning challenge than those with a predominately micro-level perspective, such as implementing agencies. Donors need a macro-level, systemic view of a social system that helps them operate a series of micro-level programs, which, in turn, contribute to macro-level, sustainable improvement in a society's level of peace. This is a macro-micro-macro planning challenge (macro-level perspective, micro-level operations, and macro-level goals).

However, donors and implementing agencies can both benefit from a systemic planning process, though each may use the basic tools of systemic planning differently. For example, donors have more leeway to listen to the system in establishing macro-level goals and objectives than implementing agencies, which are usually asked to operate programs consistent with a donor's goals. However, there is the potential for implementing agencies to do their own exercise in listening to the system, both at the local level (e.g., to better understand how the social system of a village works) and to have input into a donor's attempt to listen to the macro-level system. Ideally, donors, implementing agencies, and aid beneficiaries should be part of the analysis and planning process. Both donors and implementing agencies need to understand how to best work with the system in order to bridge the micro-macro gap. And both entities need to cooperate to maximize their ability to learn from the system to improve peacebuilding programming over time. All of this requires diverse peacebuilders to form networks of effective action to manage their respective planning challenges and to bridge the micro-macro peacebuilding gap (see "SAT Response: Networks of Effective Action" in Chapter 4).

SYSTEMIC PLANNING STEP 1: LISTEN TO THE SYSTEM

In order to deal with the contradictions and conundrums systemic planning can pose, planners need to (1) structure an ongoing process of learning, (2) make discussions of values and ethics inclusive of diverse voices and ongoing, (3) help structure responsible choices for peacebuilders, and (4) form networks of effective action. Figure 7.1 provides an overview of how the systemic planning process works to meet those four challenges.

The first step in this process is to listen to the system. From a systems perspective, systems change best when they change themselves, and it is less effective when agencies try to impose change on a system or ignore how their change efforts affect, and are affected by, the dynamics within a system. There are a few basic steps for listening effectively to a system:

Figure 7.1 Systemic Planning Flowchart

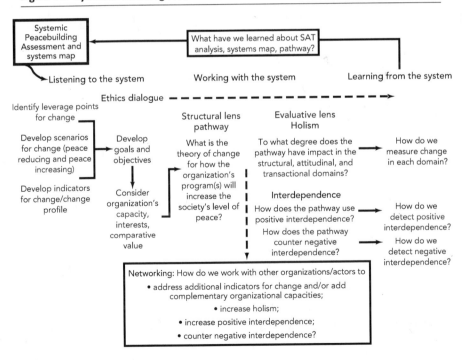

1. Identify potential leverage points for change.
2. Develop possible scenarios for change.
3. Develop indicators for change.

Identifying Potential Leverage Points for Change

The key to creating more cost-effective and sustainable peacebuilding programs is to magnify the impact of funds by working with the existing power of a system. For example, consider the difference between rowing a boat with the current or against it. The same amount of energy expended to move the oars will move the boat much further if one rows with the current (e.g., the current adds energy to the force supplied by the rower) than if one rows against the current (e.g., the energy of the current subtracts from the energy supplied by the rower).

Like the current in a river, the dynamics that make up a social system have movement and energy. A reinforcing feedback loop, such as the vengeance-retaliation archetype (Figure 6.7), can take a violent attack by members of group A on members of group B and amplify it so that it increases the level of attacks by group A on group B. The energy of this initial attack is increased by the energy supplied by the feedback loop.

A key goal of listening to a system is to find a *leverage point,* a place in the system where the dynamic energy of a feedback loop is likely to augment the impact of a peacebuilding program. Unfortunately, because systems maps are hypotheses or mental images of how a social system works, it can be difficult to spot potential leverage points. Several clues can help a planner spot potential leverage points in a systems map:

- Are there factors or causal relationships that are currently in flux?
- Are there factors that are part of "bright spots" or "attractors"?
- Are there factors or causal relationships that may have strong ripple effects?

Factors in flux. A good clue for finding a leverage point is to look for factors that are already in a state of change, organically. Factors that are in flux supply the initial energy to a dynamic feedback loop. If change is already happening in the system, this decreases the amount of effort interveners must expend because they focus their efforts on affecting the direction of that change rather than expending the energy (and resources) to create the change in the first place. By analogy, it is easier to affect the direction of a boulder rolling down a hill than it is to cause a stationary boulder to start rolling in the first place.

For example, in Cambodia in 2009, our Interagency Conflict Assessment Framework (ICAF) team identified the elite patron-client system as a core dynamic that explained Cambodian politics at the national level (see Figure 7.2). This reinforcing feedback loop depended on the ability of the ruling Cambodia People's Party (CPP) to distribute "rents" in the form of patronage or economic concessions to elites who in turn supported the CPP. This dynamic was enabled by the strong growth of the Cambodian economy, which had seen 10 percent plus growth rates for a decade. However, the ability of elites to realize rents from the concessions they were given depended, in large part, on the health of the global economy. Given the severe drop in global economic growth in 2008 and 2009, the Cambodian economy was not likely to maintain the strong growth rates that fueled the elite patron-client subsystem. The declining economic growth rate was likely to have a significant impact on the overall system, so this factor stood out as a potential leverage point for change.

Bright spots. Another clue to finding a leverage point is to look for instances in which people or communities are having success when most others who face similar challenges are not able to succeed. In technical terms, this is known as positive deviance.[10] Dan and Chip Heath call such phenomena "bright spots," or "successful efforts worth emulating."[11] In systems terms, bright spots are important because they may indicate existing changes that, if nurtured, could help the system change itself by either changing the polarity of a feedback loop (e.g., a vicious to a virtuous dynamic) or creating a new feedback loop.

Figure 7.2 Key Economic Leverage Point, Cambodia

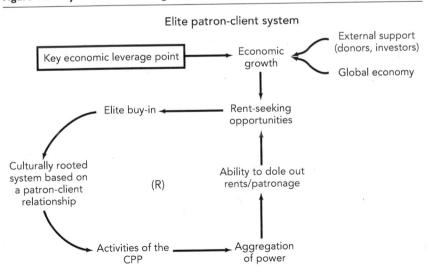

For example, the Heath brothers cite an example from Vietnam in which a small, underresourced effort was trying to reverse malnutrition in rural villages. They were told that the root causes of malnutrition where complex and change would take years to effect. Jerry Sternin, working for Save the Children, started by asking why certain children were healthy in villages where there were high rates of malnutrition. They studied the families of these children and found that relatively modest differences in how they were fed had a marked effect on the children of those families.[12] These practices were spread to other families and other villages. Sternin and his Vietnamese partners were able to find a leverage point: an existing dynamic that, with a bit of encouragement, was able to effect sustainable, cost-effective, and self-replicating macro-level change. Moreover, by using a leverage point, the program did not need the massive resources that would have been required to reverse more obvious root causes, such as chronic rural poverty. In fact, healthier children may very well be a driver of countering poverty in the long term.

Attractors. In his seminal book on systems change titled *The Five Percent: Finding Solutions to Seemingly Impossible Conflicts,* Peter Coleman advances the argument that all systems have dynamics that serve as "attractors." Coleman defines attractors as "somewhat stable patterns or tendencies in systems that draw us in and resist change."[13] These might be thought of as dominant or central dynamics in a systems map that have a powerful impact on the overall performance of a social system (e.g., they may drive stability or violence or have a marked impact on other dynamics). For example, an attractor would be the elite patron-client dynamic in the Cambodia ICAF systems map (see Figure 6.4). Attractor dynamics are good places to look for potential leverage points. If peacebuilders can affect factors that are already in flux or bright spots that exist within an attractor, then the power of the attractor dynamic might amplify the impact of a modest change and cause additional changes throughout the rest of the system.

Ripple effects. Attractors are an important example of the more general phenomenon of ripple effects. When a pebble is dropped into a pond of calm water, ripples emanate from the spot where the pebble struck the surface. Similarly, in a system, a ripple effect refers to all the subsequent changes that result from a change to one particular factor. In a detail complexity systems map (see Chapter 6 for a discussion of detail complexity), one identifies all the impacts a particular factor has on other factors in a system. These are drawn as arrows leading out of a particular factor and into other factors or leading out of a dynamic and affecting other dynamics in the system. This is similar to what Coleman refers to as "out-degree," or factors that serve as "key sources of stimulation or inhibition in the conflict or other elements."[14] In short, a factor or dynamic will have greater ripple effects (more potential leverage) if it has a higher level of "out-degree." (Ripple effects will be discussed more later in this chapter.)

Developing Scenarios for Change

Once one has identified a potential leverage point, it is helpful to understand the potential vectors that changes already happening in the system might follow so that a peacebuilder can encourage that change in ways that increase the society's level of peace. For example, the likelihood that Cambodian economic growth rates would slow or even decline meant that there would be change in the elite patron-client dynamic, but it did not predict what that change would be. A systems map (or any particular feedback loop) is not like a mathematical equation where if you change one variable, you can predict the impact on the product of the equation. Similarly, knowing that the economic growth rate will change does not imply a specific consequence for the level of peace in Cambodia. Rather, once a potential leverage point for change has been identified, the next task is to envision some likely ways the system might respond to this change. Because it is impossible to envision every likely future scenario, it is enough to look at two reasonably plausible scenarios, one representing a more pessimistic and the other a more optimistic outcome.

In the Cambodian ICAF, the potential economic leverage point was likely to result in some degree of challenge to the CPP's hold on power, which was critical to the level of stability in the country.[15] Thus, the optimistic scenario looked at ways the system could respond to lower economic growth rates in order to minimize the levels of instability. We labeled the optimistic scenario the "Economic Green Scenario" and the pessimistic scenario the "Economic Red Scenario."

The red scenario includes multiple feedback loops (see Figure 7.3). The first is the same as the original elite patron-client dynamic, except instead of being a reinforcing loop that increases the CPP's hold on power, it becomes a reinforcing loop that decreases the CPP's hold on power:

- *Economic Red Scenario, Loop R1:* Declining economic growth means that there are fewer rent-seeking opportunities. In turn, having fewer rent-seeking opportunities leads to a weakening of elite buy-in and the basic client-patron mind-set, which constrains the activities of the CPP and lowers its aggregation of power. As the CPP's hold on power lessens, it has greater difficulty doling out rent-seeking opportunities, which further lessens the number of rent-seeking opportunities given to elites, and the cycle continues to deteriorate.

- *Economic Red Scenario, Loop R2:* Fewer rent-seeking opportunities also kicks off another reinforcing loop that further challenges the CPP's hold on power. Declining elite buy-in kicks off a potential search for alternative rents, which can lead to a search for alternative patrons, be they domestic challengers to the CPP (such as disaffected elites) or foreign powers. The search for alternative patrons leads to more fragmentation of political power, which further lessens the rent-seeking opportunities the CPP can dole out. More ominously, the fragmentation of power can lead to the CPP's asserting control through more authoritarian rule, which leads to even greater levels of elite dissatisfaction, and the loop continues and intensifies.[16]

The Economic Green Scenario begins with the same initial outer loop (R1) as in the red scenario, where lower economic growth leads to fewer rent-seeking opportunities, less elite buy-in, more fragmentation of power, and ultimately even fewer rent-seeking opportunities (see Figure 7.4). In the red scenario, the CPP responds to R1 by using more authoritarian rule, which

Figure 7.3 Economic Red Scenario

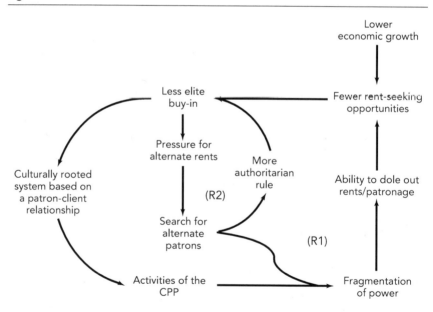

creates another reinforcing loop (R2) that further erodes the CPP's hold on power and increases instability. However, in the green scenario, the ICAF group posits that the CPP could respond to the decline in economic growth by regularizing the policy-making environment as a step toward promoting more manageable long-term economic growth. The World Bank did a study of the habits of the economies that grew by 10 percent or more per year for twenty years. An important finding was that a key to sustaining economic growth was to increase investment, from domestic sources, in infrastructure and education, as well as to build government capacity and credibility in economic policy making.[17] The CPP would also need to invest in more in-clusive growth and retreat from the more egregious forms of land grabbing that benefit a small group of elites and create broad economic inequities. However, this investment in a more regularized policy-making environment could bring Cambodia in line with other countries that have maintained strong economic growth and help blunt the impact of a decline in economic growth. The investment in a regularized policy-making environment could lead to moderate, long-term economic growth, which in turn would help increase the number of rent-seeking opportunities, which would initially decline as economic growth declined. This causal chain forms a balancing loop (B1).

Figure 7.4 Economic Green Scenario

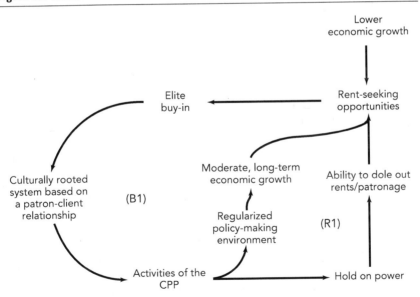

Developing Indicators for Change

The red and green scenarios for change provide two contrasting visions of how change in the system can play out. They provide a set of bookends within which planners can now ask what direction of change they want to support. Of course, this brings us back to the ethical question concerning the right of any peacebuilder to influence change in the system and the moral and ethical implications of working for any specific change. The rest of this planning process discussion assumes that these ethical issues are debated in an open and inclusive way but does not attempt to draw a universal, bright-line rule that might apply in every circumstance, subject of course to generally accepted principles of human rights.[18]

A critical question is, How will a peacebuilder know if a particular social system is following the red or the green scenario? To do this, it is helpful to develop indicators of change for both scenarios. For example, in the Cambodian ICAF, the team developed two sets of indicators to help US government planners understand whether Cambodia was responding to the change in the economy in ways that would push the country more toward the red or the green scenario. The team developed seven indicators for each scenario, such as "macro-economic indicators" and "investments in creating a better policy environment." These indicators were suggested as signposts for gauging how Cambodia was responding to the decline in economic growth. For each of these seven indicators, we developed two sets of measures, one for each scenario. Table 7.1 lists the indicators and measures we developed. In total, the ICAF team developed nineteen indicators of change associated with the economic leverage point for change. Taken together, these indicators for the red and green scenarios constitute a change profile that can serve as a reference point for peacebuilders to use in determining their own programmatic goals and objectives, or, in more systemic terms, how they can best work with a system to nurture long-term change.

SYSTEMIC PLANNING STEP 2: WORK WITH THE SYSTEM

The change profile paints a picture of the enormity of the macro-level changes needed to increase a social system's level of peace. However, no one intervener, or network of interveners, is able to implement a macro-level approach to creating all the changes identified in the change profile. This means that the biggest challenge peacebuilding planners face is how to bridge the gap between the complexity of macro-level change and the reality of micro-level programming. To make matters worse, as Chapter 4 argues, "adding up," the traditional approach to bridging the micro-macro gap that assumes many micro-level impacts will amalgamate into macro-level change, does not work.

Table 7.1 Change Profile for the Key Economic Leverage Point

Economic Dynamics

Red Scenario	*Green Scenario*
1. Macro-Economic Indicators	
• Shrinking pie/low or declining levels of economic growth • Rapidly increasing levels of poverty	• Moderate/stable rates of economic growth • Stable, small increases in poverty levels
2. Level of Pragmatism in Government Statements on Economy	
• Denial, obliviousness to economic challenges and trends • Misleading, inflated, and/or irregular indicators to support predetermined political goals	• Recognition of problems • Use of credible economic statistics and economic indicators
3. Economic Investments	
• Investments in the mineral sector • Concessions to economic interests that build large corporate operations (fishing, farming, etc.) that deliver very little value to local Cambodians	• Investments in the agricultural sector • Development projects that strengthen the value chain and spread the benefits of economic development to more Cambodians
4. Public Investments in Rural/Social Infrastructure	
• Selective show projects that have little strategic development value or thinking behind them	• Strategic investments in projects that support overall development goals and build rural capacity for self-sufficiency (e.g., health, education, etc.)
5. Security of Property Rights	
• Greater predatory use of government entities (e.g., land grabbing) with impunity • Inadequate land laws that are subject to abuse	• Predictability, confidence in security of property ownership • A legal approach that balances the interests of those with no formal land title with interests in economic development • Credible recourse to courts

(continues on next page)

While systemic peacebuilding may present obstacles, it also presents opportunities. While no one group of interveners has the power to do it on its own, the key to making systemic change is to harness a system's inherent dynamism. Social systems are constantly in motion and constantly changing. Whether a peacebuilder is aware of it or not, the dynamic feedback loops within a system are working with or against (or possibly both) the changes he or she is trying to make. The tools for working with the system are designed to help peacebuilders maximize the chance that they will work with, not against, it.

Table 7.1 (continued)

Economic and Institutional Dynamic	
Red Scenario	*Green Scenario*
6. Investments in Creating a Better Policy Environment	
• Lack of qualified staff to support key functions • Further marginalization, undercutting of opposition parties by ruling party • Expansion of patronage jobs into key policy-making positions • Uncoordinated, fragmented responses to key policy challenges • More government secrecy and impunity • Passage of key laws with no government enforcement capacity • Long delays in passing key laws (e.g., anticorruption laws)	• Training for key ministry staff/sufficient resourcing for key functions (especially legislative) • Collaboration of ruling party with opposition to produce key legislative initiatives • Qualified hires/appointments to key policy-making positions • Formation of cross-ministry teams to deal with cross-cutting issues like the environment • More government transparency/accountability • Development of government vision/strategy in key sectors and more regular policy reviews
7. Stability Within Ruling Elite Portfolios	
• Frequent shifting of elites from one political/economic portfolio to another • Increased competition for short-term rents • More open elite disagreements, retaliations, disaffection (especially among the military)	• Stable and predictable allocation of portfolios to elites • Increased support for long-term economic development versus short-term personal gain • Effective dispute-resolution abilities among elites

In order to work with a system to foster Peace Writ Large, peacebuilding planners need to do the following:

1. *Articulate a pathway:* Where should peacebuilders focus their attention, and what theory of change, or pathway, describes how the changes an intervener aspires to nurture will contribute to increasing the society's level of peace?
2. *Strengthen their pathway:* This is accomplished by
   • maximizing holism—increasing the sustainability of micro-level impacts by ensuring that they effect change in each of the structural, attitudinal, and transactional domains;
   • maximizing positive interdependence—using the power of dynamic feedback loops in the system to amplify micro-level program impacts in ways that help bridge the gaps between the micro, meso, and macro levels;
   • minimizing negative interdependence—reducing the potential for dynamic feedback loops or other causal factors in the system to undermine the impact of micro-level programs.

3. *Build their network:* How can interveners work effectively with other peacebuilders to strengthen their systemic impact?

4. *Structure feed-forward to get good feedback:* What key lessons produced by the systemic assessment and planning process need both to guide implementation and to be tested in light of field experience?

For many peacebuilding organizations, a funding agency defines their programs, such as building roads, demobilizing child soldiers, or training human rights monitors. These organizations may not have the leeway to define their own program goals or select what types of changes they will support. However, even for these peacebuilders, there is still a benefit in understanding how their assigned program relates to the process of systems change (as defined in the change profile) and harnessing the power of working with a system to the extent that they can.

Articulating Their Pathway: Structural Lens[19]

A change profile, as in the Cambodia example above, can help peacebuilders get a preliminary idea of how to focus their efforts (e.g., which indicators of change they are best able to work on). One way to do this is to survey the environment to understand what indicators other peacebuilders may be working on and where one's organization might enjoy a comparative advantage. For example, a peacebuilder might

- *map* the peacebuilding environment to understand which peacebuilders might be addressing other indicators of change in order to avoid duplication of efforts, spot unaddressed needs, and identify potential partners and collaborators;
- *inventory* the skills, capacities and resources, areas of expertise, relationships and networks, and interests of the organization(s) involved in the effort;
- *identify* areas of comparative value, where the organizations and their networks enjoy a relative advantage in nurturing particular changes in the system;
- *consider* what actions the organizations could take that best align with their collective values and ethics.

Once an organization or network has an idea of where it might best work to nurture change in a system, the next task is to refine and assess how those changes might contribute to PWL. Often, an organization's theory of change, or how an impact at one place in the system will lead to macro-level change, is left unarticulated. The theory of how a particular program or group of programs will affect a society's level of peace using a systems map is called a *pathway*. For example, in the Cambodian case discussed above, the peacebuilding organization GoX is hoping the Cambodian government will follow the pathway illustrated by the Economic Green Scenario in Figure 7.4. By promoting a more regular policy-making environment, GoX hopes to change how the Cambodian government works to maintain its power. Rather than making Cambodia less democratic as part of the process of doling out rents, GoX is trying to encourage the Cambodian government to respond to the global economic slowdown with measures that will both encourage stability and increase the level of democratic governance.

In order to better illustrate how to articulate a pathway and, more importantly, how to strengthen it through an understanding of interdependence, it may be more helpful to take a more difficult example, that of a micro-level actor trying to increase the potential that its micro-level programs will contribute to macro-level change. It is a bit easier for an actor with a macro-level perspective, like GoX, that is planning meso-level programming to see a connection to change at the macro level in Cambodia. It would be harder for an NGO working in a few villages in Afghanistan to see how to maximize the chance that its efforts might contribute to increasing the level of peace in that country.

Specifically, assume that a fictitious NGO, People Talking to People (P2P), has been asked by a donor to run a program called Dialogue in Afghan Communities (DAC). Even though the goals of the program are being set for P2P, it is still essential that the organization do an SPA and systems map. Ideally, the donor sponsoring the DAC program will have done this as well and listened to the system in order to decide that the DAC program was worth funding.

The challenge for P2P is to use a systems map to articulate how the DAC program can contribute to PWL in Afghanistan. For example, if P2P is using the systems maps of Afghanistan, what pathway can explain how the impacts of the DAC program might increase the level of peace in Afghanistan? Just articulating a possible or desired pathway from the impacts of a particular local project to PWL at the societal level does not ensure the connection from the micro to the macro will happen. However, evaluating and strengthening that connection will be impossible if it remains unarticulated. Articulating a pathway is just the first step—one that is necessary to assess the viability of that pathway or increase the chances that it will make a lasting contribution to peace.

Developing a pathway starts by asking whether the intended impacts of the DAC program affect any of the key factors that appear in the Afghanistan systems map (from Chapter 6). For example, DAC is intended to strengthen peaceful reconciliation and the capacity to mitigate conflict in Afghanistan.

In terms of the Afghanistan systems map, the program is especially relevant to two key factors: "conflict in communities" and "ethnic tensions/politics." If the program were successful in addressing these two factors, reducing the level of conflict in communities and ethnic tension in Afghanistan, how would that affect the level of peace? Figure 7.5 is based on the Afghanistan systems map and shows how affecting these two factors might impact the level of peace. For example, reducing the level of conflict in communities would help lower the level of unmet expectations, which in turn would help improve respect for the rule of law in Afghanistan and reduce the activity of armed groups. These two factors might help reduce the level of insecurity, which is a proximate driver of the level of peace. In addition, less insecurity would improve the economy, helping to increase the level of peace and further reducing the level of conflict in communities. This last connection forms a reinforcing loop (R1) that will further amplify the initial reduction in the level of conflict in communities.

Figure 7.5 Illustrative Macro-Level Program Pathway: Dialogues in Afghan Communities Project (DAC)

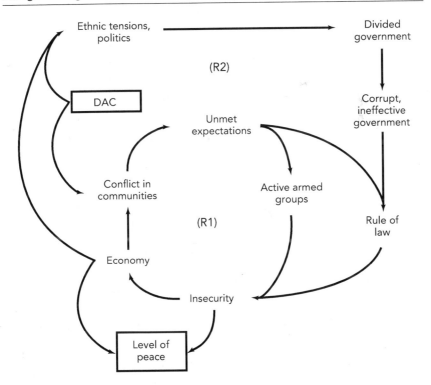

The DAC program also aims to lessen the level of ethnic tensions and politics. A reduction in the level of ethnic tensions forms part of a second reinforcing loop. Lower ethnic tensions will help reduce the level of divided government, which helps reduce the level of corrupt, ineffective government. In turn, this will help improve respect for the rule of law, lessen insecurity, and help the economy, which will further reduce the level of ethnic tensions (R2).

Again, just articulating these linkages does not mean that the DAC program will increase the level of peace in Afghanistan. There are large logical and logistical leaps between the DAC program lessening conflict in ten or even one hundred of the thousands of villages in Afghanistan, thereby lessening the overall level of conflict in communities and affecting peace at the macro level. However, identifying a pathway is meant to correct one simple problem with existing peacebuilding practice: the tendency to assume, with little critical thought, that good work at the local level will add up to peace at the societal level. The pathway is a minimum requirement if peacebuilders are going to have a macro-level impact. It is a way of saying, If our program is to make a contribution to PWL, this is how it will have to work given the social system as we understand it. A second contribution of the pathways analysis is that it forces peacebuilders to think about their impacts in systemic rather than linear terms. Lastly, the pathways analysis is important because it forces peacebuilders to contextualize their programs and their impacts in light of a particular society and its unique dynamics.

Strengthening Their Pathway: Holism Analysis

A pathways analysis is a necessary step for peacebuilders, but it is not sufficient in itself. A pathway is a structural description of how a micro-level impact might potentially affect a society's level of peace. Stopping the planning process at this stage is a bit like the "If you build it, he will come" school of wishful thinking. In order to evaluate and improve the potential for a program to make a sustainable contribution to Peace Writ Large, peacebuilders need to assess the degree to which it is affecting change across the three SAT domains: structural, attitudinal, and transactional. According to the SAT model, sustainable change processes require a dynamic interaction between changes in the three SAT domains. Further, the SAT model holds that transactional peacebuilding can be used as the catalyst to effect structural and attitudinal change.

A peacebuilding program is more holistic, and its impacts more sustainable and systemic, to the degree that it complies with these two tenets of the SAT model. The first step to increasing a program's holism is to fine-tune not just a program's desired impacts but how it tries to create them. For example, the purpose of the DAC program is to affect two key factors: "conflict in communities" and "ethnic tensions." Rather than trying to eliminate these factors, the DAC program should seek to change the relationship between them and other factors in the system (see Chapter 4). Currently, conflict in communities contributes to the level of unmet expectations, which in turn undermines the rule of law and increases the activity of armed groups. Both of these factors contribute to insecurity and lower Afghanistan's level of peace. To be more holistic, the DAC program needs to change how communities deal with conflict so that instead of increasing, the level of unmet expectations is lowered.

In order to change the polarity of the impact of conflict in communities on unmet expectations, the DAC program needs to have impact across the three SAT domains because there are likely to be structural, attitudinal, and transactional reasons for why conflict in communities increases unmet expectations. For example, conflict in communities has an obvious transactional dimension: Key people from rival families in a village are unable to resolve interfamilial disputes. These unresolved disputes may mean that needed development projects cannot take place (e.g., the community is unable to organize itself to work with a donor) or the development projects that do take place are not sustainable (e.g., crops are burned because one clan takes revenge on another due to an unsettled dispute). Unresolved disputes can lead to a strong sense of distrust and tension between families in the village (an attitudinal driver), giving rise to further transactional breakdowns, and the cycle starts over again.

The purpose of the holism analysis is to assess the degree to which the DAC program is having impacts in the SAT domains. Table 7.2 presents an analysis of the extent to which the DAC program, as originally conceived, is having structural, attitudinal, and transactional impacts.

Like many programs, the DAC program was primarily designed in one of the three SAT domains: transactional. As a result, it is strong on making transactional impacts. The glaring omission of the DAC program is the absence of explicit structural activity or impact. There are some residual impacts on attitudes in villages where the DAC program operates. However, without any associated structural changes, attitudinal changes tend to be short-lived. Dialogue can be a powerful tool in building trust and changing intergroup perceptions in the short term. Without longer-lasting structural changes resulting from dialogue, old levels of mistrust and suspicion may quickly reemerge as participants find life in the village to be as difficult as always and conclude that talk is cheap.

Without creating a dynamic interplay between structural, attitudinal, and transactional changes, the DAC program may actually increase the level of unmet expectations. Dialogue is usually an empowering experience, and participants often leave the process with increased hope and expectations for

Table 7.2 Illustrative Holism Analysis

Intended Impacts of the DAC Program	Lower the Level of Conflict in Communities and Reduce Ethnic Tensions		
	Structural	Attitudinal	Transactional
Desired impact	?	Increased trust between families and lower levels of tension	Communities able to manage conflicts productively
Activity	Reestablish traditional community dispute-resolution structures ?	Interfamily dialogue Interfamily confidence-building measures	Reestablish traditional community dispute-resolution structures Provide dialogue and facilitation training Community mobilization
Indicators of change	?	Lower levels of tension as measured by a survey Less antagonistic, more collaborative statements from one family toward another	Lower levels of community violence Greater community satisfaction with dispute settlements Sustainable dispute settlements/ reemergence of fewer settled disputes

the future. However, dialogue can also be risky as participants might create suspicion and distrust among members of their own community who disapprove of talking to the "other side." And if dialogue is not seen as leading to tangible improvements on the ground (structural change) or lasting attitudinal change, then participants and the broader community may become even more cynical and pessimistic about the future.

The holism analysis identifies a major weakness in the pathway from the DAC program to macro-level change. In response to this weakness, the DAC program planners need to find ways to integrate structural activity and impact. A simple response would be to add structural activity into the DAC program, such as using community dialogue to identify needed structural improvements (such as rebuilding irrigation canals or building a health clinic) and to provide the resources needed to implement these programs. However, many programs either do not have the financial recourse to add new activities to their projects or are precluded by donor restrictions from diverting resources from one use (e.g., dialogue) to other activity (e.g., building a health clinic). These restrictions leave one potential source for the DAC program to increase its holism: networking with other organizations that have a mandate and resources to do structural peacebuilding (more on this below).

Strengthening Their Pathway: Increasing Positive Interdependence

The holism analysis examines how well a program affects the relationship between factors in a social system (e.g., how well does the DAC program change the relationship between conflict in communities and the level of unmet expectations). Rather than looking at the relationship between a program and particular factors in a system, the interdependence analysis looks at how a program affects, and is affected by, the dynamic feedback loops in a social system. In general terms, the relationship between a program, such as the DAC program, and the dynamics of a social system like Afghanistan can be of two types: positive or negative. Positive interdependence is the degree to which a dynamic in the system amplifies the impact of a program, while negative interdependence is the degree to which dynamics in the system counteract the impacts of a program.

More importantly, positive interdependence is the primary means for bridging the micro-macro gap. Because micro-level program impacts do not add up linearly, there are two primary ways to bridge the gap between local impacts and macro-level change:

- *Replication:* If a program works in one village, then reproducing that program in many villages should expand its impact to the meso and macro levels.
- *Interacting out:* The way to expand the impact of a local program is to use the power of a reinforcing feedback loop or loops in the system to amplify positive impacts.

The practice of replicating, or scaling up, a successful program is the more common approach to bridging the micro and macro levels, but it is much more difficult than commonly assumed to repeat the success of a program that works well in one context, or one village-level social system, in a different context. Each project must be tailored to the particular social system in which it takes place. The means of creating a positive dynamic between structural, attitudinal, and transactional change will differ in each community, as will the key people that must be engaged. This does not mean that replicating successful programs is impossible. Lessons learned in one context should inform the implementation of similar programs in another. However, the need to tailor programs to specific village-level social systems means that replication is not as cost-effective as currently assumed; nor is it assured that even a properly replicated program will succeed in a new context.

Therefore, maximizing a program's positive interdependence, or the likelihood that positive program impacts can be amplified by dynamics within a system, may be the more efficient way to bridge the micro-macro gap. Assessing positive interdependence means identifying which feedback loops are impacted by a program and assessing how strong those impacts are. For example, the DAC program has direct impacts on conflict in communities and ethnic tensions. Therefore, DAC has ripple effects on every other factor and feedback loop that these two factors affect.

However, a central problem in articulating a connection between a micro-level program and macro-level change is how attenuated impacts become. In other words, even if a program does what it says it will do at the local level, such as lowering the level of conflict in communities and the level of ethnic tensions in a few villages, it is likely to have a much smaller impact on conflict in communities and ethnic tensions in a province that may contain dozens of villages or, on the macro level, in a country like Afghanistan that has several thousand villages.[20] The problem of attenuated impacts is illustrated by the fact that a connection between the direct, micro-level impacts of the DAC program and macro-level change in the level of peace takes five steps. For example, affecting (1) conflict in communities affects (2) unmet expectations, which affects (3) active armed groups, which affects (4) insecurity, which then affects (5) the level of peace. If micro-level program impacts are reduced with each step it takes to make a connection to macro-level change, then even large micro-level successes will have miniscule impacts at the macro level.

Fortunately, it is not as simple as that. Impacts do not necessarily travel through a system in a linear fashion. It is impossible to know, with mathematical certainty, how impacts at the micro level will reverberate through a system. The best peacebuilders can do is to increase the chances that the dynamics in a system will amplify a program's micro-level impacts (positive interdependence) and to minimize the dynamics' potential to counteract a program's micro-level impacts (negative interdependence). In order to understand and potentially augment the positive interdependence between the micro-level impacts of the DAC program and Afghanistan's level of peace, it is necessary to understand the strength of the program's impacts. A program's positive interdependence can be assessed and enhanced by improving its

- cumulative impact
- ripple effect
- amplifier effect

Cumulative impact. Many factors in a system have multiple arrows going into them, meaning that multiple factors often affect any one factor. For example, using the detail complexity systems analysis of Afghanistan that I did with Mercy Corps (see the discussion of detail versus dynamic complexity in Chapter 6), the factor "unmet expectations" is influenced by five factors: "conflict in communities," "economy," "corrupt/ineffective government," "rural versus urban divide," and "lack of voice for communities."[21] These factors do not have the same relative influence on the level of unmet expectations; in other words, each of the five causal factors does not account for 20 percent of unmet expectations. Some factors are more important drivers of unmet expectations than others. While it may not be possible to know precisely the relative importance of each causal factor, there is a tipping point beyond which changes in them will change the nature of the relationship between the five causal factors and unmet expectations. At some point, a lower level of conflict in communities plus changes in the other four causal factors will turn the "+/+" relationship between conflict in communities and unmet expectations into a "−/−" relationship: Instead of more conflict in communities increasing the level of unmet expectations, a lower level of conflict in communities will decrease the level of unmet expectations.

In order to maximize the chances that the DAC program will succeed in finding this tipping point, the program should seek to affect either as many of the causal factors that affect unmet expectations as possible or the most important causal factors that lead to unmet expectations. For example, doing more to impact the economy, remedying a community's lack of voice, and strengthening governance would help build the cumulative impact of reducing conflict in communities and increase the likelihood of finding a tipping point in the relationship between this factor and unmet expectations. The cumulative impact analysis should be done on all the important causal relationships in the DAC program's pathway, including the program's intended initial impact on conflict in communities. For example, the DAC program should pay special attention to the impact of lack of infrastructure and lack of voice for communities, two important causal factors that affect the level of conflict in communities. All of these potential ways to increase the DAC program's cumulative impact should be included in the program planning chart (see below).

Before we move on to the other methods for increasing positive interdependence, it is necessary to reflect on how to assess the importance of a causal factor. The relative importance of a causal factor can be assessed in either qualitative or quantitative terms. A qualitative approach means using one's intuition, informed by as much research as possible, to assign relative weights to causal factors. This is the approach used in the dynamic complexity map of Afghanistan (see the discussion of managing detail versus dynamic complexity in Chapter 6). For example, corrupt/ineffective government is assigned a larger weight in affecting unmet expectations (represented by a thicker arrow) than conflict in communities, which is assigned more weight than lack of voice for communities or the rural versus urban divide.

This may seem dangerously imprecise in comparison to a more quantitative method. It is possible to sharpen these intuitive assessments by assigning precise values to represent the importance of various factors. For example, each causal factor could be assigned a relative weight to represent its impact on a factor, such as determining that corrupt/ineffective government is responsible for 40 percent of unmet expectations while the rural versus urban divide accounts for only 5 percent. Another approach is to assign a value to each factor to represent its general impact on the system. For example, in the article "Planning for Systemic Impact," an "impact value" is assigned to each factor in a systems map.[22] These values are calculated by using a detail complexity map and assigning each factor a certain number of points based on both the number of impacts it has on other factors in the system and on the importance of the factor affected. For example, factors with direct impacts on the system's level of peace are worth more than those with a secondary impact on the level of peace, and so on.

While more quantitative approaches may seem to provide harder and more definitive assessments, these judgments are still subjective. Assigning a numeric value to them may be dangerous as analysts often confuse numeric value with objective certainty. Whether one uses a qualitative or more quantitative approach, an analyst's assessment about which causal factors are important and the nature of the relationships between them is still an educated hypothesis that must be tested in light of experience and new information.

Ripple effect. Another way to think about a factor's importance from the perspective of maximizing positive interdependence is to look at how many factors any given factor affects: The more factors any one factor affects, the better. For example, "rural versus urban divide" affects two other factors in the detail complexity systems map of Afghanistan. On the other hand, "insecurity" affects eight other factors. A program will generate a bigger change if it has a significant impact on insecurity than if it has a significant impact on the rural versus urban divide. Said another way, a significant impact on insecurity has a greater ripple effect. Of course, it is more difficult to have a significant impact on a factor like insecurity because, in addition to affecting many factors (eight), it is also affected by many factors (seven). Therefore, it is especially helpful to look at the cumulative impact of a program on factors that have a high ripple effect.

In the case of the DAC program, a wise investment of resources might be to strengthen the program's cumulative impact on the factor "corrupt/ineffective government" because it has a high ripple effect. In addition, as noted in the holism analysis, it may also be a good investment to expand the

DAC program to affect the factor "economy," both because of its ripple effect and because doing so would strengthen the program's cumulative impacts on other key causal factors.

Amplifier effect. Both cumulative impact and the ripple effect deal with the relationship of a program to other individual causal factors. The amplifier effect deals with the relationship of a program to a feedback loop as a whole. It refers to the potential for the micro-level impacts of a program to be augmented, or amplified, by a reinforcing feedback loop within a social system. This phenomenon is best illustrated by the butterfly effect, a metaphor from chaos theory for how small and seemingly inconsequential events can have catastrophic impacts. In the story, the small impact of a butterfly flapping its wings in a South American jungle is amplified by the interrelationships of a dynamical system and causes a tsunami in Asia. Similarly, micro-level impacts can be amplified by dynamic feedback loops and create macro-level impacts.

For example, the DAC program affects two reinforcing loops in the Afghanistan dynamic complexity systems map (see Figure 7.5). One of those dynamic loops is R1 in Figure 7.5. Currently, this loop is a vicious cycle: Conflict in communities leads to higher levels of unmet expectations, which increases the activity of armed groups and lowers respect for the rule of law. In turn, these factors increase the level of insecurity, which worsens the economy and increases the level of conflict in communities. In addition, both insecurity and a worsening economy lower the level of peace. Just as with the relationship between two causal factors, there is a tipping point at which this vicious cycle can become a virtuous cycle, where a reduction in conflict in communities, though a dynamic interplay with the same feedback loop, results in an improving economy, lower levels of insecurity, and an increasing level of peace.

It is probably impossible to know precisely what kinds of impacts or changes to this feedback loop will cause it to turn from a vicious into a virtuous cycle. However, the chances of finding this tipping point are most likely increased with each positive change to the other causal factors in the loop and the relationships between them. In other words, the chance of this feedback loop amplifying the impacts the DAC program has on conflict in communities is increased if the levels of unmet expectations and the activity of armed groups are lowered, the respect for the rule of law increased, the economy improved, and so on. The need to harness the power of the amplifier effect in order to bridge the micro-macro gap means that the sponsors of the DAC program must be aware of programs that are trying to impact the other causal factors that are part of the same feedback loop of which conflict in communities is a part. This argues for forming a network of effective action with other programs and organizations that operate in the same feedback loop as the DAC program.

The result of the positive interdependence analysis is to identify ways the DAC program can increase its cumulative impact on the factors it is trying to affect directly (conflict in communities and ethnic tensions) and those that these two factors affect, increase the program's impact on factors that have a large ripple effect on the system, and increase the potential amplifier effect of feedback loops in the system to help bridge the gap between micro- and macro-level impacts. The output of this analysis is captured in a systemic program planning chart (see Table 7.3).

Strengthening Their Pathway: Countering Negative Interdependence

Negative interdependence represents the power of systems to undermine the sustainability of program impacts or even to turn micro-level successes into unintended negative consequences. For example, remember the example of the island nation of Kiribati from Chapter 4. In response to the problem of declining fish stocks, the government of Kiribati and aid organizations subsidized coconut farming as an incentive to get residents to fish less. The program, however, had the opposite outcome: Fishing increased. The Kiribati experience is an example of negative interdependence. The government and aid organizations assumed that by making coconut farming more profitable than fishing, more people would grow coconuts and fewer would fish. So, the government provided a subsidy to coconut farmers in order to increase incomes from coconut farming. It was believed that more revenue from coconut farming would reduce the need for (and amount of) commercial fishing, which would both increase fish stocks and reduce the amount of income from fishing. This drop in income would then lead to more need for coconut farming, and the cycle would reinforce the draw toward coconut farming and away from commercial fishing. This dynamic is represented as R1 in Figure 7.6.

What the government had not counted on was that increasing the profitability of coconut farming would increase disposable incomes, which in turn would increase the amount of leisure fishing and improve the productivity of fishing (both commercial and leisure) by increasing the quality of fishing equipment and technology. This is represented as R2 in Figure 7.6. The strategy of increasing the profitability of coconut farming might have worked to reduce the amount of commercial fishing and increase fish stocks if not for the impact of leisure fishing and improved fishing technology. The level of fish stocks was dependent on three factors: the level of commercial fishing, the level of fishing technology, and the amount of leisure fishing. The government and aid organizations ignored the impact of two of these three variables. The level of leisure fishing and fishing technology had a negative

Table 7.3 Systemic Program Planning

Holism Analysis	
Program Need	*Possible Responses*
• Add structural and additional attitudinal impacts to the DAC program.	• Consult communities to identify structural needs; map other agencies that are doing or could do structural peacebuilding work in DAC communities. • Network by sharing information with agencies to explore coordination or expansion of the DAC program into the structural area.

Positive Interdependence Analysis	
Program Need	*Possible Responses*
Cumulative impact • Improve DAC's impact on factors that affect conflict in communities (lack of voice for communities and lack of infrastructure, resources, and skills) and ethnic tensions and politics (economy and international interference).	*Economy* • Info sharing: Share information with NGOs doing economic-development work about economic needs in communities with the DAC program. • Coordination/collaboration: Develop a model collaboration with an NGO doing economic-development work in Afghanistan to link the DAC program with its economic-development activity. • Advocacy: Lobby donors to fund economic-development work in communities with the DAC program. Lobby DAC funders to include additional resources for economic development. [continue the analysis with *lack of voice* and *infrastructure*]
Multiplier effect • Improve DAC's impact on corrupt, ineffective government and economy.	*Corrupt, ineffective government* • Modify and expand DAC to increase skills training in dialogue and negotiation to local governments; hold dialogue sessions between villagers and local governments. • Network (coordinate/collaborate) with other agencies with programs and expertise in improving the effectiveness of local governance. • Network (advocacy with other agencies) to lobby donors to expend resources for improving local governance. [continue the analysis with *economy*]
Amplifier effect • Improve DAC's impact on factors in the R1 loop: unmet expectations, active armed groups, rule of law, insecurity, and economy.	*Multiple factors* • Monitor and map other agencies working on the R1 factors. • Explore networking opportunities (information sharing, coordination/collaboration, and joint advocacy).

Negative Interdependence Analysis	
Program Need	*Possible Responses*
• Understand and counteract the potential for key factors that are unaddressed by DAC to undermine the value and/or sustainability of DAC impacts, such as international interference, economy, and active armed groups.	*International interference* • Monitor how international actors' activity in Afghanistan affects the DAC program and the villages where DAC is working. • Work with other NGOs to advocate for greater protection for civilian populations and the cutting off of support for nonstate armed groups. [continue the analysis with *active armed groups* and *economy*]

Figure 7.6 Negative Interdependence: Kiribati Example

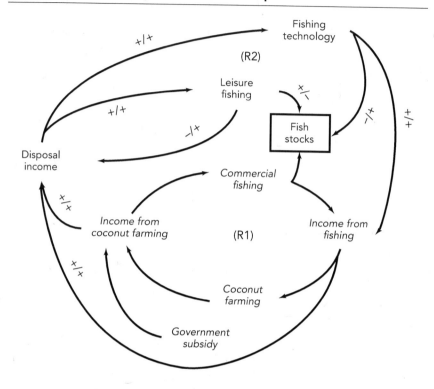

impact on the ability of a partial reduction in commercial fishing alone to increase the level of fish stocks.

By ignoring the impact of disposable income on the amount of leisure fishing and the level of fishing technology, the program had unintended negative impacts. The negative interdependence analysis is meant to prevent this type of problem. The analysis is the inverse of the cumulative impact and amplifier effect assessments. Negative interdependence asks two questions:

1. Are there factors outside the scope of the planned project that could frustrate or counteract the intended impacts of the project?
2. Are there dynamics in the system that might frustrate or counteract the project's intended pathway from micro- to macro-level impacts?

In the case of the DAC program, efforts to rehabilitate traditional community dispute-resolution structures and improve their problem-solving and facilitation skills are intended to reduce the level of conflict in communities. This addresses part of one of the three drivers of that factor: a lack of skills. It does not address the lack of infrastructure and resources in general; nor does it affect economy or the lack of voice for communities in addressing community development and other needs. The risk is that even if the DAC program achieves its intended objectives, setbacks in the economy, the lack of other infrastructure, or frustration over the lack of community voice may undermine any positive impacts. Peacebuilders need to decide whether—and if so, to what extent—to address these other factors in their program planning.

Moreover, conflict in communities is part of several feedback loops. The DAC program risks negative interdependence with other factors in these broader loops. For example, the pathway from conflict in communities to level of peace depends heavily on reducing the level of insecurity in Afghanistan. The DAC program has a rather attenuated affect on insecurity. Moreover, the DAC program does not have a strong impact on three of the four factors that affect the level of insecurity: international interference, economy, and armed groups.

In addition, the DAC pathway relies heavily on reducing unmet expectations and improving respect for the rule of law. Corrupt/ineffective government and the economy have a stronger impact on these two key factors, yet the DAC program has a relatively weak impact on governance and the economy. Here again, the DAC program risks negative interdependence if these two factors, which are largely outside the scope of the DAC program, worsen and work to lower the level of peace in Afghanistan.

Strengthening Their Pathway: Networking[23]

The holism and interdependence analyses are designed to spot needs and opportunities for developing a program in ways that increase the lasting impacts of a program and, thereby, a program's impact on Peace Writ Large, or a system's level of peace. For example, Table 7.3 provides a list of the issues identified in the holism and interdependence analyses that need additional attention (e.g., how to increase the program's need for greater cumulative and/or ripple effects). There are three basic ways planners can address program needs in the hope of bridging the micro-macro gap (i.e., three ways to improve holism, increase positive interdependence, and lessen negative interdependence):

1. *Monitor and map:* The minimal way to address needs for program development is to find out who is working on a particular issue that is relevant to one's own program. It may not be necessary to make changes to a program if other organizations are addressing a particular programmatic need.

2. *Modify/expand:* Another way to address program needs is to take direct action by modifying or expanding a program to address variables not addressed or insufficiently addressed by the program as currently structured.
3. *Network:* An alternative to modifying a program is to work with other organizations to address a programmatic need.

Monitoring and mapping should be done as part of aiming efforts, but having a specific idea of which factors are most critical to the success of a particular program or set of programs will help focus efforts. Certainly programs can be modified or expanded depending on organizational resources and expertise. Often, however, the holism and interdependence analyses suggest a need to address issues that are outside of an organization's funding mandate, available resources, or area of expertise. Therefore, the much more frequent response to the program needs spotted in the holism and interdependence analyses is to do some form of networking. There is a range of possibilities for networking with other organizations:

1. *Information sharing:* In addition to identifying organizations working in related fields, an organization can share important information (e.g., program descriptions and updates, analyses, best practices, evaluation data, etc.).
2. *Coordination/collaboration:* A step beyond information sharing is deciding to act on this information by working together. This could include joint analysis and planning, coordinating activities, partnership, and the like.
3. *Advocacy:* In addition to programmatic coordination or collaboration with others, organizations can work together to advocate for policies, funds, or programs that address holism or interdependence problems. For example, if a certain type of economic-development work is needed but not currently funded, organizations can advocate for the development of such a program by donors.

Table 7.3 provides examples of how planners can address the needs for information sharing, coordination/collaboration, and advocacy through networking. It may not be possible for a program to address each of the factors identified because of resource or time constraints. At a minimum, however, planners should look through the chart to spot priority needs. For example, broadening the DAC program to address economic and related infrastructure needs should be a high priority because doing so would address program needs to add holism, maximize positive interdependence, and counter negative interdependence.

Further, networking can be a way to maximize resources by expanding impact but not increasing costs at the same rate. Chapter 4 provides some useful parameters for setting up networks of effective action:

- Create horizontal integration so that programs generate change in the SAT domains and involve participants with expertise in those domains as well.
- Create vertical integration so that programs span the local (micro), regional (meso), and societal or national (macro) levels.
- Follow an iterative planning, acting, and learning (PAL) cycle so that peacebuilders can gauge their progress against their target measures of change, test and revise their systems map of the situation, and capture both successes and failures.

Further, networks also increase the potential for learning, both about the system and its multiple dynamics and about which strategies and projects work well and which do not. In Easterly's terms, networks are much more efficient at "searching" than individual peacebuilders because networks increase the number and diversity of programs being tested and can collect best (and worst) practices. In this regard, peacebuilders could learn from examples in the corporate world where companies have set up forums whose explicit purpose is to learn from failures.

SYSTEMIC PLANNING STEP 3: LEARN FROM THE SYSTEM (FEED-FORWARD)

Ultimately, the goal of planning is to produce learning about how peacebuilders can work more effectively for systemic change. If the planning processes described above are done well, then peacebuilders should be in a good position to learn from a social system. Plans are really hypotheses to be tested against feedback from field experiences (which are the indicators of how a system is responding to changes in it).

However, the process of feedback is often short-circuited because the process of planning, from assessment to implementation to learning from experience, inevitably involves complex handoffs from person to person, department to department, and organization to organization. This could be from analyst to policy maker, donor to implementing agency, or international NGO to local NGO, and vice versa. This is especially true when peacebuilders are working in extended networks that are vertically and horizontally integrated. Jeremiah Pam, a Jennings Randolph Guest Scholar at the US Institute of Peace, argues that the complexity of the process makes it imperative to err on the side of simplicity in setting strategies for complex activities such as peacebuilding, while preserving a complex and nuanced analysis.[24] In order to do this, planners who are handing off peacebuilding strategies across a network of actors need to pass on clear guidance to those involved in the later stages of planning and implementation. This is the purpose of effective feed-forward.

Good feed-forward requires that analysts and planners (such as donors) hand off a few pieces of critical guidance to implementers by doing the following:

1. Setting priorities by
   - focusing attention on affecting dynamics, not just individual factors in a system;
   - identifying potential leverage points for change and developing a desired change profile;
   - aiming efforts by evaluating how the donor or implementing organization, with its resources and networks, can add comparative value to affecting the change profile;
2. Developing strategies for maximizing holism (e.g., integrating structural, attitudinal, and transactional changes);
3. Developing strategies for maximizing positive interdependence and minimizing negative interdependence;
4. Advising about potential networking with other programs or actors to strengthen the link between micro- and macro-level impacts;
5. Enabling good feedback by identifying indicators for macro-level change and key hypotheses to be tested in light of on-the-ground experience. Learning from the system is essential to helping peacebuilders better understand the social systems they are trying to affect.

This last point, identifying key hypotheses to enable better learning from the system, deserves some elaboration. A systems map is a hypothesis about how a social system works. Are the structural, attitudinal, and transactional factors initially included in the systems map important? What factors were underestimated or missed completely? What about the causal relationships identified between factors? For example, the Afghanistan dynamic complexity systems map analysis in Chapter 6 (see discussion of managing detail versus dynamic complexity) showed a parallel relationship between the level of conflict in communities and unmet expectations, where more of one led to more of the other. If the level of conflict in a community declines, do we see a drop in the level of unmet expectations as predicted? Why or why not? Does a particular village-level system differ in important ways from dynamics identified in a national-level systems map?

The change profile contains a list of indicators that can help test whether a map, and the factors, causal relationships, and feedback loops within it, reflect reality. Have assumptions about the organization, the capacity of its network, and how it can best add value to systemic change proved correct? Have hypotheses from the holism analysis about how to enhance the sustainability of program impacts by creating a dynamic interplay between SAT factors proved correct?

There are hypotheses about what will enhance positive interdependence and increase the potential for micro-level impacts to contribute to macro-level change and how to counter negative interdependence. Peacebuilders must be aware of whether they see evidence of micro-level impacts having meso- or macro-level impacts. Most traditional approaches to monitoring and evaluation of peacebuilding programs look only at whether a program is having micro-level impacts. Peacebuilders also need to identify and monitor evidence of meso-level impacts. For example, is there evidence that the DAC program's positive impact in a village or group of villages is having an impact at the district or even the provincial levels? Are other villages, districts, or even the national government taking notice of the DAC program and the possibility of replicating it? Do they see fewer unmet expectations in the province as a whole or increased acceptance and improved relationships between local governments, police forces, villages? Is the economy or level of security improving in the village, district, or province?

The DAC program and its sponsors must also be watchful for indicators of positive or negative interdependence not anticipated in their planning. Do they see unintended positive benefits of the DAC program, especially in the structural and attitudinal areas (where the program was weak at the outset)? Unfortunately, factors that lead to negative interdependence, or counteract the impacts of a program, are easier to spot after the fact than before. The negative interdependence of increases in disposable income were more obvious after the Kiribati program failed. Learning from the system means learning from failures as well. For example, are negative interactions impeding or counteracting positive impacts of the DAC program?

Complicating matters is the fact that systems themselves are constantly changing. This means that even if our initial analysis and planning were correct at one point, natural changes in the system may require changes to programs meant to affect it. So, along with learning about whether a program is engaging effectively with a system, there is a need to update the underlying analysis itself, including the SPA assessment and systems map.

In short, good feed-forward provides planners with an assessment of a context that is comprehensive, comprehensible, and portable. *Comprehensive* refers to the ability to provide a holistic view of a social system that does not oversimplify the situation by leaving out elements outside of an organization's interests or expertise. However, that comprehensive view also has to be *comprehensible* and avoid overloading planners with too much information, or what Peter Coleman eloquently refers to as "parsimony informed by complexity."[25] And that comprehensive and comprehensible feed-forward has to "travel well," or be *portable*. It needs to crystallize the assessment's main insights and implications for the many individuals who need to learn from and act on the assessment, especially when those individuals were not part of the initial assessment process.

CONCLUSION: THE NEED TO PRESERVE FLEXIBILITY AND ADAPTABILITY

Systemic planning requires different kinds of thinking and acting from those peacebuilders are currently familiar with and, hence, may seem more onerous and complex than it actually is. At its essence, the mind-set of a systemic planner focuses on these basic concepts: listening to a system, working with a system (holism, interdependence), networking, and learning from the system (feed-forward and feedback).

The bigger challenge is to do planning in a way that supports peacebuilding programs that are as flexible and adaptive as the social systems in which they operate. In turn, the key to being flexible and adaptive is to learn from experience. This requires many of the mind-set shifts identified in Chapter 4, such as creating an error-embracing culture that does not rely on overly controlling linear approaches, such as insisting on rigid, preset objectives to control the activity of implementing agencies. The key to making these mind-set shifts is for peacebuilders to put a value on learning—to make testing analytic hypotheses a central goal of any peacebuilding program. This comes back to Eisenhower's quote that started this chapter—plans are not important, but planning (assessment, action, and learning) is an essential, ongoing process.

CHAPTER 7 SUMMARY

- Systemic program planning requires peacebuilders to think of planning as a structured process for learning that needs to include an ongoing and inclusive dialogue about intervention ethics, help decision makers make responsible choices, and facilitate the formation of networks of effective action.
- Systemic planning starts with peacebuilders listening to the system in order to aim their efforts effectively, find areas where they add comparative value to making systemic change, and develop a change profile to inform their ongoing efforts.
- Working with a system means

- ○ understanding and enhancing the holism of programs in order to increase sustainability and systemic impacts;
- ○ harnessing the dynamism of a system to amplify micro-level impacts by maximizing positive interdependence through enhancing a program's cumulative impact, ripple effect, and amplifier effect;
- ○ avoiding negative interdependence by understanding how causal factors and/or feedback loops outside the immediate scope of a project can counteract positive local impacts;
- ○ building a network of effective action to help increase holism, maximize positive interdependence, and minimize negative interdependence.
- Good feed-forward is essential to getting good feedback. The ultimate purpose of systemic planning is to structure an effective process of learning about a system and how to effectively work with a system to increase its level of peace. A systems map and systemic planning techniques are designed to provide testable hypotheses about a system and to increase effectiveness over time.

PART III

CATALYZING SYSTEMIC CHANGE

CHAPTER 8

HELPING SYSTEMS CHANGE THEMSELVES

ॐ

> Catalyst: an agent that provokes or speeds significant change or action.
> —Miriam Webster's dictionary

Part II of this book is designed to help peacebuilders understand the social systems in which they work and to spot opportunities to engage those systems in ways that increase the potential for their programs to have a sustainable and systemic impact. If Part II is about understanding where to engage a system (the *P* in the planning, acting, and learning [PAL] project cycle), then Part III is about how to engage a system in ways that best nurture changes that will increase the society's level of peace (the *A* in the PAL cycle). The structural, attitudinal, and transactional (SAT) model lays out the basic strategy for promoting systemic change—using transactional peacebuilding to effect changes in the structural and attitudinal domains, which will increase the transactional ability of key actors moving forward. The key is to understand which transactional interventions will best catalyze structural, attitudinal, and further transactional change in the system. This was a lesson I learned the hard way.

As noted in Chapter 1, the Democratic Republic of the Congo (DRC) witnessed what has been called the world's worst humanitarian tragedy. After the genocide in neighboring Rwanda in 1994, the DRC saw multiple internal wars, the presence of seven foreign armies on its soil, and devastating natural disasters. This resulted in the loss of an estimated 6 million lives between 1996 and 2009. A formal peace process was started in 1999, but a final settlement proved elusive. In 2001, I was asked to join a team of returned Peace Corps volunteers (RPCVs) to help the three main combatant parties resolve their differences and resurrect the stalled peace talks.[1] On the margins of official talks, which were supported by the United Nations, the African Union (then the Organization of African Unity), and governments like the United States, the RPCV team worked on an unofficial basis with representatives of the DRC government (Kinshasa), the Movement for the Liberation of the Congo (MLC), and the Congolese Rally for Democracy (RCD). As described later in this chapter, our team had some success.

However, by the fall of 2002, our team, as well as the governmental interlocutors, were finding the stop-and-go, one-step-forward-two-steps-back nature of the negotiations to be maddeningly frustrating. Around this time, I participated in a workshop on systems thinking hosted by the Alliance for Peacebuilding. As part of the session, members of our team did a causal loop diagram (systems map) of the Congolese peace process. We zeroed in on trying to understand why periodic gains in the peace process were offset by equal or greater setbacks. While the map would not meet the standards of the SAT model, or any good systems map, we did discover a surprising and sobering insight into the problem: The efforts of those trying to improve the negotiations among the combatant parties, including our team, were most likely counterproductive.

The causal loop map we created was crude, but it did contain SAT components (although not deliberately so). As people coming from a conflict-resolution (transactional) background, we gravitated toward developing a hypothesis for why the negotiations were constantly stop-and-go. The analysis (see Figure 8.1) helped us tell the following story:

> Setbacks in the negotiations prompted third parties to offer assistance. If third parties helped the combatant parties make progress in the negotiations, it threatened the position of the many war profiteers in Congo for whom war was good for business. If these powerful people felt threatened, they would work to foment conflict by shipping arms to various militia groups in the parts of the eastern DRC that were controlled by the RCD rebels. This would provoke fighting between the militias and the RCD, who in turn would blame the DRC government for supporting the militias. In turn this would reduce trust between the government and the RCD and inevitably cause a setback in the negotiations.

The message from the analysis for our team was clear: Simply working to strengthen the national-level negotiations was not going to help the process. We needed to change tactics. Our actions up to that point had been well intentioned, even logical, but they were not based on a systemic understanding

Figure 8.1 Causal Loop Map of DRC Negotiations

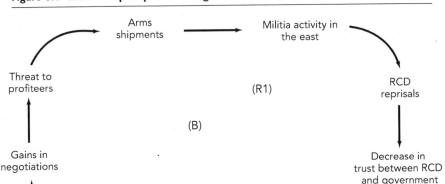

of the situation. We fell into two common traps. First, we took a linear approach: If national-level negotiations were going poorly, then we needed to help "fix" them by working with the three national-level combatant parties (the DRC government, MLC, and RCD).[2] Second, we accepted the fact that the national-level negotiations were largely being forced upon the parties and worked within that framework. As unofficial actors, we heard many complaints by the parties regarding the process and the arm-twisting that went on in order to get them to participate in it.

Creating a crude systems map of the DRC helped us correct the first error. The map of the negotiation subsystem helped us see that the real driving force was a regional subconflict. The second fix to our approach was to step away from the national negotiations. This was critical because the national-level talks were largely an attempt to impose change on the DRC system. From a systems perspective, imposing change from outside a system is less effective than working with the system. Noted systems thinker Donella Meadows encourages those working to make systemic change to "aid and encourage the forces and structures that help the system run itself."[3]

Chapter 2 (see "The SAT Model: A Systemic Theory of Peacebuilding") holds out transactional peacebuilding as the best means to help systems change themselves. To recap, Meadows posits three ways to encourage system change: change the elements in the system, change the interconnections between the elements, or change the purpose of the system. Of these, Meadows feels that just changing individual elements will have the least impact on changing the system. Changing the purpose has the greatest potential to change the system but is the hardest to accomplish. Changing the interconnections has the highest potential to effect change in a shorter time frame. Transactional peacebuilding, improving the ability of key actors to manage conflict and solve problems collaboratively, is a powerful tool for changing those interconnections.

To begin this potential change process, our team needed to analyze the key actors involved in the stuck negotiation subsystem. Our goal was to gauge the feasibility of a transactional intervention designed to change the interconnections between these key actors (and thereby help the system change itself). We focused in on two key parties, the RCD leadership and the leadership of the largest of almost two dozen Congolese militias collectively known as Mayi-Mayi.[4] The key to deciding whether—and if so, how—to make a transactional intervention is to assess the willingness and ability of these key actors to engage in collaborative, problem-solving negotiation (hereafter referred to simply as "negotiation"). The remainder of this chapter details a framework for assessing a party's willingness and ability to negotiate. Chapter 9 elaborates on the intervention tools that can be used to affect a party's willingness and ability to negotiate.

Why Willingness and Ability?

Because the purpose of the intervention was to be a catalyst for the system to change itself, we needed to start with the system—or rather, with key actors in the system. In order for these actors to own any change, we needed to look at whether they were willing and able to do so in order to avoid imposing a change on them.

It may seem that willingness and ability are separate concepts, but they are very much related. A practical example will help illustrate the interaction between the willingness and ability to negotiate and their collective impact on the decision to negotiate. In 1990, I was part of a team that led a negotiation-training session for a group of more than forty leaders of civic organizations from black townships throughout South Africa. These civic organizations were usually the unofficial, but widely legitimate, governments in black townships and were formed in opposition to the "official" local governments established by the National Party, the white government that had implemented South Africa's apartheid policies.

During the first morning of the five-day workshop, the main activity was an exercise intended to demonstrate the value of good negotiation. Just before breaking for lunch, the participants made a request. They politely asked that the training team leave the room so that they could decide whether they wanted to proceed with the training. This was certainly not the impact we intended to have on the group. When we were called back into the room, the group made their concerns known using a common South African saying: "In South Africa, there are two ways that the white man steals from you: One way is with the gun, and one way is with a smile. Negotiation is the way they steal from you with a smile." And because we, the trainers, were seen as encouraging the civic leaders to negotiate, we were basically telling them to surrender their cause to their enemies—to lie down and let the white authorities, whom many of them had risked their lives to oppose, steal from them. Negotiation was seen as a white man's game, and the civic leaders neither knew the rules of that game nor had any confidence that they could play it well. If you know you are going to lose, why play the game in the first place? Their lack of confidence in their ability to negotiate drove their unwillingness to do so.[5]

Many groups that are unwilling to negotiate are wrestling with some weakness in their ability to negotiate. This might be a lack of skills or experience (as in the case of the South African civic association leaders), internal divisions, or a lack of opportunities or mechanisms to talk. Of course, it is also true that a group can be, or believe itself to be, quite able to negotiate and yet decide not to. For example, some leaders may feel that they are much more powerful than the other party and thus believe that they can get what they want without negotiating (e.g., through escalating a war or simply waiting the other side out). In either case, it is essential to look at the key drivers of a decision to talk or not—to look at the interconnected issues of the willingness and ability of key people to negotiate.

In general, a party's willingness and ability to negotiate with any other party in the system is a function of three questions[6]:

1: What is the party's negotiation frame—its mind-set toward the situation in general and negotiation in particular?

2: How does the party see the value of talking versus not talking?
- Does it have an understanding of interests versus positions (its own and other parties')?
- Does it see possible options for mutual gain that could be pursued through negotiation?
- How does it value alternative ways to meet its interests other than through negotiation with a specific party?

3: Does the party have the means to negotiate?
- Does it have sufficient working relationships with potential interlocutors on the other side? Is it legitimate to talk to the other side?
- Does it have the means to communicate effectively? (Are there channels of communication? Does it have the needed negotiation skills?)
- Does it have the ability to deliver on commitments that it might make in a negotiation?

Caution: To Analyze Is to Intervene

Unfortunately, it is very difficult to get a reliable understanding of a key actor's true attitudes about negotiation. Gathering this data is part of the analysis process, which is very different from, and meant to be a precursor to, intervention. However, it is not that simple. Collecting information on the willingness and ability of key people to negotiate inevitably requires face-to-face contact with people in the system. This contact means that an analyst will cross the line between neutral observer and engaged intervener.[7]

Why? Whether or not to negotiate is a critical strategic question, and views about it are often closely guarded. A leader's willingness to negotiate, if communicated openly at the wrong time, might signal weakness to opponents or demoralize fighters on the front line. As such, gathering the data needed to make an in-depth diagnosis of a party's willingness and ability to negotiate is much harder than understanding structural or attitudinal factors. There are usually fairly objective indicators of structural factors such as poverty and economic-performance levels. There are also indicators for levels of freedom, health care, good governance, and security.

Measuring important intergroup attitudes is more difficult, but there are generally accessible indicators for the attitudinal drivers of a conflict, such as for levels of group trauma, intergroup tensions, and social capital.[8] The dehumanization of Tutsis by extremist Hutus was not a guarded secret but was in fact broadcast over radio stations in Kigali. Catholic attitudes toward Protestants in Northern Ireland were not just the subject of private conversations but the topic of public murals in Belfast and Derry.

However, the best information about a key actor's willingness and ability to negotiate comes directly from the individual in question. More importantly, that information will ideally be given in a context in which one can trust the honesty of the individual being interviewed. Short of that, there are varying proxies. There are public statements by a key person and by other people in his or her organization. There are the views of "informed" proxies who know, or have reason to know, what a particular key person thinks. There are experts who know the context and history of the situation and the players.

But because gathering data on the willingness and ability of key people to negotiate inevitably necessitates face-to-face contact with people in the conflict zone or society, it blurs the line between more clinical analysis and more applied intervention. More importantly, the entrance of interveners into the system they purport to be studying has ripple effects throughout the system.

For example, in the 2002 DRC case, our team had been working with the RCD leadership for more than a year and had already become part of the DRC system (albeit a small part). We knew of the RCD's general opposition to negotiating with any Mayi-Mayi leaders. More importantly, however, we had established relationships with key individuals and had access to many others. The Mayi-Mayi militia was a different question. Our team needed to consider carefully any plan to make contact with the Mayi-Mayi because contact alone would have ripple effects. For example, it would affect our relationships with the main combatant parties. The DRC government regarded contact with the Mayi-Mayi with great suspicion, and the RCD saw it as an illegitimate, even hostile act. After carefully considering the potential impact of contact with the Mayi-Mayi and developing a plan to manage any negative fallout, our team moved ahead. We decided to work though another NGO that was trusted by the RCD leadership and had also established contact with the particular Mayi-Mayi group in question. Having found a means to gather information, we set about trying to understand three key questions: (1) What was their negotiation frame? (2) How did they see the value of talking versus not talking? (3) Did they have the means to talk effectively?

STEP I: ASSESSING KEY PEOPLE'S NEGOTIATION FRAME

Years of research and practical experience suggests that certain assumptions, or beliefs, make it more likely that an individual will be able to negotiate effectively and/or be more willing to do so. Collectively these assumptions and beliefs make up an individual's negotiation mind-set, or negotiation frame. These basic mind-sets are hypotheses about the way the world works and determine how one should act in order to be effective. For example, the classic assumption discussed in negotiation courses around the world is the "win-win" versus "win-lose," or "zero-sum," assumption, which holds that in every human interaction there is necessarily a winner and a loser, and for any gain one might make in a negotiation, there must be a corresponding loss for someone else. If I gain a dollar, you must lose a dollar. For me to get what I want, I must deny you what you want.

This assumption contrasts with a belief that rejects the zero-sum view of the world and posits the opposite, that in most human interactions it is possible for both (or all) sides to attain their interests or satisfy their needs (i.e., to win). Rather than my gain necessitating your loss, the opposite is true: I am more likely to get what I want if I help you attain what you want. Having conducted hundreds of negotiation trainings around the world and been involved as an advisor or facilitator in several international negotiation efforts, I have witnessed firsthand the power these two sets of assumptions have on the willingness and ability of key people (and thereby the groups they represent) to negotiate effectively.[9]

If it is assumed that the world is a zero-sum, win-lose contest, then negotiators will most likely pursue an adversarial strategy (e.g., get them before they get me) and adversarial tactics (e.g., intimidation, bluffing, posturing, issuing of extreme demands). The problem with this approach to negotiation is that if the other parties to the negotiation play the same zero-sum game, the talks often break down in frustration over the lack of progress and a worsening relationship. It is also common for people who believe negotiation is a win-lose contest and that they have less power than their adversary to decide not to negotiate at all.[10]

On the other hand, a "win-win," or joint-gain, mentality is much more likely to produce negotiation strategies and behaviors that will greatly improve the ability of key people to negotiate effectively and increase their willingness to do so. There are many examples of how win-lose versus win-win assumptions play out in real negotiations. Perhaps the best example of the power of a negotiation frame comes from South Africa and concerns the relationship that developed between the two chief negotiators for the two main parties in the talks: the National Party government of F. W. DeKlerk (represented by Roelf Meyer) and the African National Congress (ANC) headed by Nelson Mandela (represented by Cyril Ramaphosa).[11] Roelf Meyer told a story that illustrated the value of approaching the negotiations from a "mutual-gain," or joint-problem-solving, frame. He recounted the first negotiating session between Cyril Ramaphosa and himself. Meyer entered the meeting room to find Ramaphosa sitting at the end of the table with a place for Meyer to sit opposite him, in the traditional adversarial negotiation position. Not wanting to step into this "me versus you" frame for the negotiation, Meyer took the chair opposite Ramaphosa and swung it around beside him, thereby framing the negotiation as something to the effect of "We are facing a big problem in South Africa. How are *we* going to deal with it?" According to Meyer, Ramaphosa responded immediately by laughing, then saying, "You took the same negotiation workshop I did didn't you."[12]

Obviously, this move did not settle the negotiation. However, it was a key symbol of the kind of collaborative relationship Meyer and Ramaphosa would build—one based on a mutual-gain negotiation frame (us versus the problem) as opposed to an adversarial win-lose frame (me versus you). Cyril Ramaphosa said the attitude of the two negotiators was that "there is not a problem without a solution and that *our* job is to find the solution."[13] The negotiators said that without this attitude, they might not have reached an agreement that set the stage for South Africa's historic transition from apartheid to democracy.

I saw a similar dynamic when I visited Iraq in March 2006 to work with newly elected members of parliament and other political party officials from the Sunni, Shia, and secular political coalitions. We began by working with politicians from each group separately. In each session, we used an exercise designed to illustrate the value of a mutual-gain versus a "win-lose," zero-sum mind-set. For each group, it was an eye-opening experience to see that although their positions or demands were incompatible, their underlying interests did not necessarily conflict.

Again, this insight did not end the conflicts in Iraq. However, when we subsequently brought representatives of the three political coalitions together for a joint workshop, the Iraqi participants from different sects reported that they were able to deal with each other much more easily than they had previously. This was due in part to changing their adversarial negotiation frame into one that saw issues like security not in zero-sum terms but as a joint problem. The shift was from a mind-set that said, In order for me to have security, I must deny you your security, to a one that said, I am more likely to achieve my need for security if I help you achieve your need for security. In a short, two-day session, the joint group of Iraqi politicians worked out a rather detailed plan for a "relationship-management mechanism" that would help reduce tensions, build confidence, enhance their ability to negotiate with each other, and ultimately improve security for all. In the eyes of the participants, this was a significant accomplishment, especially given their preexisting hostility toward each other. And this was attributed in part to a shift in their negotiation frame.[14]

So, the negotiation frame or mind-set of key people toward the situation and toward the other parties to the conflict is a critical variable to assess in determining a person's willingness and ability to negotiate. Any number of negotiation frames will dispose a key person toward or away from negotiation; however, there are five key negotiation frames to look for:

1. Mutual gain (win-win) versus win-lose (as defined above) mind-set
2. Moralistic versus structural view
3. Compelling positive vision for the future versus backward-looking, reactionary stance
4. Positive versus negative identity statement (e.g., "We are for x" versus "We are opposed to y")
5. Empowered versus disempowered/victimized stance (e.g., a hero with the ability to affect one's destiny versus a victim with no choice but to ...)

The mutual-gain and win-lose mind-sets are described above, but the other key negotiation frames deserve some elaboration.

Moralistic Versus Structural View[15]

Often, key people involved in a difficult situation or conflict tend to describe it in terms of who is right (themselves) and who is wrong (the adversary). This is a moralistic frame. Considerations of morality and justice are critical. And in terms of helping key people work together to deal with these difficult situations, it is also critical for them to see the situation in structural terms—to be able to describe a situation in terms of cause and effect, without attributing fault or blame. Moreover, the ability to view a situation structurally supports key actors' ability to adopt a "we versus the problem" negotiation frame.

For example, in the context of South Africa's historic transition from apartheid in the late 1980s and early 1990s, Roelf Meyer's statement, "We are facing a big problem in South Africa," serves as a kind of structural frame. It does not ascribe blame for the situation; nor does it speak to the moral standing of any group. It simply says, "Whites and blacks in South Africa face a big problem of how to manage their future together." Another version of a structural frame is, "South Africa is a case of different racial groups that each fear dominance by the other." In contrast, a moralistic framing would be, "Black violence against whites means whites cannot trust blacks with political power," or "White oppression means that blacks must protect themselves using violence." Neither of these statements is necessarily wrong. In fact, they probably accurately reflect how some whites and blacks perceived the situation. However, if the task is getting key people to work together better, then a contest over who is right or who is to blame for South Africa's problems is likely to be less productive than trying to manage a common problem, like avoiding a race war or finding a new political system that works for both white and black South Africans.

Compelling Future Vision Versus Reactionary Stance

It is no secret that working through complex problems collaboratively can be difficult, especially when doing so involves parties that have been in armed conflict with each other. It takes persistence, creativity, and a level of commitment that will justify making short-term sacrifices, be they political, military, or personal, in order to achieve long-term gain. That level of persistence requires individuals to have a compelling vision of what they hope to achieve in the process. Participants who lack that compelling vision are much less likely to engage in a difficult negotiation process or have the ability to persist even if they start.

In my mediation work, a standard early objective is to help the parties develop a compelling vision of what a better future looks like in order to move them away from being stuck in a reactionary spiral precipitated by the conflict.[16] For example, I once mediated a dispute between an international refugee-resettlement organization and a small social-service organization that was running a local resettlement program. The conflict involved a dispute over a $40,000 contract. So much animosity had developed between the two sides that they were on the verge of going to court and severing their long-standing relationship. I started by working with each party to articulate what a positive future relationship between the organizations looked like and if it was something each desired.

When it was clear that both sides saw potential value in a good future relationship (politically and financially), they worked together to define practical steps toward achieving it. In light of this vision of a better long-term relationship, the current dispute over a mere $40,000 looked insignificant and was settled in a few hours. On a small scale, this mediation demonstrates the power that a positive vision for the future can have in terms of drastically changing the behavior of combatants in favor of cooperation over competition. With no shared vision, or worse, if the parties see the other as motivated by antithetical ends, then negotiations become an adversarial contest. If they share a vision, they can work collaboratively to reach an end state that both desire.

In the initial stages of our work with the combatant parties in the DRC peace process, the RPCV team brought together representatives from two of the combatant groups, the DRC government and the RCD, for an off-the-record, unofficial dialogue. At the time there were attempts to get the DRC peace process back on track after it had languished for two years. The Inter-Congolese Dialogue (ICD) was established by the 1999 Lusaka Accord and intended to produce a final peace among the warring Congolese parties. However, by mid-2000, the parties were mired in disagreements, and the ICD process had not yet started.

Through existing contacts with the government and the RCD, we put together an informal dialogue. One of the first orders of business in our informal meeting was to help each side articulate its vision for a better future. With some work, the parties were able to define largely shared future visions; to the degree that they diverged, the differences reflected not inconsistencies but rather distinct yet compatible concerns. Based on this compelling future vision, they were able to define some concrete steps toward achieving that shared goal. One of these steps was to develop an agenda for the next round of the ICD peace talks, which was the subject of an upcoming preparatory meeting, sponsored by the Organization of African Unity, in Gaborone, Botswana. Until the informal dialogue, the parties had been deadlocked on setting an agenda for Gaborone. During the informal meeting, on seeing that they actually had strong common visions for a better future, they were able to define a draft agenda for the upcoming talks. The Gaborone meeting was a success, and the parties gave some credit to the informal discussions and the progress they made there.[17]

There are similar experiences in other processes. Take for example this account by Martti Ahtisaari, former president of Finland and facilitator of the peace talks between the government of Indonesia and the Free Aceh Movement, of the lessons learned in the Aceh peace process: "In order to move on and to achieve our jointly agreed goal, it was necessary that the focus was shifted towards the future, instead of trying to solve all the past wrongdoings around the negotiation table."[18] Therefore, one of the key negotiation frames to assess in trying to gauge the willingness and ability of key people to negotiate is the degree to which they have a compelling vision for a better future or are trapped, as Ahtisaari says, "trying to solve all the past wrongdoings." To determine this, you can look at the parties' statements. Do they focus on the past and accusations of wrongs perpetrated on them by others, or do they speak about their hopes for the future? Do they talk about what motivates them in terms of settling old scores and reacting to the last perceived provocation or in terms of what they hope to achieve and the values they are trying to serve? If asked, "Why are you acting as you are?" do they respond by saying, "Because they did *x*" or "We want to build *y*?" These questions and others like them can help determine the degree to which a person is motivated by a desire to create a better (more just, prosperous, secure) future or a need to seek revenge.

Positive Versus Negative Identity Statement

As noted in Part I, identity and conflict can be strongly interlinked. Identity is a basic human need, one that, if threatened, can lead an individual or a group to use violence to protect it. An individual's identity is made up of several traits, including values, experiences, and the differences and commonalities shared with others. As an Italian American, my identity is made up of my relation to my immigrant grandparents, the importance of service to others, a belief in justice and fair play, a quirky sense of humor, and my commitment to my family. My identity is formed both by fixed variables, like my ancestry, and by a dynamic interplay with my environment. Getting married and having children changed my self-image from being an up-and-coming young professional to being, first and foremost, a devoted husband and father.

When intergroup violence and ethnic tension defines a person's environment, the conflict affects his or her identity. This is not necessarily a bad thing, unless the conflict becomes a defining element of one's identity, in which case it can create an odd situation where an end to the conflict would, itself, become a threat to one's identity. For example, if I exist to beat my enemies, and one day there is no longer an enemy to oppose (because of a peace settlement), then I have lost my reason to exist. In order to prevent this threat to my conflict-dependent identity, I may actually work to prevent the conflict from being transformed.

A practical example will help here. In the mid-1990s, when working for the Conflict Management Group, I was asked by the US Department of the Interior to mediate between a Native American tribe and some neighboring towns over a land dispute. Before we were involved, the conflict had become extremely polarized between angry local, nonnative community groups and angry tribe members. Negotiations had been tried and failed, and neither side wanted any part of more negotiations or to participate in mediation. Our team started by meeting with members of the communities and the tribe. When we asked people to describe themselves and the conflict, they said things like, "We are here to stop the injustices perpetrated by the [tribe]," or "We are here to oppose the racism of the [townspeople]." One member of the nonnative community pointed to how his fundamental rights were being denied and said that he was ready to "fight the Revolutionary War all over again."

This dispute, which developed in the context of three hundred years of native/nonnative conflict and had been escalating for many years, had become a defining force for many. Opposing the other side became their reason for being. If they are cruel, we are just. If they are deceitful, we are honest. As much as they all regarded the conflict as a problem, it was also very difficult for them to give it up or to conceive of a situation in which the tribe and the towns worked together as allies, not adversaries. Peace between the towns and the tribe would mean that several key leaders would no longer have a reason to be. Unfortunately, one of the reasons the mediation did not produce a settlement, in my opinion, is that some hard-liners on each side could not buy into a process aimed at settling the dispute because doing so would undermine their position and sense of identity. The proximate cause for the end of the mediation was the leak of some very sensitive information by one of the key people involved in the process.

The title of Chris Hedges's book *War Is a Force That Gives Us Meaning* reflects the truth that when something is a profound source of meaning, it is hard to give up. When one's identity is defined in terms of what or whom one opposes, this is termed a negative identity statement—not negative in terms of being bad but in terms of negating something. So in the case of the conflict between the tribe and the neighboring towns, some key people on both sides worked to undermine the process intended to end the dispute, which had become an important part of their reason for existing. Having a negative identity statement will greatly reduce the willingness or ability of key people in a conflict to negotiate or work to create a peaceful transformation.

Fortunately, the opposite is also true. Someone with a positive identity statement is more likely to be willing and able to negotiate. A positive identity statement is framed in terms of what someone is for or what positive values he or she is hoping to achieve. For example, in South Africa, as the transition from apartheid was starting back in 1989 and 1990, I remember talking with several leaders of what were collectively called the black liberation movements, such as the ANC, Pan-African Congress, Azanian People's Organization, and others. All of them could recount stories of how loved ones had been killed and they and their friends had been tortured, beaten, and imprisoned by the security forces of the white government. Yet, many of them had a positive rather than a negative identity statement. I expected them to say that they existed to "defeat the white government" or to "end white racism." Although some of them did, many others said they existed to "create a nonracial South Africa." The ability of Nelson Mandela and other leaders "to bring an end to division, an end to suspicion and build a nation united in our diversity" shows the power of a positive identity statement.[19]

Whether a key person has a positive or negative identity statement can be very difficult to ascertain directly. You cannot just walk up to a militia leader and say, "Excuse me, but do you have a positive or negative identity statement?" Some clues can be gleaned from public statements, though these can be misleading and not reflective of what a person is truly thinking. This highlights the need for trust and personal contact in the process of gathering information. An analyst cannot just trust the words used. It is easy to use the language of a negative identity statement in the guise of fiery rhetoric designed to motivate supporters. It is also easy to mimic the words of a positive identity statement as part of political correctness designed to appease the international community. It is crucial to square words with actions and to cross-reference data gathered directly from the person, from people in the know (e.g., confidants of the key person in question), from public statements, and so forth.[20] Is there consistency between words, actions, and third-party assessments? Does the person's thinking show a consistent evolution over time? Formulations of one's identity can change, but they rarely do so in the short term.

Empowered Versus Disempowered Stance

As noted by Clem McCartney, veteran of efforts to deal with several intergroup conflicts, "Armed groups often feel that violence seems to be an inevitable aspect of their struggle."[21] He refers to this mind-set as a "council of despair" that affects both nonstate armed groups and state actors. This council of despair is a powerful impediment to building a key person's willingness or ability to negotiate. McCartney elaborates on the reasons why: "This [council of despair] could be a political stance to justify violence but more often is a genuine … belief that other options such as democracy, dialogue and negotiations will achieve nothing and conversely undermine the struggle."[22] It may seem obvious, but a prerequisite for a key person's choosing to deal with conflict through negotiations or other nonviolent means is seeing this decision as a choice that he or she is empowered to make. Those who see only one option, violence, do not have the power to choose a different course of action.

A disempowered negotiation frame is detectable by looking at whether the key person involved uses the language of victimhood in describing the conflict. How does he or she talk about the choices available (if any)? In every conflict I have worked on, at some point and from some key person involved in the process, I have heard phrases like, "We have no choice but to do *x*" or "The only way to deal with [people like them] is to do *y*." These and similar phrases are indicators of a disempowered negotiation frame. This is not to say that such statements are illegitimate rationalizations. Rather, they illustrate a mind-set that will make it very difficult to get key people to participate in a negotiation process.

There are lots of examples of parties being coerced into sitting down at the table, even if they have a disempowered negotiation frame. However, these talks rarely produce a good outcome as the parties are constrained by a deep distrust of each other and a belief that the chances of a successful outcome are minimal. Returning to the peace process in the DRC, when the ICD started, hosted by South Africa in February 2002, our RPCV team was present. The presence of the parties at the ICD had required, among many things, lots of international pressure from donor governments, such as the United States, France, Belgium, and the United Kingdom, as well as the African Union and the United Nations. While the parties made the political commitment to participate, the main combatant parties lacked trust and confidence. I can remember a very definitive conversation with a general from the DRC army who said in reference to the MLC and RCD rebel movements, "How can we negotiate with people like this?" The general was not speaking on behalf of the government, but his view reflected what we heard from people on all sides, that negotiations simply were not possible, despite their presence at the talks.[23]

Months later, as our team was exploring the willingness and ability of the RCD leadership to negotiate with a Mayi-Mayi militia, we heard echoes of this same disempowered negotiation frame. To our surprise, the leadership of the Mayi-Mayi militia was rather willing to negotiate. Although they too showed signs of having a disempowered, win-lose negotiation frame, they were frustrated with the lack of progress militarily and were willing to consider negotiations. The RCD leadership presented a much more difficult case. One faction saw a genuine opportunity in negotiating with the Mayi-Mayi, but it struggled to overcome a very deep-seated negotiation frame that was part disempowered stance and part strong negative identity statement based on years of struggle.

Eastern Congo has been the source of instability in the DRC for many years, especially in the period from 1997 to 2004. The RCD based in Goma (on the border with Rwanda) claimed to be the protectors of the Congolese Tutsis (or Banyamulenge). The RCD saw many of the Mayi-Mayi militias as aligned with Hutu militias from Rwanda who fled into Congo after the 1994 genocide against Rwandan Tutsis. Complicating matters further, the RCD claimed (with verification from some international observers) that the DRC government was providing support to both the Mayi-Mayi and the Hutu militias.

Like the Congolese general mentioned above, a group within the RCD leadership felt that there was no choice but to fight the Mayi-Mayi who were in league with their mortal enemies, the genocidaires from Rwanda. The opposition to the Hutu militias was so strong that, for some, it had become part of their identity—they existed to ensure that genocide against Rwandans or Congolese of Tutsi origins would never happen again. The idea of negotiating with genocidaires or their allies was inconceivable. Again, if the negotiation frame toward this Mayi-Mayi militia did not change, there would be little chance the RCD would own a negotiation process with them.

In sum, negotiation frames—or one's view of a situation and whether (and if so, how) to deal with other key people—are a significant determinate of key people's willingness and ability to negotiate. This frame is the lens through which every important decision in the peace process is viewed and has a powerful impact on the transactional ability of leaders at the national and local levels. While the five discussed here are not the only negotiation frames, they deserve special attention as few processes can succeed, or be sustained, if any of them is present among key people.

STEP 2: ASSESSING THE PERCEIVED VALUE OF TALKING VERSUS NOT TALKING

Even if the president of a country, a rebel leader, a tribal sheik, or a local cleric has a negotiation frame that disposes him positively to negotiation, he will not necessarily decide to negotiate or negotiate effectively. The decision of whether to negotiate (or to persist in negotiations once begun) can be thought of as a fairly basic calculation of whether the perceived value of talking (or pursuing a nonviolent, peace-enhancing strategy) outweighs the perceived value of not talking (or pursuing violence or another peace-reducing strategy).

Some might deem this idea naive, for one might argue that once a group has made the decision to pursue violence, it has forsworn the path of negotiation. Not true. In discussing factors that would cause a group leader to support negotiation instead of violence, McCartney argues that a leader would need to "be able to show that more could be gained from negotiations and dialogue than from continuation of the struggle."[24] In fact, members of armed groups who participated in the ACCORD project on engagement with armed groups, sponsored by Conciliation Resources, all reported that the issue of whether to pursue negotiation or armed confrontation was constantly before the leadership of their group. One armed group member voiced a sentiment that was fairly typical of the others. He said that the group's current strategy of pursuing a negotiated settlement was "the product of a long process of internal debate and political maneuvering on the costs and benefits of such a strategy."[25]

While it may be common for leaders to weigh, on an ongoing basis, the costs and benefits of talking versus not talking, this calculation is a complex one that surely varies in its specifics from situation to situation. However, certain variables exist to some degree in each of these deliberations. In assessing how a particular key person may be weighing the decision to negotiate or not, it is helpful to analyze three important variables.

Assessing how an individual sees the value of talking versus not talking:

- Does the individual have an understanding of interests versus positions (his or her own and those of other parties)?
- Does the individual see possible options for mutual gain that could be pursued through negotiation?
- Does the individual believe negotiation with a specific party is the best way to serve his or her interests versus trying to satisfy them through means other than negotiation (e.g., war)?

For each of these questions, a yes answer increases a key person's perceived value of talking versus not talking, which in turn increases his or her willingness and ability to negotiate in general.

Interests Versus Positions

Measure: To the degree that individuals are able to think in terms of interests and not positions, they will generally be more willing and able to negotiate.[26]

The concept of interests in negotiation is the subject of much debate, particularly the difference between interests and basic human needs and values.[27] The basic distinction is that interests tend to be more specific, shorter term, and more issue focused as compared to basic human needs. As discussed at the beginning of Chapter 3, human needs, defined as identity, community, security, and vitality, are irreducible requirements, while interests can be traded off or even compromised. Interests here refer to more proximate motivators, the reasons a negotiator negotiates—his or her concerns, hopes, or other requirements that can be satisfied or settled. Interests are driven, at some level, by basic needs. For example, a renter has a range of interests when seeking an apartment—affordable rent, location, room for his family, and so forth. These can be satisfied in the short term by finding the right apartment. These interests are related to deeper needs for security (adequate shelter) and vitality (an affordable place to live that will allow one to work, earn a living, and provide for one's family). Finding the right apartment does not mean that these basic needs cease to exist; rather, they are a constant throughout the renter's life. Their expression at any one time and in particular situations can be thought of as interests.

This distinction holds in the peacebuilding context. For example, during the DRC peace process, when an agreement was reached to form a transitional government of national unity, the RCD and MLC were given vice presidential posts. I spoke with the RCD's vice president, Azarius Ruberwa, prior to his agreeing to go to Kinshasa to take up a post in the government. I came away from the conversation with the following understanding:

> The RCD rebel movement had interests (the ministries they would control in a power sharing government, security for their representatives in the capital city, how the army was to be reformed, etc.), needs (e.g., the broader need for security for themselves and the people they purported to represent, etc.), and values (e.g., acceptance of Congolese Tutsis, etc.). All three—interests, needs and values—provide motivations for the RCD, as well as the other parties, during the peace process. But while interests can be said to be satisfied in the context of a transaction, needs and values have to be pursued over time.[28]

Putting attention on the interests of particular key people does not mean that one should disregard their basic needs. Understanding a key person's needs and values is critical to understanding his or her motivations, and those needs and values are often uncovered in the process of understanding that person's negotiation frame (e.g., a compelling vision of the future is usually phrased in terms of basic values). In addition, an analyst can generally assume that a key person will always have some form of basic needs involving security, identity, community, and vitality, as well as corresponding values related to justice and dignity. And because interests are shorter term and defined in relation to specific issues, they are a necessary part of the picture and a means by which conflict is managed, agreements reached, and problems solved.

Why is it important to understand interests as opposed to positions? Positions can be very difficult to reconcile, while interests are much easier to satisfy through a range of options. Earlier I referred to a mediation I participated in between a Native American tribe and three local towns. The starting positions of the two sides were starkly incompatible: The tribe sought to add 10,000 acres of land to its relatively small reservation (land that would be taken away from the three towns); the towns were willing to give the tribe exactly zero acres of new land. There was little chance that negotiations were going to bridge the gap between the two sides' positions: 0 and 10,000 acres. Instead we asked the parties about their interests in the land (e.g., what land should be used for residential areas, what for commercial development, what for recreational use, what for green space, etc.?). When we compared their respective interests in the land, we found that they were largely compatible. This potential compatibility of their interests helped make the parties more willing to negotiate.

When it comes to assessing the ability of key people to understand and deal with interests, there are a few basic questions:

- How well do they understand and represent their own interests?
  - Group interests:
    - Are they focused on positions or on the underlying interests of their group?
    - Do they, or can they, represent their group's interests accurately? If not, why?
  - Personal interests:
    - Do they understand their personal interests? Can they distinguish between personal and group interests?
    - Do they know what they want versus what they do not want to happen?
    - Do they or others in their group have a vested interest in keeping the conflict going (e.g., war profiteering)?
  - Third-party interests:
    - Are there influential external parties (patrons, sponsors, donors, diasporans) whose interests affect individual key people or their group?
- How well do they understand the interests of others?
  - Do they have an empathetic, accurate sense of the other side's interests, or are they focused on positions?
  - Do influential external parties, sponsors, or constituents have critical interests at stake?

Options for Mutual Gain

Measure: The more creative key people can be in devising different ways to satisfy interests, their own and others', the more willing and able they will be to negotiate.

Simply put, options are ways of satisfying interests. Options can be substantive terms (e.g., money, a power-sharing arrangement, a joint business plan, etc.) or processes (e.g., arbitration, referral to a council of elders, mediation, etc.). One reason that peace processes become stalemated is that key people on various sides get stuck on positions. A conducive negotiation frame and the ability to understand and deal with interests are helpful in overcoming such impasses. Another key ingredient for addressing these situations is the ability to develop creative options. And the inability to do so is often at the heart of the stalemates in negotiation. Similarly, the inability even to conceive of creative options can be at the heart of a party's unwillingness to negotiate.

For example, Ecuador and Peru fought a border war, on and off, for over forty years. Between 1941 and 1999, there were three armed conflicts, a disputed treaty (the Rio Protocol), and an arbitration case concerning the disputed territory; yet, the dispute continued, and the positions of the two countries remained firm and irreconcilable. In 1998, there was little willingness on either side to return to the negotiating table. That year, Professor Roger Fisher of Harvard Law School led a team to explore possibilities for resolving the conflict. He met with Presidents Alberto Fujimori of Peru and Jamil Mahuad of Ecuador to understand the impasse. Fisher described the situation as one in which both countries held firmly to a position unacceptable to the other side; yet, there was no process in place to develop new options. And this was not just a case of personal intransigence on the parts of two presidents. Public opinion in both countries made many options nonnegotiable. Opinion polls in both Peru and Ecuador asked people about a particularly sensitive issue, possession of the symbolically important village of Tiwintza. When asked if their country should agree to give up Tiwintza if they got everything else they wanted from the negotiations, large majorities in both countries said no.

Fisher understood that if the two presidents held firmly to their positions and saw no potential for finding new options that benefited both, there was little chance either would support negotiations. As a way of changing these perceptions, Fisher won the support of both presidents for an informal "facilitated joint brainstorming session" between key people from the two sides. The session produced a recognition of the deep differences between the sides but also developed several creative approaches to seemingly intractable problems like what to do with the village of Tiwintza. The results of the meeting helped the presidents see the futility of their positional approach to the negotiations and to recognize the potential to develop new options for mutual gain. Subsequently, the two held face-to-face discussions, and then formal negotiations.

Eventually, the parties reached an agreement to resolve their dispute, including a decision as to who got ownership of Tiwintza. In the end, they agreed that Tiwintza would be in Peruvian territory, but one square kilometer of the village (nearly all of Tiwintza) would be owned by Ecuador.[29] In addition, the sides agreed that both countries would set up "ecological parks" on both sides of the border where only "ecological police," not military forces, would be allowed. Although there were many reasons for the Ecuador-Peru settlement, a key cause of the turnaround in the negotiations was the ability to find creative options that satisfied the interests of the two sides and their publics.

As in the Ecuador-Peru case, the ability to deal with options creatively is a key determinant of a key person's ability and willingness to negotiate. Questions that are helpful in determining a person's ability to deal with options include:

- Is the individual stuck on positions? How wedded is he or she to past positions?
- Is the individual able to see opportunities for mutual gain (e.g., the Tiwintza option)?
- How creative is the individual in thinking of ways to satisfy the interests of multiple parties?
- Have important issues become nonnegotiable (e.g., has public sentiment turned against a possible settlement or has compromise become illegitimate)?

Alternatives to Negotiation

Measure: The more realistically key people understand and can accurately value their ability to satisfy their interests through means other than negotiation, the better able they will be to negotiate effectively.

Alternatives to negotiation, as defined by Roger Fisher, Bill Ury, and Bruce Patton, refer to the ways people can satisfy their interests if they choose not to seek a negotiated settlement with a particular party.[30] For example, if I cannot reach agreement with my current boss for a raise, then my alternative might be to get a similar job with better pay with a different employer. Fisher and Ury term this other job offer as my best alternative to a negotiated agreement (BATNA).[31]

Key people often overestimate the value of their alternatives to negotiation. If they think their BATNA is good (even if that belief is unrealistic), then they are less willing to negotiate.[32] If a party thinks it can attain total victory on the battlefield, then why go through the painful process of negotiation, which will inevitably involve compromise?

In 1990, as part of the South Africa project mentioned earlier, the Harvard Negotiation Project/Conflict Management Group team held a negotiation session with key leadership from the ANC, including the ANC's chief negotiator and negotiation team. As part of that session, the team led the ANC leadership through an analysis of their alternatives to negotiation with the National Party government. At the time, both the ANC and the government had taken hard positions on the preconditions necessary to start constitutional talks, both had rejected the preconditions of the other side, and there had been no talks to overcome this impasse.

The basic outcome of the BATNA analysis had a significant impact on the participants: Though confident of its nonnegotiating position, the ANC realized that if there were no talks, they were unlikely to achieve a new constitution or elections that they deemed fair. And if there were no new elections, then the National Party would still be in power, and the ANC would be denied its fundamental goal, unless the situation turned violent, which the ANC wanted to avoid. This realization seemed to occasion at least a temporary reassessment of the value the ANC placed on the nonnegotiation alternative.[33]

In addition to the effects of leaders overvaluing their alternatives, there is the danger of leaders using ethnic, religious, or other intergroup differences to foment public support for their political positions. The US Agency for International Development's conflict assessment handbook warns of the violence that often erupts as a result of leaders exploiting intergroup tensions to "gain, maintain, or increase their hold on political or economic power."[34] Manipulating ethnic or religious passions is a way for leaders to strengthen their nonnegotiation alternatives—either through violence (a way of protecting one's interests without negotiating) or insulating themselves from any criticism for not engaging in negotiations.

Lastly, another prominent way in which alternatives can affect key people's willingness and ability to negotiate is whether the prospect of a negotiated peace actually threatens their position. For example, the prospect of being subject to war crimes trials has led some leaders either to reject peace agreements or to refuse peace talks.[35] There are also examples of leaders who have vested interests in keeping conflict going because of war profiteering or other stakes.[36] In these cases, the prospect of peace is much worse than the alternative to any peace deal, even though they quite commonly participate in talks because doing so is politically expedient and puts them in a strong position to ensure that no peace deal is ever reached. For example, the initial chief negotiator for the Kinshasa government through much of the DRC peace process was named as one of the chief war profiteers in two UN reports. Spoilers are usually key people who have reason to fear a peace deal.

In order to understand how key people are thinking about alternatives to negotiation and how this affects their willingness and ability to negotiate, the following questions are helpful:

- Do they have a realistic sense of their alternatives to negotiating with the other parties? Do they know how they will attain their interests if they do not negotiate?
- Do key people fan intergroup tension to bolster their own political position?
- Do key people see peace or a negotiation process whose goal is a peace settlement as a threat to their staying in power?

In the 2002 DRC example, the split in the RCD leadership with regard to negotiating with the Mayi-Mayi militia mirrored a split on these basic questions of interests, options, and alternatives. On the question of interests, there was a split between those who felt the interests of the movement would be best served by supporting the peace process and even joining a transitional government in Kinshasa and those who saw the negotiations as doomed to failure. On the issue of options, many had never even conceived of the idea of negotiating with the Mayi-Mayi, let alone thought about potential options for mutual gain. They saw the interests of the Mayi-Mayi through the same prism that they saw the interests of the Hutu militias; their only interest was to kill Tutsis. As for alternatives, there was a general confidence that the RCD could win a military battle with the Mayi-Mayi, but, at least privately, individuals voiced a preference for ending what seemed like an endless war. Lastly, there were definite spoilers who had a vested interest in maintaining the status quo, which included the conflict. For the RCD to own any process that changed its interconnections with the Mayi-Mayi (and thereby the stuck negotiation subsystem), there would need to be a change in its somewhat muddied internal calculus about the value of talking versus not talking with its Mayi-Mayi adversaries.

STEP 3: DETERMINING WHETHER KEY PEOPLE HAVE THE MEANS TO NEGOTIATE

Lastly, even if key people have a negotiation frame conducive to negotiation and see a greater value in talking than not talking, they may still lack the means for negotiating. As noted above, a few key components determine key actors' ability to negotiate:

- Do they have sufficient working relationships with potential interlocutors on the other side?
- Do they have the means to communicate effectively? (Are there channels of communication? Do they have the needed negotiation skills?)
- Do they have the ability to deliver on commitments that they might make in a negotiation?

Relationships

Measure: The better the working relationship between individual key people, the more likely they are to be willing and able to negotiate (the weaker the relationships, the less likely they are to be willing or able to negotiate).

In a working relationship, parties are able to deal constructively with their differences.[37] A good working relationship exists independently of agreement on issues. In fact, the best relationships often exist between people who disagree on many issues. Senators Orrin Hatch (R-UT) and Edward Kennedy (D-MA) had what they and others regarded as a strong working relationship—despite the fact Hatch was regarded as one of the most conservative and Kennedy as one of the most liberal politicians in the United States. Hatch acknowledged the vast policy differences he had with Kennedy but said that the two of them were able to find common ground on many important legislative initiatives. Hatch always trusted Kennedy to keep his word. After Kennedy's death, Hatch wrote,

> With the loss of such a liberal legislative powerhouse who spoke with conviction for his side of the aisle, but who was always willing to look at an issue and find a way to negotiate a bipartisan deal, I fear that Washington has become too bitterly partisan. I hope that Americans in general and Washington politicians in particular will take a lesson from Ted's life and realize that we must aggressively advocate for our positions but realize that in the end, we have to put aside political pandering, work together and do what is best for America.[38]

The existence of trust between parties and the ability to work collaboratively while remaining firm in advocating for their own interests are hallmarks of a good working relationship in negotiation. Hatch and Kennedy exemplified a key quality of a good relationship: the ability to separate substantive issues (e.g., particular policy disagreements) from process issues (e.g., level of trust, ability to talk respectfully and keep agreements, etc.).

All working relationships between individuals exist within the context of the general relationship between the groups to which those individuals belong, be they corporations, communities, religious sects, political parties, clans, or ethnic groups. This analysis assumes that those group relationships influence, but do not determine, relationships between individuals and that it is possible for individual key actors to form good working relationships even in the context of poor intergroup relations. Indeed, Hatch and Kennedy maintained a good working relationship despite the growing divide between their respective political parties. However, the intergroup relationship can set the parameters for the relationship between key people from each group. For example, if the broader groups feel it is illegitimate to talk to anyone from the other side, then public meetings between key people will be difficult or impossible.

Assessing the working relationships between key people means looking at the individuals' ability to work together effectively within the context of the relationship between the group (or groups) they represent or belong to. In particular, the following issues are important to examine:

- Working relationships between key groups:
  - Is there sufficient trust between groups to allow for effective communication or negotiation?
  - Do group members see negotiation between their leaders, or a peace deal itself, as legitimate? Why or why not?
  - Are relations between groups getting worse (e.g., is there more tension, less trust), or are groups stuck in a downward-spiraling dynamic?
- Working relationships between particular key people:
  - Are key people able to talk despite their personal and group disagreements? Are they able to separate relationship issues (e.g., trust, emotions) from substantive issues (e.g., cease-fire, governance, security, etc.)?
  - Are there informal contacts between key people from different groups? Do indirect channels exist (e.g., a chain of people or network of relationships that can be used to carry messages from one key person to another)?
  - Is there sufficient trust between key leaders to allow for effective negotiation?
  - Is it legitimate to talk with the other side in the eyes of the group's leadership and its constituents?

Communication

Measure: The greater the ability of key actors to communicate, the more likely they are to be willing and able to negotiate. The ability to communicate includes both skills (e.g., negotiation skills) and opportunities (e.g., channels of communication).

It seems obvious that the ability to communicate information and meaning accurately back and forth between individuals is essential to negotiation. Yet, the process is not as simple as speaking. People speak all the time without accurately communicating either information or a particular intended meaning.

In 1991, Roger Fisher and I met with members of the UN Security Council as part of an effort to draft a resolution aimed at removing Saddam Hussein from Kuwait without fighting a war. We met with several ambassadors then on the UN Security Council, including the US and Iraqi ambassadors. As the political climate intensified up to the start of the war, Hussein issued a statement that said, in effect, if the United States makes us an offer, then we are prepared to listen. We met with the Iraqi ambassador to the United Nations the next morning, and he was quite excited by Hussein's speech. "Did you hear what the president said?" he gushed. To him Hussein's statement was a huge concession as previously Hussein had rejected any talk of a compromise with the United States. The ambassador felt this was an enormous opening for diplomacy. A short time later, we met with the US ambassador to the United Nations. Regarding the same speech from Hussein, he said, in effect, "Did you hear what that [—] said? If he thinks we are going to come to him with a proposal . . ."[39] The United States heard the speech not as a concession or a diplomatic opening but as an insult. The message as received was not the message as intended. Not long after, the war started.

Two basic kinds of communication obstacles can impede a key person's ability to communicate. The first, as in the Hussein example, involves more subjective issues related to the content of what is said, the manner in which it is delivered, and how it is interpreted. The second involves more objective or mechanical issues related to the existence and quality of channels of communication. It may seem that with the spread of technology, whereby people can communicate to the world from the middle of a riot in Tehran or Nairobi, people should never lack the means to talk or exchange information. Not so. The fact of communication, especially in the midst of a conflict, is a highly symbolic act, regardless of the content of that communication, and can be politically impossible even if technologically possible. Our highly interconnected world also means that it is very difficult to hide the fact that communication has taken place. Cell phones can be monitored, e-mail records retrieved, and so forth.

Early on in our involvement with parties in the DRC, one of our most significant contributions, at a very politically sensitive time, was simply to arrange a private cell phone conversation between two key people from different combatant groups. These two people had known each other before the war but were now prevented from talking directly by the boundaries imposed by the conflict. Our contribution to the process was to open up a channel of communication, which meant that we had to prearrange a time when both key people would be in an isolated place (so they could talk freely) and would be holding their cell phones (which were normally in the possession of one of their many aides) so that they could answer the call. In various processes I have been involved in or heard about, the lack of channels played a significant part in hindering communication, or the existence of confidential channels strengthened the ability of key people to talk. There are also times when communication channels exist but are ineffective. For example, a formal negotiation process might exist, but because it is badly structured or facilitated, the existence of the channel may actually be worse than if there were no channel at all.

As for the content of the communication, there are lots of excellent books on what makes for effective communication, and I cannot summarize them here.[40] However, there are some points to look for in assessing the ability of people to communicate effectively. The first is their capacity to deal with perceptions. A Russian proverb says, "Everyone views the world from the bell tower of their own village." As human beings, it is impossible for any one of us to have a totally objective view of the world. Each person has a unique, and at least partially valid, perspective. Good communicators acknowledge this fact and behave accordingly. They know that their perceptions, while valid for them, are only part of the complete picture and that others will have different perceptions, even of the same event (like the US and Iraqi ambassadors to the United Nations in relation to Hussein's speech). Good communicators acknowledge the limits of their own perceptions and actively seek to understand the perceptions of others.

The ability to acknowledge differing perceptions and to accept them as at least partially valid (as a statement of what another believes to be true) is key to good communication. And it is linked to a second indicator of good communication: the ability to have an empathetic understanding of others' concerns, feelings, and the stories they would tell of the conflict or situation. Skillful communicators are able to achieve an empathetic understanding of another's perceptions without necessarily agreeing with them or accepting them as true (or as invalidating of their own perceptions). Some people, especially those in a conflict zone, can find it quite difficult to hold two different, even diametrically opposed, stories in their head at the same time. For example, during the Troubles, a Catholic resident of Northern Ireland might have found it hard to hold his perception of Protestants as the perpetrators of the violence at the same time that he tried to see many Protestants' perception of the Catholics as the perpetrators.

Unfortunately, the opposite of good communication often precipitates conflicts. Poor communication starts from the premise that the speaker's perceptions are "the truth" and that those who disagree are at best wrong and at worst evil or perhaps delusional. Sometimes, though rarely, key people acknowledge that they have poor communication skills and that this deficiency makes them less able to negotiate. More often, one-sided perceptions, misperceptions, distortions, and a lack of empathy for the other side make people less willing to negotiate because they just think it is pointless to talk with someone so [fill in the blank (e.g., irrational, twisted, etc.)]. Compounding the impact of misperceptions and the lack of empathy is their tendency to shape people's emotional state. An unempathetic, distorted story about the other side's actions and intentions tends to breed strong feelings of anger, disgust, self-righteousness, and even fear. These in turn tend to compound the original misperceptions and shape (mis)interpretations of new events.

So, in assessing the ability of key people to communicate, it is necessary to look at whether channels or processes for communication exist and at the quality of those channels, as well as at the key people's communication skills, such as their ability to deal well with perceptions and to achieve empathy. Some questions to consider are:

- What is the ability of leaders or negotiators to communicate effectively?
  - Are there functioning channels of communication (formal or informal)?
  - Are there processes available for negotiation or mediation? How good are the channels that exist (do they improve communication or exacerbate communication difficulties)?
  - Are there important misperceptions, distortions, or miscommunications? Do they shape emotional reactions, behavior, or decision making?
  - Are leaders or negotiators able to hold different, even opposing, perceptions in their minds at the same time? Do they have an empathetic understanding of the perceptions of others?

As with other variables, these are not questions you can ask a person directly. Rather, you need to use them to analyze what key people say and do. For example, how do they describe the perspectives of others, particularly people they consider adversaries? How do they describe others and their motives and intentions? How do they characterize their own actions and those of others? How do these characterizations and perceptions square with how other people would describe themselves, their actions, and their motives? Is there a willingness to consider differing perceptions or to acknowledge the limits of their own perceptions?

Commitments

Measure: The greater the ability to make and deliver on commitments, the greater the willingness and ability to negotiate.

One of the most overlooked barriers to effective negotiation is the inability of key actors to deliver on commitments they might make at the negotiating table. Most key actors are quite sensitive about airing internal divisions within their organization. They are also reluctant to take a politically risky move, such as participating or delivering on commitments made in negotiations, that might expose their inability to control internal factions. Perhaps the best-known example of intraparty conflicts thwarting interparty negotiations is the Israeli-Palestinian conflict. The split within the Palestinian side between supporters of Fatah and Hamas has long prevented any one Palestinian leader from being able to deliver on behalf of all Palestinians. In addition, Rabbi Marc Gopin once commented that an Israeli-Palestinian peace accord might lead to internal civil war—within the Israeli community.[41] The difficulty both sides have with delivering on a commitment made in a peace deal compromises their ability to negotiate and contributes to a lack of willingness to negotiate in the first place.

Internal difficulties can be attributed to dysfunctional processes (e.g., disorganization), internal political disagreements (e.g., power rivalries, a split between military and political leaders, etc.), or deep-seated psychological barriers. The difficulties in the Israeli-Palestinian process are fairly obvious versions of all three factors. In other cases the obstacles are less apparent. As I mentioned earlier, a colleague and I were called in to help mediate between a Native American tribe and three surrounding towns in preparation for a large land-claim negotiation potentially worth tens of millions of dollars. We were brought in by a group of advisors to the tribe who were at a loss to understand why the tribe was dragging its feet when it came to getting to the negotiation table. Then, in one session in our negotiation workshop, one of the tribal elders explained why he was reluctant to proceed with the negotiations: "I'm angry. I have three hundred years of anger inside me at the way our people were treated for so long. More importantly, members of the tribe are angry. My fear is that if we come home with an agreement to settle our land claim, even a good agreement, our people are going to throw three hundred years of anger at it, and me." There is a range of questions to consider in assessing the impact of a key actor's ability to make and keep commitments:

- Are there internal divisions that make a common position impossible?
- Are there command-and-control problems that make implementing commitments difficult? Do political leaders feel they can control all levels of field commanders (especially those who may be profiting from illegal activities, such as the drug trade)?
- Are there representational problems (e.g., who speaks for the group)?
- Are the issues framed in a "decidable" way (e.g., is the issue framed as "respect for ethnicity," which is a broad and vague notion, or are there concrete options for how the parties can treat each other more respectfully, such as guaranteed seats in a transitional parliament or protections for issues of language and culture)?
- Are there deep-seated wounds or traumas that make the idea of "agreement with the enemy" irrational?
- Are there processes for airing and deciding difficult internal disagreements, or are internal conflicts forced underground, where they remain unresolved?

So, how did we assess whether the key people on the RCD and Mayi-Mayi sides had the means to negotiate effectively? As for the ability to make commitments, there were some command-and-control concerns about whether the political and military leadership could manage all the fighting units under the command of the RCD. This issue was not discussed openly, but credible reports from the region gave us some insight. On the positive side, even though there were obvious internal splits, there was a healthy culture within the RCD leadership of airing disagreements and trying to resolve them through a respectful process. The biggest issues entailed a lack of working relationships between key actors on both sides and the absence of any effective channels of communication. There was some unofficial contact but nothing that could support delicate negotiations. And there was a very strained group-to-group relationship between the RCD and Mayi-Mayi in general, which led to important misperceptions and distortions between the groups and often generated very strong emotional attachments to seeing each other as mortal enemies. Again, significant work needed to be done to change the willingness and ability of the parties to negotiate when it came to having the means to talk effectively.

Taken together, the analysis we did of the willingness and ability of key actors from the RCD and this particular Mayi-Mayi militia gave us a rich understanding of the obstacles to the parties' changing their interconnections and thereby potentially changing the stuck negotiation subsystem. It also illuminated some potential assets that the parties could draw on to improve their ability to work together. The process of gathering this information was itself a kind of intervention into the system, which I discuss in more depth in Chapter 9. This more detailed understanding of what it would take for the parties themselves to own a change process multiplied the potential ways that our group or others, including the parties themselves, could serve as catalysts for change. More importantly, these potential interventions do not aim to insert an outsider directly to mediate an agreement between the parties. Rather, the purpose is to put the parties at the forefront of any potential change process. The analysis of their willingness and ability to negotiate is intended to develop an understanding of how to encourage the forces and structures that help the system change itself.

CHAPTER 8 SUMMARY

- The key to nurturing change in a system is to improve the ability of key actors to address important structural and attitudinal factors. In turn, the ability of key actors to work for change depends on their willingness and ability to negotiate or work together collaboratively
- Three components shape key actors' willingness and ability to work together:
  - Their negotiation frame, or how they think about the situation and their relationships with other key actors
  - How they perceive the value of talking (working collaboratively with others to pursue their goals) versus not talking (pursuing their goals unilaterally)
  - Whether they have the means to work collaboratively

- There are structured approaches to assessing each of these three variables that affect a key person's willingness and ability to work collaboratively. However, gathering this information means that an analyst needs to come into contact with the system he or she is trying to assess. This means that in assessing the willingness and ability of key people to collaborate, the analyst is already making an intervention and has to plan and implement that intervention with care.

CHAPTER **9**

TRANSACTIONAL PEACEBUILDING
A TOOLBOX

⋻

> In negotiation, the time might not be ripe for resolution, but the time
> is always ripe to do something.
>
> —Roger Fisher

In the early 1990s, forces from the Georgian government and the ethnic en-
clave of South Ossetia (in the north of Georgia) fought a war. By late 1994,
the active fighting had stopped, though there was sporadic violence, and it
was unsafe to travel across the battle lines. In addition, the two sides were
at an impasse in terms of finding a political solution. In 1995, I was part of
a team from the Conflict Management Group (CMG) that began a series
of informal brainstorming meetings between delegations from Georgia and
South Ossetia designed to find ways to break the impasse. The sessions were
unofficial and off-the-record and included many exercises and discussions
aimed at finding new ways to look at the situation and the conflict. Despite
a high degree of skepticism among the participants that there was any hope
of moving beyond the stalemate, the sessions did succeed in developing
new possibilities and momentum for change. At the end of one session, a
participant explained why the meeting had been a success: "You opened our
eyes to possibilities to which we had blinded ourselves."

This quote captures the value of transactional peacebuilding as a catalyst
to help systems change themselves. However, it may be difficult for many

organizations to use transactional peacebuilding techniques because they are seen as narrowly centered on negotiating political settlements as opposed to broadly helping key people build their willingness and ability to work together. For example, in the middle to late 1990s, relief and development organizations began trying to incorporate conflict resolution skills into their organizations in response to increased donor demand for such activity. Even those organizations that took the lead in this regard tended to treat conflict resolution as a discrete program area, only suited to specialized situations, rather than as a core competency with a role in program delivery in general.

Official negotiation and mediation form a small subset of transactional peacebuilding but have become emblematic of the field. As such, it is easy to see why many would be reluctant to embrace transactional peacebuilding as a core competence of their organizations. First, formal agreement making between parties in conflict is usually not the business of most organizations that contribute to peacebuilding (e.g., those that do structural and attitudinal peacebuilding). Second, formal agreement making is also inconsistent with the ideal of humanitarian and development practice as being apolitical.

However, as with the participant in the Georgia–South Ossetia dialogue, the answer may be to "open people's eyes" to the full range of transactional peacebuilding practice. As the epigraph by Roger Fisher at the start of this chapter indicates, there are many more transactional peacebuilding options besides seeking a formal agreement. Chapter 8 breaks transactional peacebuilding down into its component parts—that is, the varied factors that drive the ability and willingness of key actors to work together to address issues of common concern. This chapter further expands the notion of what it means to do transactional peacebuilding by exploring the myriad of potential transactional interventions that can be used to accomplish that end. My hope is that more peacebuilders will find ways to incorporate transactional peacebuilding into their practice as a part of a holistic approach to systems change.

A first step in this direction is to appreciate that transactional peacebuilding is useful in most situations, even those without a formal conflict or even easily identifiable parties. For example, Chapter 7 used the 2009 Interagency Conflict Assessment Framework (ICAF) systems map of Cambodia to illustrate how to listen to a system. It identified the need to regularize the policy-making environment within the Cambodian government in order to nurture change in the system that would increase Cambodia's level of peace. This may seem like a classic structural peacebuilding problem, but it has a critical transactional component: whether to implement a more regularized policy-making environment, and if so, how to make critical decisions. Outside actors, such as donors, diplomats, and international NGOs, could try to impose decisions on the Cambodian government, but these approaches are unlikely to work well in the long term. The alternative, providing support to key Cambodians to address this problem on their own, is a transactional intervention.

Another example of the wide applicability of transactional approaches is the use of participatory development (PD) or community-driven development (CDD).[1] Basically, PD/CDD is a methodology that puts communities in a leading role in defining their development needs, designing the implementation of programs, and overseeing and owning development outcomes. There is evidence that PD/CDD increases the quality and sustainability of development outcomes. And the use of transactional techniques distinguishes PD/CDD from regular development processes.

It is probably impossible, and certainly tedious, to try to catalogue every potential transactional intervention technique. A better way of conveying the richness of transactional techniques is to explore the key dimensions along which transactional peacebuilding practice can vary:

- *Purpose:* the objective of the transactional activity
- *Role:* the function a transactional peacebuilder plays in pursuit of a specific purpose
- *Style:* the way in which a transactional peacebuilder implements a particular role

The many possible ways to combine purpose, role, and style mean that there is a limitless range of potential forms of transactional peacebuilding. Many of these combinations are well suited to the less political, unofficial nature of traditional humanitarian and development practice. This chapter elaborates on each of these three dimensions of transactional peacebuilding and provides examples of transactional techniques that organizations may incorporate into their peacebuilding practice.

GAINING ENTRY

As helpful as these individual transactional techniques are, much of their usefulness derives from the context within which they are employed. For example, Chapter 8 gives examples of helping groups of key people (in South Africa and Iraq) appreciate the difference between a zero-sum, or "us versus them," mind-set and a mutual-gain, or "us versus the problem," mind-set. The specific technique used in both cases was a form of a "prisoner's dilemma" exercise. In both cases, the participants saw, first through a generic training exercise and then through a discussion of their current situation, how a mutual-gain negotiation frame might serve them better. However, if the relationship between the third party, in this case the training team, and the participants was one of hostility and distrust, then there was little chance the technique would be effective.

The key to using any of these transactional techniques well is to build an underlying relationship with the key people involved that is based on a level of trust sufficient to allow them to take what the third party says at face value: They might not be predisposed to accept everything the third party says, but neither do they discount it from the start. Building this sufficient level of trust between a third party and a group of key people is known as gaining entry. Often the easiest way to gain entry is not to formally "enter" at all. Rather these techniques work best if they can be used in the context of a preexisting relationship between the third party and the key people. For example, a colleague and I worked with the political parties in Iraq in 2006 at the request, and under the auspices, of the National Democratic Institute (NDI), which had worked with many of the political parties in Iraq for years. In fact, NDI had actually supported the establishment of many of these parties. Even though my colleague and I had no preexisting relationship with the Iraqi politicians, we were able to gain the trust of these key people because of the trust they had in NDI.

By the same token, transactional techniques can be built into existing programs and take advantage of existing relationships with key people, whether at the village, provincial, or national level. In addition, much of the work of gaining entry may already have been done as part of gathering data about a key person's willingness and ability to negotiate in the first place. In either case, in advance of their participation in a transactional process, key people need to know the answers to a few basic questions in order to build their trust in the process:

- Who is the third party and under whose auspices is the activity taking place (e.g., who is the sponsoring organization, where is the funding coming from, etc.)?
- What is the purpose of the activity?
- Why is the key person being included?
- Who among the key person's community, constituency, or superiors will know about the activity and what will they think?
- What will happen with the key person's participation (e.g., will there be a report, is he or she representing anyone, etc.)?
- What role will the sponsoring agency play in the future?

In 2007, Mercy Corps in Afghanistan decided to build the capacity of its Afghan staff to incorporate communication and conflict resolution skills and training into the wide array of development programs the organization delivers. For example, a Mercy Corps team might provide conflict resolution training to key people in a village to help them set up a mechanism for allocating aid resources to families there. In that case, the above questions would largely be answered through Mercy Corps's long-standing relationship with that particular village and the details of the particular development project.

In situations where a systemic planning process might lead to the initiation of a new program, it is nearly impossible to gain entry without forming some sort of collaboration or using some form of networking to take advantage of a preexisting relationship between the partner organization and the key people involved.[2] Assuming that an organization, one way or another, manages to gain entry to the key people they need to work with, then peacebuilders can find the right transactional technique (or mixture of techniques) to fit the situation by combining and tailoring the purpose, role, and style to fit the specific context.

PURPOSE

Chapter 8 provides a detailed breakdown of the factors that contribute to whether a key person is willing and able to work collaboratively with other key people. The results of this analysis provide a menu of potential purposes for transactional peacebuilding that fit under the rubric of "ripening" a situation, or making it more likely that key people will be willing and able to work together. For example, a transactional intervention might target changing a particular key person's negotiation frame, building relationships between key people, or helping them clarify their interests and understanding of the interests of others. In general, the purposes of transactional peacebuilding mirror the basic components that drive a key person's willingness and ability to negotiate:

1. *Negotiation frame:* techniques designed to affect the negotiation frame of key people
2. *Value of talking versus not talking:* techniques designed to affect how key people see the potential value of a collaborative process for achieving their objectives versus pursuing an adversarial, nonnegotiation strategy
3. *Strengthening the means for negotiation or collaborative problem solving:* techniques designed to improve the ability of key people to engage in collaborative problem solving

Negotiation Frame

A key person's negotiation frame usually takes time to truly change. Often this change, if it happens, results from many different experiences, new interactions, and improved working relationships. However, certain techniques can play a critical role in this change process. For example, in 1998, as part of the CMG's work on the negotiations between Ecuador and Peru over their border conflict, CMG held a "facilitated joint brainstorming session" with six unofficial but influential representatives from each side.[3] Toward the start of the session, the participants were given an assignment as part of an ice-breaking exercise. They were paired up, one Ecuadoran with one Peruvian, and each person was asked to interview his or her partner for the purpose of introducing that person to the group.

The exercise aims to help participants find personal connections so that they may begin to see each other in terms outside their official titles (e.g., presidential advisor, admiral, or newspaper editor) or even their nationality (e.g., Ecuadorian or Peruvian). The goal is to have them discover some common identity, value, or purpose that might shift them out of viewing themselves as adversaries (e.g., an "us versus them" frame). After a period of discussion, each pair did their introductions. The exercise had gone well enough; the atmosphere was cordial, even a bit jovial. Then the last pair went. According to one of the facilitators in the session, the last group at first demurred, saying that they could not participate in the introductions because they had not completed the assignment. When pressed, they said they had "failed the first assignment" because their discussion quickly went to matters "too personal to discuss" with the rest of the group. When pressed again, the pair said that early in their discussion the two men had discovered that they were both fathers of mentally handicapped daughters. They had talked about how strongly they loved their daughters, how difficult it was for them, and how concerned they were as parents.

Far from failing the exercise, the two had taken an important step toward reframing their view of each other and the conflict: Instead of seeing each other as an Ecuadoran and a Peruvian fighting a win-lose battle for land, they began to see each other as concerned fathers facing a common problem. While this small step did not settle the border dispute, it did help these two, and the larger group, work better together. It will be easier for two concerned fathers to work collaboratively then it will for two adversaries, from rival countries, to do battle in a forty-year-old dispute. A common variation on this exercise is to ask participants, who have given their time to attend a meeting like the Ecuador-Peru brainstorming session, to address the question, Why are you here? Often this prompts participants to bring their best selves forward—to articulate their nobler aspirations, such as to leave a better future for their children or to end suffering. A cynic may regard such statements as hollow rhetoric; however, the commitment and emotion behind these words add credibility to them and, more importantly, help focus the group's attention on their common aspirations, even if they also harbor some less-than-collaborative emotions.

It is not possible here to catalogue all the different techniques for addressing the negotiation frames of key people. However, another kind of exercise has been useful, in one form or another, in most transactional interventions in which I have participated: exercises that help participants understand and grapple with perceptions. For example, one exercise, which is now difficult to use because it has been used so much, involves a group looking at a line drawing of a woman, who can be seen as either young or old. There are variations on the exercise, but generally participants see one or the other. When participants from these two groups attempt to reach a consensus on the age of the woman, it soon becomes evident that battling over who is right is not useful.

This experience is helpful in making the shift from seeing the world only in a moralistic frame and debating who is correct to seeing it also in a structural frame and defining the problem without attributing rightness or wrongness. One community activist in South Africa, who went through this exercise, reframed the conflict there from black versus white battling over legitimacy to one in which "there are two realities in South Africa, one for the white and one for the black, and our job is to first understand each other's reality." Almost any dispute, conflict, or important issue involves differing perceptions. As such, the situation can be framed as a group of people struggling to overcome their differing perceptions in order to find a common answer to a difficult problem. Again, this does not solve the issue, but it often helps key people work together collaboratively.

Value of Talking Versus Not Talking

Another set of purposes for transactional peacebuilding is to target the variables that affect how key people assesses the value of talking, or engaging in a collaborative process with others, versus pursuing a unilateral, adversarial, or even violent strategy. One of these key variables is the degree to which key people understand their own interests, the interests of their group (e.g., clan, organization, political party), and the interests behind the positions of other key actors. It is difficult to discuss interests directly with key people because they often see a risk in disclosing the things they truly care about and are reluctant to signal any willingness to change or abandon a preexisting position. Even in circumstances that may not be conflictual, like designing a process for aid delivery in a village or creating a more regularized policy-making environment, people are often wary of change or will want to be sure that any change benefits or does not hurt them. In these situations, key people will form a position based on what they think will be best for them and adhere stubbornly to it. When key people form entrenched positions, they see less value in negotiating, or if they become stuck on positions, they will be less able to work collaboratively.

Helping key people reflect on their own interests and those of others is a way to get past the difficulties posed by positions. For example, in the Georgia–South Ossetia dialogues referred to earlier, the official negotiations were deadlocked over inconsistent positions (e.g., independence versus no independence), and the sides were refusing to negotiate with each other. In one of the sessions, participants were taken through an interests exercise.

The group was divided in half, with Georgians in one room and Ossetians in another. Each was asked to list the interests of the other party. The lists were written on large flip chart pages and then posted in a common room. Each group could then make edits to the list of its interests prepared by the other side (e.g., the Georgian participants edited the list of Georgian interests originally prepared by the Ossetian participants and vise versa). The exercise may seem convoluted, but in the end, it produces a more in-depth and honest discussion of each side's interests than tends to happen otherwise. Often key people are reluctant to disclose their interests for fear of revealing too much. However, they have an incentive to correct a misperception of their interests and are much more willing to do so.

After exploring interests, it is useful to help groups brainstorm creative ways to satisfy them. As the quote from the Georgian participant at the beginning of this chapter indicates, brainstorming a range of creative approaches to managing problems or opportunities can have an empowering effect. Diana Chigas, in writing about the impact of unofficial processes in general, concludes that "exploring creative ways of addressing the conflict" is one of the steps necessary to "bridge the polarization of positions and escape stalemate."[4]

It is also helpful for groups to winnow down options and make decisions. This can turn an upbeat brainstorming session into an adversarial battle over each person's favorite idea. One way out of this potential trap is an exercise known as affinity diagramming. In the initial Georgia–South Ossetia session, the group came up with over ninety options for how to improve the relationship and negotiation environment between the two groups. Affinity diagramming asks the participants to take their myriad of ideas and to group like ideas together into a much smaller number of categories. The Georgia–South Ossetia participants organized their ninety-plus ideas into about a dozen categories and, from these, picked six categories deemed the highest priority. The group then developed a hybrid idea for each of the six categories and, out of these, picked four ideas to implement. Affinity diagramming helped the group move from more than ninety ideas to a decision to implement four ideas that the whole group regarded as the most promising. Again, the ability of key actors to see concrete ways to take collaborative action greatly increases the likelihood that they will do so. Brainstorming and affinity diagramming are important transactional techniques that allow peacebuilders to intervene on this specific aspect of bolstering the willingness and ability of key actors to work together.

Strengthening the Means for Negotiation

In addition to the factors discussed above, three key factors can improve the willingness and ability of key actors to negotiate: the quality of their working relationship, their communication skills and opportunities, and their ability to make and keep commitments. Again, there are transactional techniques whose purpose is to affect each of these three variables.

For example, from 1996 to 1998, I was part of a CMG team asked to help improve race relations in the city of Springfield, Massachusetts. A key event in the process, which took almost three years, was a meeting CMG facilitated in the early spring of 1997. The purpose of the meeting was to bring together a racially diverse cross section of the city, such as business leaders, the chief of police and rank-and-file officers, the head of the local chapter of the National Association for the Advancement of Colored People (NAACP), community activists, high school students, and elected officials. The meeting was held over four days, the first two days of which were devoted to various activities and conversations designed to improve the working relationships among the participants.

However, two participants in particular, a leader of the city's African American community and a member of the district attorney's office, repeatedly wanted to "get down to it" and debate whether the city (the police and law enforcement) was racist. The two, one black and one white, maintained a combative demeanor and confronted each other whenever possible. After dinner on the second day, we held an open forum to let the participants discuss any topic they wanted. The two antagonists tried to seize the opportunity and began debating, but they were interrupted by an elected official. The official, who was black, asked the prosecutor, who was white, why he chose to join the district attorney's office in the first place. In response

the prosecutor's demeanor changed. He began to tell an emotional story about being assigned to defend a white suspect who had shot a black manager in cold blood. His story was told with intricate detail and he began to become more and more emotional, as did all those listening. He finished by saying, "that's why I became a prosecutor, so I didn't have to defend guys like that. If you want to talk about racism, what they did to that man [the manager] was racism and I didn't want to be part of it." The room was silent. The prosecutor's main antagonist, a leader in the African-American community, broke the silence by saying that while he reserved judgment about the system, he could work with this prosecutor as someone he could trust.[5]

If the session had ended that evening, it would have been a success in that it had helped to improve the working relationship between two people critical to the future of race relations in Springfield. The session also underscores that relationships among key people are both one-to-one and communal. It made a difference that the exchange between the two key antagonists happened in the midst of a group of about thirty-five fellow community members. It was a reminder that their relationship affected not just the two of them but the community as a whole.

The Springfield meeting, as well as the overall process, helped to deal with the emotional and identity components that affect the quality of the working relationship between key people. There are also skills associated with communication and negotiation that are critical to managing working relationships. For example, I helped to lead a joint training for negotiation teams from a First Nations band and the government of Canada, which were in the midst of a drawn-out and adversarial land-claim negotiation. The session was devoted to exploring the potential for a collaborative, interests-based process to help the parties move beyond their negotiation impasse. After a few days of the workshop, we facilitated an open discussion on the potential for using an interests-based approach. One of the First Nations negotiators said that the interests-based approach was their preferred style of negotiation because it was more consistent with their culture. A government negotiator was incredulous and objected, "The Band is one of the most positional bargainers we work with." At that, the negotiator from the band said, "Yes, and who do you think we learned that from?"

Contrary to being an incendiary remark, the negotiator's statement led to a common acknowledgment that neither side was happy with how the negotiations were going, and both wanted to find a way out. This marked a positive turning point in the ability (and willingness) of the two sides to work together. Later in the session, they worked together on redesigning the process so as to increase their ability to use a collaborative approach. They even went so far as to work together to help each side negotiate more effectively with its internal bosses. For example, representatives of the band agreed to help the government negotiators persuade other relevant ministries in the Canadian government to allow the team more flexibility in the talks. By building the skills of these key actors and helping them to improve the process they used to negotiate, the intervention helped rebuild their willingness and ability to work together.

Lastly, another key purpose for a transactional intervention is to help key actors manage internal disagreements and improve their ability to make and keep commitments. Chapter 8 discusses the relationship between the Congolese Rally for Democracy (RCD) and one of the largest Mayi-Mayi militias in Eastern Congo, two key actors in the peace process. At an important point in the process, the potential existed for these two key actors to negotiate a cease-fire, which our crude systems analysis at the time suggested was critical to the overall peace process. However, a critical obstacle to encouraging these two key actors to change their relationship with each other, hence their impact on the overall system, was that they were mortal enemies.

As such, the RCD executive was split between those who wanted to try negotiations and those who felt that they had no choice but to fight and defeat the Mayi-Mayi. A member of the RCD leadership asked us to help. The split within the leadership meant that they could not enter into negotiations because they could not deliver on any commitments made in the process. After we facilitated conversations among members of the RCD executive and met with members individually, the group decided to give negotiations a chance and eventually concluded a cease-fire agreement. Again, while mediators played a critical role in helping the parties reach an agreement, an important step along the way was a transactional intervention for the more limited purpose of helping the RCD improve its ability to make and keep commitments, which in turn increased its willingness and ability to talk with the Mayi-Mayi in the first place.

ROLE

Just as transactional peacebuilding has many different purposes other than agreement making, third parties can also play many different roles beyond that of mediator. For example, Christopher Mitchell has argued that mediation is a complex process that requires more than the efforts of a single mediator. Indeed, Mitchell identifies thirteen different functions or roles that are important to the success of a mediation effort.[6] In 1999, William Ury published *The Third Side,* in which he argues that essential to dealing with any dispute is the presence of a third side that can play any one of ten different roles.[7]

These different roles identified by Mitchell and Ury vary by the amount of power and involvement of the third party. Figure 9.1 provides a list of possible third-party roles along a continuum from those that are least involved and have the least power over the participants to those where the third party is highly involved and has a high degree of power over the parties. For example, the role of witness entails no interaction with the key actors other than observing what happens and letting one's presence be known. The presence of a third party as a witness might encourage key people to be on their best behavior, or a witness may be able to provide early warning of potential violence. However, the witness has no direct involvement with the process of interaction between key people or the substance of their discussions. Contrast this role with that of arbiter at the other end of the spectrum. An arbiter can determine what process the parties will use in addressing a substantive issue or conflict, and in binding arbitration, the arbiter has final decision-making authority and can impose a solution.

Just as the purpose of agreement making may be inconsistent with the mission of most peacebuilders (e.g., human rights organizations, relief and

Figure 9.1 Spectrum of Third-Party Roles

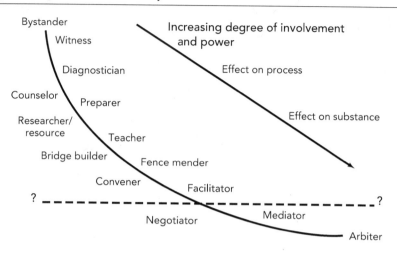

development organizations, trauma healers), so might the roles at the high-power and high-involvement end of the spectrum. This is represented by the dotted line in Figure 9.1. However, the many roles above the dotted line, such as the following, may be quite useful for peacebuilders to play:

- *Diagnostician:* interviewing key actors to understand their perspectives and/or the situation
- *Counselor:* helping key people consider their options for addressing an issue or handling a dispute
- *Preparer:* helping key people or organizations prepare for key meetings or negotiations
- *Researcher/resource:* providing key people with needed information, analysis, or logistical support
- *Teacher:* providing one or more key people with needed skills
- *Bridge builder:* making connections between key people
- *Fence mender:* helping repair relationships between key people
- *Convener:* hosting a meeting, providing "good offices," or constructing a process for dialogue
- *Facilitator:* running meetings and managing the process of interaction between key people

Roles that invest less power in the third party are also more consistent with the notion that systems change best when they change themselves. Roles that delegate more power over the substance, and to a lesser degree over the process, take ownership away from the key actors involved and make it more likely that any change resulting from the process will be the product of the intervener instead of the key actors in the system. The roles at the less powerful end of the spectrum are better suited as catalysts for nurturing change from within a system. A few of these roles deserve elaboration.

Diagnostician

Despite its cumbersome label, the role of diagnostician helps key actors to think in different ways about their situation and the potential for change. A diagnostician interviews key actors for the purpose of understanding the situation from their perspective. In addition to helping a peacebuilder understand a particular social system (e.g., as part of a Systemic Peacebuilding Assessment), a diagnostic process often helps key actors think through familiar problems and situations in new ways. Further, if key actors are going to behave differently in the context of a complex system, be it to resolve a dispute, make new policy, or set up a community development council, then that shift in behavior needs to be preceded by a shift in thinking. A diagnostician can serve as an important catalyst for this change.

A standard tool for diagnosticians is the four-step thought process of the Circle Chart, developed by Roger Fisher, William Ury, and colleagues at the Harvard Negotiation Project. Using the Circle Chart, the interviewer starts with Step 1, asking a key actor to describe, generally, what a better future would look like: Is there peace, economic development, security, and so forth? What attributes or developments would let them know that the situation had improved (e.g., Muslim and Christian children attending a common school, villagers working out disputes peacefully using traditional mechanisms, etc.)? Key actors then articulate the extent of the gap between this preferred future and the disliked aspects of the current situation that depart from it. This sets up what Peter Senge calls a "creative tension" that acts as a force for change.[8] Focusing only on the difficulties of their current situation may deter people from acting at all. If they focus only on what might be, they risk becoming stranded in dreamland. However, if people can hold both ideas in mind at the same time, they become both motivated to change their current reality by the prospect of a brighter future and grounded by the need to deal with the practicalities of the current situation.

In Chapter 8, I describe a land-dispute mediation involving a Native American tribe and the neighboring nonnative towns. Emotions ran high on all sides. Accusations of racism flew back and forth. People on each side felt that the other threatened their fundamental rights. At the outset of our involvement, we played the role of diagnostician, meeting with key people and groups from the tribe and the towns, and we started with Step 1 of the Circle Chart. Starting with the question, What does a better future look like? had a strikingly profound impact on people. For example, when we held open forums in the nonnative communities, the audience was ready to unload a barrage of complaints against the tribe. Rather than pursuing these complaints at the outset, we asked the audience to form small groups and share their visions for a better future. At first, some members of the audience seemed stunned by the question. They had been mired for so long in what they did not like that they had lost sight of what they wanted. They had focused for so long on what was wrong about "them" that they had lost sight of what was right for themselves.

As the groups reported out, we developed a hybrid desired-future vision. When we then asked people to describe the disliked aspects of the current situation, we received less emotional intensity, more objectivity, and sharper analysis than we had at the start of the meeting. In addition, defining the current situation as a gap between a disliked present and a desired future allowed the group to grapple more productively with the second step of the Circle Chart: diagnosing why the gap exists. Again, this provided us, as third parties, with valuable insight into the situation, but it also helped the audience members focus on why they had been unable to move beyond the current situation rather than remaining resigned to it. We asked the group members to give special attention to framing their diagnoses in terms of things they (or someone) could do something about. For example, "bad history" was often cited as a reason why the current conflict existed. However, it is impossible to go back in time and change history. On the other hand, an addressable diagnosis for the gap might be "an inability to move beyond a troubled past" or "distrust between the communities fueled by a difficult history." "Distrust" and "moving beyond" a bad history are things the community could do something about. Step 2 of the Circle Chart has the impact of focusing people's attention on new ways of addressing their situation. It encourages them to take responsibility for improving the situation and empowers them by identifying things they can do something about.

Taking individuals and groups from both the tribal and town communities through Steps 1 and 2 of the Circle Chart helped inform our thinking and also began to change how key actors in the situation thought about the issues and each other. Our team then took another step that can be added to the role of diagnostician: We played back what we had learned to the two communities, which had additional positive impacts. First, it helped show that despite the angry conflict between the communities, they had remarkably similar future visions—not in terms of the particulars (e.g., who owned what land) but in terms of the values they wanted to see realized and the quality of life they hoped to enjoy and leave for their children. This opened the possibility of key actors from each side changing the nature of their relationship.

Second, reporting back also helped identify some common traps that key actors on both sides fell into. For example, one of the Step 2 diagnoses we heard from both sides was that key people felt the media regularly misquoted or misrepresented what they said. Yet, both sides also accepted that what they read about the other side's comments or actions was completely accurate. Key actors on both sides smiled when they realized that these two beliefs could not both be true, and this recognition provided an impetus for these key actors to improve their channels of communication—to talk directly to each other and not through the media!

Of course, playing the role of diagnostician can be as simple as perspective taking, or listening to the views of key actors regarding their situation. This helps third-party peacebuilders gain information, satisfies an important interest of key actors to be heard and understood, and assists with building a working relationship between an intervener and the key actors. Whatever version is used, the diagnostician role can help build the willingness and ability of key actors to work together. For example, helping key actors focus on their desired future, instead of just the disliked present, can help shift them to an empowered negotiation frame. Putting key actors in the role of diagnostician (having them diagnose the drivers of the gap between their current and desired-future states) helps them shift to a more structural frame. Developing options to address diagnoses (Step 3 of the Circle Chart) helps them to see more potential options for mutual gain. Lastly, the role of diagnostician can be an intervention in itself, or it can be used as part of a longer-term change process.

Researcher

Often, when faced with difficult decisions, key people do not have the time to do extensive research. A transactional peacebuilder can help fill in this gap. For example, in the Democratic Republic of the Congo peace process, as talks turned to issues of power sharing and transitioning to one national army, questions arose about ways to structure a power-sharing government and to protect minority groups—or whether it was even possible to do this. One key person in the negotiations questioned why they were even talking about power sharing because it was not the "African way." "In Africa," he said, "the president is all powerful; he is the leader of the government, leader of the army, sports hero, sexiest man."[9] In response, our team developed two memos, one that included about a dozen different strategies taken by governments around the world to protect minority groups and another that pulled together a range of diverse power-sharing arrangements included in peace treaties from other conflicts. While neither memo solved the problem, the parties who saw them reported that they helped organize their group's thinking on the subject and allowed them to grapple more effectively with the issue. In other words, the memos seemed to advance the key actors' willingness and ability to negotiate.

Teacher

There are many examples and assessments of training used as an intervention technique in conflict and peace processes.[10] Training in conflict transformation and communication for key people from one group or joint training for key people from multiple groups can improve skills, strengthen relationships, and affect basic attitudes. It can be a powerful technique to build the willingness and ability of key people to work together, as evidenced by several examples already cited in this book, among many others. Rather than returning to ground that has already been well covered, I want to highlight two specific uses for training as a transactional peacebuilding role.

First, the role of trainer provides a transactional peacebuilder with a way to help key actors grapple more easily with divisive or sensitive issues. For example, in the training session with the negotiators from the First Nations band and the government of Canada cited above, each side was having difficulty dealing with its internal constituents (such as the Tribal Council for the band and representatives from other ministries for the government negotiators). These difficulties posed significant obstacles for each side at the negotiation table and contributed to a deteriorating relationship. However, neither side felt comfortable discussing this point with the other for fear that doing so would signal weakness. As a trainer it is possible to ease in to a discussion of this issue by talking about it generically. Specifically, we did a presentation on the general research into difficult internal dynamics and the problems they pose for negotiators. This frame allowed us to identify nearly all the issues each side said it was facing. Framing the issue in generic terms made the issue discussable and allowed us to move into a session on how negotiators from opposite sides can help each other manage difficult internal negotiations. As discussed above, this strengthened their relationship and the negotiation process—key elements that affect key people's willingness and ability to work together.

Second, the role of trainer allows a transactional peacebuilder to structure an experiential exercise that can help key actors more easily grapple with controversial or divisive issues. In 1989, the Wilgespruit Fellowship Centre, with some assistance from our team from the Conflict Management Group, hosted a negotiation workshop outside Johannesburg, South Africa, for community activists and representatives of the main black liberation movements. This was a significant event. In fact, we were told it was the first time that the liberation movements had sent representatives to a meeting knowing that the other movements would also be sending representatives.

A direct discussion of the need for and benefit of greater interaction among the liberation movements would not have been politically appropriate; nor was there much potential for it to succeed. However, we ran a generic exercise on the difficulty of multiparty negotiations and the danger of a bad multiparty process frustrating the attainment of important interests. In this exercise, the group gets a prize if it can reach a consensus but loses the prize if it does not. As with most groups that participate in this particular exercise, the group struggled and lost the prize. In the review and discussion of the exercise, a colleague, Charles Barker, made explicit a powerful analogy: If the liberation movements could not reach a consensus among themselves about what direction a future South Africa should take, what hope did they have of negotiating that future with the National Party government? And if they could not, they might lose the prize: South Africa. The room was silent. The group was given another chance to find a consensus and win the prize (which they did), but more importantly, after that moment, there was a different spirit of camaraderie and sense of purpose among the group.

Convener

The role of convener, as someone who provides good offices, is nothing new. It is said that the war between the Lydians and the Medes ended in 585 BCE when the factions negotiated a peace agreement "owing to the good offices of Nebuchadnezzar of Babylon and Syennesis of Cilicia."[11] Conveners provide an essential element in the transactional process: a secure space for key people to meet plus logistical assistance and the political cover needed to discuss sensitive topics. Provider of good offices, however, is often portrayed as a passive role and one better suited to formal peace processes.

The notion of a convener encompasses much more than just good offices and can make an essential contribution in situations where there are no well-defined parties or issues and settlement is not the goal. For example, in the case of race relations in the city of Springfield, Massachusetts, referenced earlier, there were no clearly defined parties—there was not one representative for all African Americans, Latinos, or Caucasians in the city. Racial tension and racism are not decidable questions in the same way as determining whether to have a cease-fire or to adjust a disputed boundary.

In these situations, the convener can play an indispensable role in "building a container," or establishing a process, to deal with unwieldy social issues. In Springfield, it took months of interviews with members of the community to find a convening issue that would bring people together. For example, framing the issue as police-community relations automatically put participants into one of two camps: on the side of either the police or the community. Some people we spoke to in Springfield said they would not participate in such a meeting. As an alternative, we settled on building secure communities as an issue all would endorse and under which the thorny issues of racism could be addressed explicitly. Further, this framing for the meeting allowed key people from the community to set the agenda for how to make their community more secure.

In addition to finding a convening issue, our team needed to identify key people to participate in this initial session. Chapter 5 provides a list of criteria for defining a key person in a specific context. However, in situations that involve issues as pervasive and unstructured as race relations, it is often difficult to identify key people. Certainly the leaders of important organizations are key people, such as the head of the local NAACP or the chief of police. However, relying only on these formal, established structures is dangerous because it misses a great wealth of informal structures and informal leaders. In Springfield, these included community activists (one such group referred to itself as the Housewives from Hell), students from the local high school, and businesspeople. A convener who helps identify both formal and informal key people makes a critical contribution to systems change by creating an opportunity for key people to meet who would not ordinarily have reason to interact.

Lastly, in addition to identifying key people, a convener can also help make it easier for them to come together. In Springfield, some organizations said they would (ordinarily) boycott any meeting attended by a rival organization. For example, certain religious leaders said they would not attend a meeting also involving the police or the district attorney's office. However, as conveners, we overcame these objections by finding a "sufficient invitation." A key part of what made the invitation sufficient was the apolitical nature of the convening issue. We were also explicit that the meeting was not a negotiation and stressed that individuals were being invited in their personal capacity and not as representatives of any group. As such, participants could not make commitments on behalf of any organization. These ground rules helped make it clear that attending the meeting on building secure communities did not represent a concession on any past position a group may have taken.

Most importantly, our team took care from the very beginning of the process to establish the legitimacy of our involvement. A diverse committee of community leaders from Springfield originally contacted CMG. After establishing the basic purpose of our involvement, which was to start a community-driven process for addressing race relations in the city, we worked to ensure that our efforts would not appear prejudiced in favor of any one party who had invited us or who was paying for our services. For example, if we had been invited and funded by the police department or the local NAACP, many in the community would assume we were partial to one of these entities. Instead, we advised the informal committee to increase its representativeness by including other key community leaders and to find funding from diverse sources that would be acceptable to the community. The legitimacy of our team's involvement in Springfield lent legitimacy to our invitation to key people to participate in the process.

In sum, the role of convener can be much more complex than simply offering good offices. A convener can provide a critical transactional intervention to make unstructured and chaotic issues or situations more amenable to key people working together.

STYLE

In addition to the panoply of roles that a transactional peacebuilder can play, third parties can also use different styles to play each role. Again, there is an infinite variety of styles, but four key dimensions define the difference between them:

- *Elicitive versus directive:* the degree to which a third party helps participants think through the situation and make their own choices about the process and substantive issues versus telling the parties what to do[12]
- *Reactive versus proactive:* the degree to which a third party acts only in response to requests from the participants versus being self-starting and taking the initiative
- *Transformative versus evaluative:* the degree to which the third party places a value on the participants improving their working relationships by letting parties work things out largely on their own versus providing assessments as to the best, most legitimate, or wisest outcome
- *Official/formal versus unofficial/informal:* the degree to which the third party is explicit and structured about its role and relies on formal agreements between the participants as to the process or substance versus neither calling attention to its role nor stressing explicit, formal agreements

As Figure 9.2 indicates, certain styles are more appropriate for transactional peacebuilders. Styles on the left of the four continua tend to be more compatible with using transactional peacebuilding as a catalyst for helping systems change themselves. Styles on the right of the continua are better suited to the role of a power mediator, who may need to strong-arm reluctant parties into an agreement. However, as discussed earlier, forced change is not likely to be sustainable or owned by the key people involved. More participant-centric styles are more consistent with the participants owning the results of the process and building the ability to work better together over time.

While styles that are less formal and more elicitive, responsive, and transformative tend to be better suited to transactional peacebuilding, interveners

Figure 9.2 Transactional Peacebuilding Styles

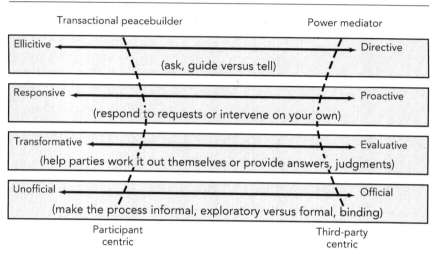

should be able to adjust their style as demanded by the context. In the Springfield project, for example, our team knew that we needed to use a more elicitive style that would encourage key people to set an agenda for managing race relations in the city. Our team was quite directive, however, both at the outset of the initial meeting in setting out the purpose of the session (building secure communities) and its ground rules and during the earlier parts of the meeting agenda (e.g., resisting the calls from some participants to debate whether the city government was racist).

For key people in tense, uncertain, or risky situations, externally imposed structure, if perceived as legitimate, can be reassuring. Structure removes much of the social ambiguity caused by bringing together people who may not often interact or introducing them to unfamiliar situations (e.g., a four-day retreat on race relations in Springfield or an off-the-record meeting of combatant leaders). Further, in more unstructured settings, key people tend to fall back into old routines and re-create old arguments. A new structure, with new ground rules, can help break them out of these old habits of mind. In addition, in a tense situation, it can be easier for key people to respond to an external initiative than to take initiative on their own.

For the Springfield meeting to be a successful catalyst for change, our team needed to shift its style. The agenda for the session started with structured exercises to help participants build or rebuild personal relationships. However, the session moved to exercises designed to elicit from the group members their vision for a better future, their diagnosis of the gap between their current reality and that vision, their ideas for moving forward, and their suggestions for key next steps. Our role as facilitators became more responsive to the participants as they became more proactive. The final part of the process we labeled "transitioning" out of the session back into normal life. The group members defined the process for how they would work together. Our role became less formal as we transitioned to serving as advisors to the group.

CHAPTER 9 SUMMARY

- An infinite variety of transactional peacebuilding roles can be tailored to fit the intervening organization, the context, and the type of changes the organization is trying to nurture from within the social system.
- The toolbox of a transactional peacebuilder includes much more than just mediation for use in producing agreements between warring combatants. Transactional tools can be focused on building specific aspects of the willingness and ability of key people to work together. The challenge, especially for organizations unaccustomed to doing transactional peacebuilding, is to find the appropriate transactional tools for their organization (or network of organizations) and the context. This requires peacebuilders to
  1. fine-tune their purpose to correspond to their analysis of the willingness of key people to work together;
  2. craft a role or roles best suited to their purpose(s);
  3. develop their style, across the four dimensions, to suit their role and purpose.

CHAPTER 10

DO ANY OF US HAVE THE POWER
TO CHANGE A SYSTEM?

⊸

No one of us is as smart as all of us.

—African proverb

In early 2000, my wife gave birth to our third child. In addition to great joy, the event brought the realization that my wife and I could no longer manage in a city, even one as beautiful as Boston, without our extended family. We decided to move to my wife's home state of Wisconsin. I started my life at an academic institution, the University of Wisconsin, Milwaukee, in the beginning of 2001. This gave me the opportunity to reflect on my experiences in the nonprofit peacebuilding world. Three questions preoccupied me: (1) Why did what we do work when it worked? (2) Why did what we do not work when it did not work? And, most importantly, (3) why, even when what we did worked, did it not *work*?

This last question deserves some elaboration. I began to focus on some of the clearest examples of instances in which the work my colleagues and I did had the most demonstrable positive impacts. For example, from 2000 to 2002, my colleague Jim Tull and I were involved in a project to provide assistance to the government of Colombia on the peace process there. At one critical point, President Andreas Pastrana was going to meet with Manuel Marulanda, the head of the Revolutionary Armed Forces of Colombia (FARC), in a last-ditch effort to save the peace process and avert a return to all-out war. On the eve of the mission, our team drafted a memo to the president with ideas for how to keep the negotiations going. The president managed to reach an agreement with the FARC leader, and the process continued—for a while.

After the agreement was announced, our contact in the president's office called to say that some of the paragraphs from our memo actually made it into the agreement. This intervention was successful in that it helped keep the peace process going in the short term. However, some ten years after this "success," the violence in Colombia still exacts a large human, financial, and social cost. In other words, even when what we did (advise the president) worked (helped lead to an agreement), it did not work (our success did not lead to Peace Writ Large in Colombia).

At first I was proud of myself for asking, Why, when what we did worked, it didn't work? The question was an admission that the work my colleagues and I did was of limited value—even when we achieved our immediate goals. This is not a question I asked (at least out loud) when I was the executive director of a nonprofit competing for funds against like organizations. Admitting that you or your organization could only have limited success is very risky. However, the more I thought about the question, the more I was ashamed of myself for not asking it earlier. Why should it be so difficult to admit that, as one person or one organization, you are limited in how effective you can be? Why should a conflict resolution organization, or a human rights advocate, or a donor funding market-reform programs find it so hard to admit that it alone cannot achieve Peace Writ Large in Colombia or elsewhere? In retrospect it seems foolish to believe otherwise.

The problem is not that we do not recognize or that we disagree with the fundamental wisdom of the African proverb "No one of us is as smart as all of us." Peacebuilders, just as people in general, know that it takes many different people working together to tackle large social problems. Rather, the problem is that we are not good at harnessing the power of "all of us." As argued in Part I, peacebuilders often proceed on the vague hope that if they do good on a small scale, it will somehow combine with other small positive changes and create big systems change in countries like Afghanistan or in relation to big social problems like poverty or climate change. Or they succumb to the financial, logistical, and political difficulty of trying to orchestrate the work of other professional but highly independent organizations.

Ultimately, the biggest disincentive to admitting that no one of us is as smart as all of us is the perception that linking your organization's success to the success of others makes you less powerful. This is true in the short term. The narrower the scope of a project, the more likely implementing organizations will be able to achieve the goals set out for them. For example, take a program to build peace in Afghanistan by reducing the level of conflict in communities. An organization has more power to accomplish a specific task, such as training community mediators, than it does to coordinate with other organizations working on economic development, interclan reconciliation, and building local governance. However, this strategy reminds me of something Roger Fisher used to say about power: Most of us tend to get better and better at less and less until we get to the point where we have the power to make whatever we say should happen, happen. Roger concluded by saying, "One day, you can proudly proclaim that when you order the wastebasket to be moved from one side of your office to the other, it gets moved!"

Reducing complex social problems to a series of linear tasks makes peacebuilders more powerful in the short term. And it greatly enhances their chances of failure in the long term. Taking a systemic approach makes us more powerful to achieve success in the long term because it helps peacebuilders harness the power of "all of us." A systemic approach to peacebuilding is more difficult than a linear approach. However, enhancing our power to get things done in the short term by only taking a linear approach means that we will be able to do very little about the issues the world cares about deeply, such as persistent poverty, violence, and injustice.

This book is really about how to make peacebuilders more powerful. It sets out a comprehensive approach to sustainable change that spans theory (the structural, attitudinal, and transactional [SAT] model), analysis and planning (the Systemic Peacebuilding Assessment, systems mapping, and systemic planning), and action (catalyzing systemic change through transactional peacebuilding). There is certainly power in being able to put all these elements together, and there is power in thinking and acting systemically in general. *There is peacebuilding power in*

- seeing wholes and the dynamic interconnectedness of our world;
- focusing on the key drivers of big systems change: structural, attitudinal, and transactional;
- doing systemic assessment and planning;
- listening to the system, working with it, and learning from it by supplying good feed-forward to get good feedback;
- building your transactional toolbox and using transactional peacebuilding as a catalyst for structural and attitudinal change;
- learning by using an iterative project cycle;
- working in networks that are vertically and horizontally integrated.

But can thinking and acting systemically really make an organization more powerful? More importantly, can individuals or networks make a difference if, as discussed in Chapter 4 (see "Using the SAT Model to Foster Change in the Current Peacebuilding System"), the peacebuilding system works against peacebuilders who use a systemic approach? Can members of a system change the very system of which they are a part?

USING SYSTEMIC PEACEBUILDING TECHNIQUES TO CHANGE THE PEACEBUILDING SYSTEM

Peacebuilders are changing the peacebuilding system. Moreover, systemic peacebuilding techniques are helping. Two current examples give me inspiration: the Global Peace Index (GPI) of the Institute for Economics and Peace (IEP) and the Reflecting on Peace Practice Project (RPP) of CDA/Collaborative Learning Projects (CDA).

Global Peace Index

In 2010, the fourth annual Global Peace Index ranked the peacefulness of 149 countries using twenty-three indictors. The highly respected Economist Intelligence Unit (EIU) compiles the data for the GPI, which is housed at the IEP. The GPI and the institute are the brainchildren of Steve Killelea, an Australian businessman and philanthropist. Killelea was inspired to form the GPI after visiting various development projects that he was funding. As a businessperson, he took a practical approach to peacebuilding: He asked, "What are the most peaceful countries in the world, and what qualities do they share?" When Killelea had a difficult time getting an answer to his question, he decided to do something about it. After talking with a friend, Clyde McConaghy, who used to manage the EIU, Killelea embarked on the idea of developing a way to measure a country's peacefulness. In addition to involving the EIU to actually compile the rankings, he convened a panel of international experts to develop a list of indicators that could be used to measure peacefulness. These indicators range "from a nation's level of military expenditure to its relations with neighboring countries and the level of respect for human rights."[1]

The first GPI came out in May 2007. In the four years since this initial index came out, the GPI has already begun to have structural, attitudinal, and transactional impacts on the peacebuilding system. Perhaps the most immediate structural impact of the GPI is that many donors and international organizations, like the World Bank, now use it and the data it generates in their analysis and planning processes. Prior to the GPI, hard data was primarily used to document what was lacking in a society instead of what was working. This shift should increase as the GPI has helped change research agendas and spurred new work on understanding the correlates of peace.

The biggest impact of the GPI has been at the attitudinal level. The GPI was founded on the belief that peace can and should be measured.[2] More importantly, measuring peace in a holistic sense is essential. "The major re-alization that I had from founding the Global Peace Index was how little we actually know about peace and yet how pivotal it is to solving the many and varied global challenges that humanity is facing," said Killelea.[3] The index has also changed how businesses value peace by helping them see the link between the success of their ventures and the peacefulness of the countries or the markets in which they operate and invest. Killelea explained this phe-nomenon: "Peace Economics is a new and exciting field. Research indicates that there is a positive relationship between peace and per capita income. This means that there is a strategic advantage for companies in learning how to factor changing peace into their business plans."[4]

More importantly, the GPI experience validates some of the core prin-ciples of the systemic approach to peacebuilding. For example, Killelea's initial inspiration for the GPI is a good example of listening to the system: He wanted to "listen" to communities that were becoming more peaceful to understand how they were able to do so. As a businessperson, Killelea was "humble before the system" in that he did not assume he knew what would make the world, or the communities where his foundation was working, more peaceful. Rather, he took his guidance from the system itself.

GPI is also working with a key leverage point for change that already existed in the system: the evolving methods for how peacebuilders do analysis and planning. Currently, one of the key impediments to peacebuilders' focusing on long-term, macro-level change is the attitude, particularly among donors, that only what can be counted counts. This hinders donors, aid recipients, and implementing agencies from seeing wholes and interconnectedness be-cause they focus on partial or more micro-level indicators, such as number of schools built, or elections held, or medical aides trained. GPI turned this dynamic on its head by using the system's need for countables to foster a macro-level view. By creating a quantifiable macro-level measure of peace, it forces donors and other key peacebuilding actors to see wholes instead of just parts.

Lastly, GPI is a good example of the power of networking and the use of negotiation (a transactional peacebuilding tool) to create structural and attitudinal change. Killelea used his networks to have a series of negotia-tions that made the idea for the GPI a reality. For example, his relationships were key to bringing in the EIU, founding the expert panel, and leveraging international media launches for the GPI. One of the most critical transac-tions was Killelea's meeting with Chic Dambach, president of the Alliance for Peacebuilding, a consortium of leading organizations that do applied peacebuilding work. As Dambach tells the story, he initially wanted to cancel his introductory meeting with Killelea. Because he could not find a number to call and cancel their lunch, Dambach went to the restaurant. "Within a few minutes of talking with Steve, I knew this concept could transform the way we think about building peace," he said. The project has become a fundamental component of the alliance's conflict analysis and advocacy initiatives, and the alliance provided a base from which the GPI could make connections in Washington, DC, and throughout the United States in order to spread the messages of the GPI.

Based on the GPI, the Alliance for Peacebuilding and the J. William and Harriet Fulbright Center joined forces to produce the Global Symposium of Peaceful Nations, which was launched in early November 2009. The global symposium was the "first time in history that countries were honored for being peaceful."[5] It divided the globe into nine regions and used the GPI rankings to identify the two most peaceful countries in each region. Representatives of the eighteen nations met in Washington, DC, to celebrate their accomplishments and better understand the drivers of peaceful change. The symposium is tangible evidence of positive interdependence—how the system can amplify the impact of a particular program. For example, without the GPI the symposium would not exist. In turn, the symposium has begun to change attitudes toward peace by validating a country's investment in its own peacefulness. Zoë Cooprider, US program manager at the IEP, quoted the ambassador from Malawi, one of the nations honored by the symposium, as saying, "Sometimes we think that because we do not have war, people do not pay attention to us. We are thankful that you are noticing us for being peaceful!" Further, it brought together countries that would not ordinarily interact, such as Chile and Vietnam, which then discovered the parallels between their efforts to overcome a violent past.

For all it has accomplished, the GPI is not perfect. But Killelea knew that the GPI was not perfect when they launched the first index in 2007 and that it will never be so. However, each year it undergoes an extensive review process and is incrementally improved. "Measuring peace is notoriously difficult and starts with a clear, simple definition of peace," Killelea said. "However accurate statistics are difficult to obtain across such a large group of countries; therefore, there is a continuing need to keep reviewing our approach." In this sense, the GPI is also a good example of the planning, acting, and learning project cycle. And even for those who debate its validity, at least the GPI has altered the dialogue from one where peace, in the macro sense, was not discussed to one where the conversation is about how best to measure Peace Writ Large.

Reflecting on Peace Practice

The term *Peace Writ Large* itself has also changed the terms of the debate in the peacebuilding system. It was generated by the Reflecting on Peace Practice

Project of the CDA. CDA was founded by Mary Anderson, author of the groundbreaking book *Do No Harm*. CDA is perhaps best known for its Do No Harm Project, which induced an important change in the humanitarian and development spheres: the creation of a systematic approach to conflict sensitivity, which has changed how field operations engage with conflict-affected communities.

RPP builds on the rich history of *Do No Harm* and is based on the same approach to evidenced-based field research focused on topics of core concern to peacebuilders. In fact, the collaborative learning model of CDA in general and the RPP project in particular are testaments to the power of learning from the system. Mary Anderson and Lara Olson guided the first phase of the RPP project, which culminated in the publication of *Confronting War: Critical Lessons for Peace Practitioners* (2003). The book was based on a process of studying peacebuilding projects and working with peacebuilders to extract lessons from those case studies: "RPP engaged over two hundred agencies and many individuals who work on conflict around the world. The agencies included international peace and conflict resolution NGOs as well as local organizations and groups working for peace in their countries. The project conducted 26 case studies that went through a process of analysis at several consultations."[6]

The findings presented in *Confronting War* also had a profound impact on the peacebuilding field, and many of these findings serve as the starting point for this book. Peter Woodrow and Diana Chigas have managed RPP as it worked to disseminate the RPP findings to peace practitioners around the world. Through this process, practitioners have largely embraced the RPP concepts and frameworks in theory, but RPP has not seen enough parallel changes in the use of conflict analysis or the development of program strategies and design. As Woodrow explained, "Just because ideas are valid does not mean that people will proceed to implement them."[7] Again, RPP learned from the system. Practitioners in the field said that, while they agreed with the ideas RPP put forward, they often felt constrained in applying them by the requirements imposed by donors, policy makers, and UN agencies. In response, RPP began working more directly with donors and UN agencies to incorporate a macro-level perspective and systems thinking into the requirements for designing, funding, and evaluating peacebuilding programs.

In a sense, RPP shifted from helping individual peacebuilding organizations improve their effectiveness in transforming social systems like Liberia or Indonesia to working for change in the peacebuilding system itself by working with donors and the United Nations—those who set the parameters for peacebuilding work both in specific settings and in broader policies and procedures. For example, RPP worked with the Development Assistance Committee of the Organization for Economic Cooperation and Development

(OECD/DAC), a major donor network, to develop guidance for the evaluation of peacebuilding and conflict prevention programs.[8] One of the central recommendations in the report was that reference to a conflict analysis is essential to evaluating the impact of conflict-related programming. Previously, many practitioners and agencies skipped conflict analysis even though it is a crucial step. Therefore, this change in the guidelines for evaluation created a new incentive for those who receive funding from OECD/DAC members. Because programs would be evaluated using a conflict analysis, it was in their interest to do a conflict analysis as part of their program design process at the outset. As Woodrow explained, "When practitioners see that donors have different, more rigorous, and systemic standards, they will respond to it."[9]

RPP's experience with the OECD/DAC is a good example of peace practitioners working with the system to amplify the impact of an initial change. RPP helped the OECD/DAC change its evaluation approach and methodology, which, over time, has led to improvements in the ability of funded programs to affect a given conflict as a whole, as opposed to just achieving preset static indicators of success (e.g., people trained, economic infrastructure built, laws passed, etc.). This change is amplified when the recipients of funds from OECD/DAC members also adopt the practice of including a conflict analysis in their program planning and implementation. This change also prompts peacebuilders to be more explicit about their theories of change, the set of assumptions or hypotheses that explain how a program intends to generate macro-level impact on the underlying conflict factors that affect the country (or context) within which they are working. RPP nurtured a change that was already happening (e.g., the OECD/DAC's reassessment of its evaluation methods), which helped the system change itself by changing the relationship between two of its key parts, the donors and implementing agencies.

CONCLUSION: HOW CAN YOU MAKE A DIFFERENCE?

Chapter 1 discusses the need for a revolution in the productivity of peacebuilding in order to address critical global challenges such as violence, terrorism, poverty, human rights abuses, and climate change. The bad news: This will require big changes on a global scale to change entrenched systems that create these problems and hinder attempts to manage them. The good news: Each of us, as members and participants in these systems, has the ability to help the system change itself. We can each be a leverage point for change.

We can each think in more systemic ways. We can look for patterns of behavior instead of seeing discrete isolated events. Every act of violence, miscarriage of justice, melting glacier, or outbreak of disease has its roots in a dynamic system. Understanding that system is the key to addressing these issues. When politicians or colleagues suggest answers to persistent and complex problems, ask yourself whether they have thought about the systemic drivers of those problems (the structural, attitudinal, and transactional drivers) and if their proposed solutions involve using transactional peacebuilding to nurture structural and attitudinal change? Are they focused on changing one piece of a system in the hope that it will magically change the entire system, or are they listening to the system to find ways of harnessing its dynamic power? Are they looking to impose or control change, or are they honest about the likelihood of failure and prepared to learn from it effectively? Are they concerned only with stopping things they do not like or also with empowering positive behavior and the dynamics that create it?

Changing how we think and act will begin to change the organizations and networks we live in. Where is there positive change happening in your slice of the world, and how can you and your networks nurture it? How can we maximize our leverage to foster systemic change? Whether you are a student entering the field of peacebuilding, an aid beneficiary, a worker for a donor organization, or a voter concerned that foreign aid budgets be spent wisely, you can help others to think and act systemically. It may be as simple as helping diverse organizations, that each try to foster societies with sustainable levels of human development and healthy processes of change, to see themselves as belonging to the field of peacebuilding.

Lastly, I hope that I have played my part in the effort to help peacebuilders think and act more systemically. In July 2005, on the sidelines of an international conference on conflict prevention, I asked several peacebuilding practitioners what they saw as their biggest challenge. One such person, Dayna Brown, then at Mercy Corps, said that she and others knew that they needed to think about how their individual development projects added up to Peace Writ Large. But practitioners lacked a calculus, an operational way, to link the micro and the macro. That was the moment I decided to write this book. The SAT model, systemic analysis and planning, and combining transactional tools with projects aimed at creating structural and attitudinal change are attempts to create operational tools for peacebuilders that will increase their productivity, create more sustainable outcomes, and bridge the micro-macro gap.

I hope this book will help nurture change from within the peacebuilding system. Now, it is up to the actors and dynamic feedback loops that comprise the peacebuilding industry.

NOTES

⟜

CHAPTER I

1. UN General Assembly, "A More Secure World" (prepared by the High-Level Panel on Threats, Challenges and Change as a follow-up to the outcome of the Millennium Summit), Fifty-Ninth Session, Official Records, 2004, A/59/565, 33.

2. T. David Mason et al., "How Political Violence Ends: Paths to Conflict Deescalation and Termination" (paper presented at the meeting of the American Political Science Association, Chicago, Illinois, August 30 to September 2, 2007), 3.

3. Human Security Centre, *Human Security Brief 2006* (Vancouver: Liu Institute for Global Issues, University of British Columbia, 2006), 4.

4. UN General Assembly, "A More Secure World," 34.

5. Paul Tongeren et al., *People Building Peace II: Successful Stories of Civil Society* (Boulder, CO: Lynne Rienner Publishers, 2005). Craig Zelizer and Robert A. Rubenstein, *Building Peace: Practical Reflections from the Field* (West Hartford, CT: Kumarian Press, 2009).

6. A. Suhrke and I. Samset, "What's in a Figure? Estimating Recurrence of Civil War," *International Peacekeeping* 14, no. 2 (2007): 195–203; P. Collier et al., *Breaking the Conflict Trap: Civil War and Development Policy* (Oxford: Oxford University Press, 2003). The approximately 50 percent figure cited (e.g., by UN Secretary-General, "In Larger Freedom: Towards Freedom, Security and human rights for All," 2005, A/59/2005, para. 114) generally has been demonstrated by Suhrke and Samset to be a misrepresentation, with a more correct finding of the Collier et al. study being approximately 23 percent.

7. Michael Lund, "What Kind of Peace Is Being Built? Taking Stock of Post-Conflict Peacebuilding and Charting Future Directions" (paper prepared for the tenth anniversary of *Agenda for Peace* for the International Development Research Centre, Ottawa, Canada, January 2003), and Cedric de Coning, "Civil-Military Coordination Practices and Approaches Within United Nations Peace Operations," *Journal of Military and Strategic Studies* 10, no. 1 (2007): 1–35.

8. Michael W. Doyle and Nicholas Sambanis, "International Peacebuilding: A Theoretical and Quantitative Analysis," *American Political Science Review* 94, no. 4 (2000): 779–801.

9. Stephen John Stedman, Donald Rothchild, and Elizabeth M. Cousens, *Ending Civil Wars* (Boulder, CO: Lynne Rienner Publishers, 2002), 668–669.

10. Mason et al., "How Political Violence Ends," 2.

11. Ibid., 6.

12. Ibid., 5, and Veronique Dudouet, Beatrix Schmelzle, and David Bloomfield, eds., *The Berghof Research Center for Constructive Management Seminar Report* (Berlin: Berghof Research Center for Constructive Conflict Management, 2005), 7.

13. Paul Collier, "Economic Causes of Civil Conflict and Their Implications for Policy," Policy Research Paper 2355 (Washington, DC: World Bank, 2000), 2.

14. Doyle and Sambanis, 12–13; Walter C. Clemens Jr., "Complexity Theory as a Tool for Understanding and Coping with Ethnic Conflict and Development Issues in Post-Soviet Eurasia," *International Journal of Peace Studies* 7, no. 2 (2002).

15. Jeffrey D. Sachs, *The End of Poverty* (New York: Penguin, 2005), 18.

16. Jordan S. Kassalow, *Why Health Is Important to US Foreign Policy* (New York: Milbank Memorial Fund, 2001), 9.

17. Michael Ryan, teleconference with the University of Wisconsin, Milwaukee's Global Studies Summer Institute, August 6, 2002.

18. Robert I. Rotberg, "The New Nature of Nation-State Failure," *Washington Quarterly* 25, no. 3 (2002): 85–96.

19. See the Assembly of WEU, Security and Defense Assembly, *Draft Resolution on Assessing the Impact of Armed Conflict on the Environment*, A/2003, 2008.

20. CNA Corporation, *National Security and the Threat of Climate Change* (Alexandria, VA: CNA Corporation, 2007), 6.

21. Comments by Aaron Salzberg at the George F. Kennan Forum, September 29, 2010, Milwaukee Wisconsin.

22. CNN, "Audit: U.S. Lost Track of $9 Billion in Iraq Funds," CNN, January 30, 2005, http://edition.cnn.com/2005/WORLD/meast/01/30/iraq.audit.

23. Ambassador Peter Galbraith, Great Decisions Lecture 1 at University of Wisconsin, Milwaukee, January 26, 2010.

24. William Easterly, *The White Man's Burden: Why the West's Efforts to Aid the Rest Have Done So Much Ill and So Little Good* (New York: Penguin, 2006).

25. William Easterly, "Introduction: Can't Take It Anymore?" in *Reinventing Foreign Aid*, ed. William Easterly, 1–43 (Cambridge, MA: MIT Press, 2008).

26. Lund, "What Kind of Peace Is Being Built?" 21.

27. Mary B. Anderson and Lara Olson, *Confronting War: Critical Lessons for Peace Practitioners* (Cambridge, MA: Collaborative for Development Action, 2003), 10.

28. Robert Ricigliano, "Can't Get There from Here: The Need for Networks of Effective Action to Promote More Effective Peacebuilding," in *Towards Better Peacebuilding Practice: On Lessons Learned, Evaluation Practices, and Aid and Conflict*, ed. A. Galama and P. van Tongeren (Utrecht, The Netherlands: European Centre for Conflict Prevention, 2003), 213–219; Robert Ricigliano, "Networks of Effective Action: Implementing an Integrated Approach to Peacebuilding," *Security Dialogue* 34, no. 4, (2003): 445–462; Robert Ricigliano, "The Chaordic Peace Process," *Journal for the Study of Peace and Conflict* (2003–2004): 1–11; Robert Ricigliano, "A Three-Dimensional Model of Negotiation," in *The Negotiator's Fieldbook*, ed. A. Schneider and C. Honeyman (Chicago: American Bar Association Books, 2006), 55–60.

29. Anderson and Olson, 45.

30. Dan Smith, *Getting Their Act Together: Towards a Strategic Framework for Peacebuilding* (Oslo: International Peace Research Institute, 2003), 11.

31. Cedric de Coning, *Coherence and Coordination in United Nations Peacebuilding and Integrated Missions*, Security in Practice 5 (Oslo: Norsk Utenrikspolitisk Institutt, 2007), 1.

32. Lund, 22.

33. de Coning, 5.

34. Alcira Kreimer et al., *The World Bank's Experience with Post-Conflict Reconstruction* (Washington, DC: World Bank, 1998), 34.

35. Julia Demichelis, *NGOs and Peacebuilding in Bosnia's Ethnically Divided Cities* (Washington, DC: US Institute of Peace, 1996), 5.

36. Chris Alden, *Mozambique and the Construction of the New African State: From Negotiations to Nation Building* (New York: Palgrave, 2001), 119.

37. Bureau for Democracy, Conflict, and Humanitarian Assistance, Office of Private and Voluntary Cooperation, *USAID-PVO Dialogue on Working in Conflict* (Washington, DC: USAID, 2003), 38.

38. Hamid Shalizi and Peter Graff, "Taliban Ready if Afghan Government Fails, Analyst Warns," Reuters, August 31, 2009, www.reuters.com/article/idUSTRE57U17020090831.

39. Smith; Neclâ Tschirgi, "Post-Conflict Peacebuilding Revisited: Achievements, Limitations, Challenges" (paper presented at the WSP International/IPA Peacebuilding Forum Conference, New York, October 7, 2004), 13; de Coning, *Coherence and Coordination*; Louis Kriesberg, "Coordinating Intermediary Peace Efforts," *Negotiation Journal* 12, no. 4 (1996): 303–314; Susan Allen Nan, "Complementarity and Coordination of Conflict Resolution Efforts in the Conflicts over Abkhazia, South Ossetia, and Transdniestria" (PhD diss., George Mason University, 1999).

40. Kofi Annan, Press Release SG/SM/6335 AFR/16 SC/6421, September 25, 1997.

41. Espen Barth Eide, State Secretary, Norwegian Ministry of Defense, speech given at the Finnish Institute of International Affairs, Helsinki, Norway, May 29, 2006.

42. UN General Assembly, "A More Secure World."

43. Smith, 37.

44. See UN Secretary-General, "Note of Guidance on Integrated Missions," January 17, 2005, para. 4. See also the revised UN Secretary-General, "Note of Guidance on Integrated Missions," February 9, 2006, para. 4.

45. Bureau for Democracy, Conflict, and Humanitarian Assistance, Office of Private and Voluntary Cooperation, *USAID-PVO Dialogue on Working in Conflict* (Washington, DC: USAID, 2003), 38.

46. Bureau for Democracy, Conflict, and Humanitarian Assistance, *USAID-PVO Dialogue,* 12.

47. Ibid.

48. Dayna Brown, director of the Listening Project at CDA/Collaborative Learning Projects, meeting attended by author, January 28, 2010.

49. Coexistence International of Brandeis University uses "coexistence" to describe "societies in which diversity is embraced for its positive potential, equality is actively pursued, interdependence between different groups is recognized, and the use of weapons to address conflicts is increasingly obsolete" (Jessica Berns and Mari Fitzduff, *Why Coexistence Is Important and Why a Complementary Approach* [Waltham, MA: Coexistence International, 2007]).

50. de Coning, 2.

CHAPTER 2

1. See Susan Allen Nan, "Shifting from Coherent to Holistic Processes," in *Handbook of Conflict Analysis and Resolution,* ed. Dennis Sandole and Sean Byrne (New York: Routledge, 2009).

2. Muhammad al-Ghazzali, *Theology Revived* (1058–1128 CE).

3. Ludwig von Bertalanffy, *General System Theory* (New York: George Braziller, 1968), 37.

4. Descartes, quoted in von Bertalanffy, *General System Theory,* 150.

5. George Richardson, presentation at the University of Wisconsin, Milwaukee, October 2008.

6. William Easterly, "Introduction: Can't Take It Anymore?" in *Reinventing Foreign Aid,* ed. William Easterly, 1–43 (Cambridge, MA: MIT Press, 2008), 10.

7. Peter Senge, *The Fifth Discipline: The Art and Practice of the Learning Organization* (New York: Doubleday, 1990), 365.

8. Michael Lund, *Preventing Violent Conflicts* (Washington, DC: US Institute of Peace Press, 1996), 40, and Chester Crocker, Fen Osler Hampson, and Pamela Aall, introduction to *Herding Cats,* ed. Chester Crocker, Fen Osler Hampson, and Pamela Aall (Washington, DC: US Institute of Peace Press, 1999), 3–17.

9. Oliver Ramsbotham, Tom Woodhouse, and Hugh Miall, *Contemporary Conflict Resolution* (Cambridge, UK: Polity, 2005).

10. Emyr Jones Parry, permanent representative of the United Kingdom Mission of Greater Britain and Northern Ireland, Security Council Open Debate on Post-Conflict Peacebuilding, May 26, 2005, http://pdf.usaid.gov/pdf_docs/PNADS841.pdf, 65.

11. Veronique Dudouet, Beatrix Schmelzle, and David Bloomfield, eds., *Transitions from Violence to Peace,* Berghof Report 15 (Berlin: Berghof Research Center for Constructive Conflict Management, 2006), 12.

12. Bureau for Democracy, Conflict, and Humanitarian Assistance, Office of Private and Voluntary Cooperation, *USAID-PVO Dialogue on Working in Conflict* (Washington, DC: USAID, 2003), 16.

13. Rosabeth Moss Kanter, Barry A. Stein, and Todd D. Jick, *The Challenge of Organizational Change* (New York: Free Press, 1992), 7.

14. Peter Woodrow, "Strategic Analysis for Peacebuilding Programs: A Modest Proposal," draft on file with author, 2002.

15. W. Warner Burke and George H. Litwin, "A Causal Model of Organizational Performance and Change," *Journal of Management* 18, no. 3 (1992): 523–545.

16. Thomas Peters and Robert Waterman, *In Search of Excellence* (San Francisco: Harper & Row, 1982), 9–12.

17. Jeffrey D. Sachs, *The End of Poverty* (New York: Penguin, 2005).

18. Ibid., 75–89.

19. Dudouet, iv, 25; Peter T. Coleman, "Conflict, Complexity, and Change: A Meta-Framework for Addressing Protracted, Intractable Conflicts—III," *Peace and Conflict: Journal of Peace Psychology* 12, no. 4 (2006): 327.

20. CDA/Collaborative Learning Projects and the Berghof Foundation for Peace Support have done pioneering work in this regard.

21. Daniel Katz and Robert Kahn, *The Social Psychology of Organizations* (New York: Wiley, 1978), 43.

22. Peter Checkland and John Poulter, *Learning for Action* (New York: Wiley, 2006), 56.

23. Paul R. Lawrence and Jay W. Lorsch, *Organization and Environment* (Homewood, IL: Richard D. Irwin, 1969); T. Burns and G. M. Stalker, *The Management of Innovation* (London: Tavistock, 1961); D. Nadler and M. Tushman, "A Diagnostic Model for Organizational Behavior," in *Perspectives on Behavior in Organizations,* ed. Richard J. Hackman et al. (New York: McGraw-Hill, 1977); R. T. Pascale and A. G. Athos, *The Art of Japanese Management* (New York: Simon & Schuster, 1981); Peters and Waterman, *In Search of Excellence,* and M. Weisbord, "Organizational Dialogue: Six Places to Look for Trouble With or Without a Theory," *Group & Organizational Studies* 1, no. 4 (1976): 430–447, Burke and Litwin.

24. Edgar H. Schein, *Organizational Culture and Leadership* (San Francisco: Jossey-Bass, 1992).

25. Burke and Litwin, 525.

26. Ibid., 527.

27. The focus on "key people" is also an important part of the RPP change model. Mary B. Anderson and Lara Olson, *Confronting War: Critical Lessons for Peace Practitioners* (Cambridge, MA: Collaborative for Development Action, 2003).

28. See note 28 in Chapter 1. I first introduced the precursor to this framework in 2002.

29. Lam Akol, "Operation Lifeline Sudan: War, Peace and Relief in Southern Sudan," *Conciliation Resources Accord* 16 (2005): 52–55.

30. Philip Gourevitch quoted on PBS, "The Triumph of Evil," *Frontline,* January 26, 1996, www.pbs.org/wgbh/pages/frontline/shows/evil/interviews/gourevitch.html.

31. Donella Meadows, *Thinking in Systems: A Primer* (White River Junction, VT: Chelsea Green Publishing, 2008), 16–17.

32. Ibid., 16.

33. Ibid.

CHAPTER 3

1. Roger Coate and Jerel Rosati, "Human Needs in World Society," in *The Power of Human Needs in World Society,* ed. Roger Coate and Jerel Rosati, 1–20 (Boulder, CO: Lynne Rienner Publishers, 1988), 14.

2. Abraham Maslow, "A Theory of Human Motivation," *Psychological Review* 50, no. 4 (1943): 370–396; J. Burton, *Conflict: Resolution and Prevention* (New York: St Martin's Press, 1990); Terrell A. Northrup, "The Dynamic of Identity in Personal and Social Conflict," in *Intractable Conflicts and Their Transformation,* ed. Louis Kriesberg, Terrell A. Northrup, and Stuart J. Thorson (Syracuse, NY: Syracuse University Press, 1989), 55; Louise Diamond, *Peacebuilding* (Arlington, VA: Institute for Multi-Track Diplomacy, 1993); Jay Rothman, *Resolving Identity-Based Conflict in Nations, Organizations, and Communities* (San Francisco: Jossey-Bass, 1997); Roger Coate and Jarel Rosati, "Human Needs Realism," in *The Power of Human Needs in World Society,* ed. Roger Coate and Jerel Rosati (Boulder, CO: Lynne Rienner Publishers, 1988), 257–274.

3. Rothman, 177.

4. Northrup, 55.

5. See the Zulu maxim *umuntu ngumuntu ngabantu* ("a person is a person through [other] persons").

6. Coate and Rosati, 10.

7. See Coate and Rosati, 7, and Johan Galtung, "Violence, Peace and Peace Research," *Journal of Peace Research* 6, no. 3 (1969): 136.

8. P. Collier et al., *Breaking the Conflict Trap: Civil War and Development Policy* (Oxford: Oxford University Press, 2003), 53.

9. Alcira Kreimer et al., *The World Bank's Experience with Post-Conflict Reconstruction* (Washington, DC: World Bank, 1998).

10. Veronique Dudouet, Beatrix Schmelzle, and David Bloomfield, eds., *Transitions from Violence to Peace,* Berghof Report 15 (Berlin: Berghof Research Center for Constructive Conflict Management, 2006), 40.

11. Peter Woodrow, "Strategic Analysis for Peacebuilding Programs: A Modest Proposal," draft on file with author, 2002, 11–12.

12. John Paul Lederach, *Preparing for Peace: Conflict Transformation Across Cultures* (Syracuse, NY: Syracuse University Press, 1995), 17.

13. John Paul Lederach, *The Little Book of Conflict Transformation* (Lancaster, PA: Good Books, 2003), 16.

14. Janet Gross Stein, "Image, Identity and Conflict Resolution," in *Managing Global Chaos*, ed. Chester Crocker, Fen Hampson, and Pamela Aall, 93–112 (Washington, DC: US Institute of Peace Press, 1996), 94.

15. Michelle Maiese, "Dehumanization," in *Beyond Intractability*, ed. Guy Burgess and Heidi Burgess (Boulder: Conflict Research Consortium, University of Colorado, 2004), www .beyondintractability.org/essay/dehumanization (accessed April 23, 2008).

16. Morton Deutsch, "Justice and Conflict," in *The Handbook of Conflict Resolution: Theory and Practice*, ed. Morton Deutsch and Peter T. Coleman (San Francisco: Jossey-Bass, 2000), 49–50; Susan Opotow, "Aggression and Violence," in *The Handbook of Conflict Resolution: Theory and Practice*, ed. Morton Deutsch and Peter T. Coleman, 509–532 (San Francisco: Jossey-Bass, 2000), 517.

17. Michael Montgomery and Stephen Smith, "The Few Who Stayed: Defying Genocide in Rwanda," American Radio Works, http://americanradioworks.publicradio.org/features/rwanda/segc2.html (accessed March 17, 2010).

18. Ed Cairns and Micheál Roe, *The Role of Memory in Ethnic Conflict* (Basingstoke, UK: Palgrave Macmillan, 2003); Daniel Bar-Tal, *Shared Beliefs in a Society* (Thousand Oaks, CA: Sage Publications, 2000).

19. Michele Alexander and Shana Levin, "Theoretical, Empirical, and Practical Approaches to Intergroup Conflict," *Journal of Social Issues* 54, no. 4 (1998): 629–639.

20. Sean L. Yom and Basel Saleh, "Palestinian Violence and the Second Intifada: Explaining Suicidal Attacks" (paper presented at the annual meeting of the New England Political Science Association, Portsmouth, Maine, April 30, 2004).

21. Michael Woolcock and Deepa Narayan, "Social Capital: Implications for Development Theory, Research, and Policy," *World Bank Research Observer* 15, no. 2 (2000): 226; Robert D. Putnam, "The Prosperous Community," *American Prospect* 4, no. 13 (March 21, 1993), www.prospect.org/cs/articles?article=the_prosperous_community (accessed September 1, 2010).

22. Nat Colletta and Michelle Cullen, *Violent Conflict and the Transformation of Social Capital* (Washington, DC: World Bank, 2000), 10.

23. Woolcock and Narayan; Colletta and Cullen.

24. Philip Gourevitch quoted on PBS, "The Triumph of Evil," *Frontline*, January 26, 1996, www.pbs.org/wgbh/pages/frontline/shows/evil/interviews/gourevitch.html.

25. Lederach, *The Little Book of Conflict Transformation*.

26. US Department of State, Office of the Coordinator for Reconstruction and Stabilization, *Interagency Conflict Assessment Framework* (Washington, DC: USAID, 2009), 5.

27. US Department of State, *Interagency Conflict Assessment Framework*, 6.

28. Mari Fitzduff, "Meta-Conflict Resolution," *Beyond Intractability*, ed. Guy Burgess and Heidi Burgess (Boulder: Conflict Research Consortium, University of Colorado, 2004), www.beyondintractability.org/essay/meta-conflict-resolution (accessed August 23, 2007); Mari Fitzduff, *Beyond Violence* (Tokyo: United Nations University Press, 2002); Mari Fitzduff, *Community Conflict Skills: A Handbook for Anti-Sectarian Work* (Cookstown, Ireland: Community Conflict Skills Project, 1988).

29. Robert Ricigliano, *Choosing to Engage Armed Groups in Peace Processes*, Accord Issue 16 (London: Conciliation Resources, 2005).

30. Chester Crocker, Fen Osler Hampson, and Pamela Aall, eds., *Herding Cats* (Washington, DC: US Institute of Peace Press, 1999); Chester Crocker, Fen Osler Hampson, and Pamela Aall, eds., *Grasping the Nettle* (Washington, DC: US Institute of Peace Press, 2005); Chester Crocker, Fen Osler Hampson, and Pamela Aall, eds., *Turbulent Peace* (Washington, DC: US Institute of Peace Press, 2001); Jeffrey Rubin, *Dynamics of Third Party Intervention* (New York: Praeger Publishers, 1983).

31. Robert Ricigliano, "The Chaordic Peace Process," *Journal for the Study of Peace and Conflict* (2003–2004): 1–11.

32. Michael Lund, "What Kind of Peace Is Being Built? Taking Stock of Post-Conflict Peacebuilding and Charting Future Directions" (paper prepared for the tenth anniversary of *Agenda for Peace* for the International Development Research Centre, Ottawa, Canada, January 2003), 36.

33. Galtung, 167–191; Johan Galtung and Carl G. Jacobsen, *Searching for Peace* (London: Pluto, 2000); D. Bloomfield and N. Ropers, "Dialogue and Social Integration: Experience from Ethnopolitical Conflict Work" (paper presented at the United Nations Expert Group Meeting titled "Dialogue in the Social Integration Process: Building Peaceful Social Relations—by, for, and with People," New York, November, 21–23, 2005).

34. Galtung and Jacobsen, 206.

35. C. R. Mitchell, *The Structure of International Conflict* (New York: St. Martin's Press, 1981), 16–34; Susan Allen Nan of George Mason University also sees similarities between the Galtung and Mitchell models and the approach of C. W. Moore as detailed in his foundational book *The Mediation Process: Practical Strategies for Resolving Conflict* (San Francisco: Jossey-Bass, 1986).

36. Galtung.

37. Bloomfield and Ropers; and Dudouet, Schmelzle, and Bloomfield, 39.

38. Mitchell, 65–67.

39. Veronique Dudouet, Beatrix Schmelzle, and David Bloomfield, eds., *The Berghof Research Center for Constructive Management Seminar Report* (Berlin: Berghof Research Center for Constructive Conflict Management, 2005), 15.

40. However, it should be noted that addressing any conflict driver in the SAT model (be it structural, attitudinal, or transactional) is most effective if the intervention combines impact, activity, or both at each of the three levels. So addressing a broken economy is best done through a transactional process that leads to economic reforms, strengthened processes and skills for future negotiations, and improved attitudes between groups.

41. Johan Galtung, *Transcend and Transform* (London: Pluto Press, 2004), 156–157.

42. Dudouet, Schmelzle, and Bloomfield, 39.

43. Mary B. Anderson and Lara Olson, *Confronting War: Critical Lessons for Peace Practitioners* (Cambridge, MA: Collaborative for Development Action, 2003), 48–56.

44. Ibid., 49.

45. Ibid., 55.

46. I have been, and continue to be, involved in the RPP cumulative impact research.

47. Lederach, *The Little Book of Conflict Transformation*, 18–36.

48. Ibid., 22.

49. Ibid., 21.

50. Ibid.

51. Ibid., 23.

52. Evaluations of peacebuilding programs are almost exclusively done at the project or micro level. The best test of the SAT model would come from looking at the success of peacebuilding programs at the macro level. Unfortunately, outside of the RPP cumulative impacts study, there is a dearth of such macro-level evaluations.

53. World Bank, Social Development Department, Environmentally and Socially Sustainable Development Network, *Community-Driven Development in the Context of Conflict-Affected Countries: Challenges and Opportunities* (Washington, DC: World Bank, 2006), 6. It is important to distinguish CDD from the concept of conflict-sensitive development (discussed in Chapter 5).

54. Lund; Ghazala Mansuri and Vijayendra Rao, "Evaluating Community-Based

Community-Driven Development: A Critical Review of the Evidence," Development Economics Research Group and the Social Development Anchor of the World Bank, September 2003, www.cbnrm.net/pdf/mansuri_g_001_cddfinal.pdf (accessed September, 2003).

55. Mansuri and Rao, 42.

56. Lund, "What Kind of Peace Is Being Built?"

57. World Bank, *Community-Driven Development in the Context of Conflict-Affected Countries*, 24.

58. Ibid., 40–42.

59. Ibid., 42–43.

60. Ibid., 44.

61. Ibid.World Bank, *Community-Driven Development in the Context of Conflict-Affected Countries*, 33.

62. Kimberly A. Maynard, "The Role of Culture, Islam and Tradition in Community Driven Reconstruction" (a study on the International Rescue Committee's Approach to NSP presented to the International Rescue Committee, New York, 2007), 14.

63. Ibid., 12–13.

64. Ibid., 10–11.

65. Ibid., 9, 11.

66. Bureau for Democracy, Conflict, and Humanitarian Assistance, Office of Private and Voluntary Cooperation, *USAID-PVO Dialogue on Working in Conflict* (Washington, DC: USAID, 2003), 15.

CHAPTER 4

1. Richard Harris, "Reef Conservation Strategy Backfires," National Public Radio, November 18, 2009, www.npr.org/templates/story/story.php?storyId=120536304.

2. Ibid.

3. Roger Fisher was fond of saying this as a way of persuading people that static, fixed negotiation settlements were less useful than ongoing processes of problem solving.

4. Donella Meadows, *Thinking in Systems: A Primer* (White River Junction, VT: Chelsea Green Publishing, 2008), 3.

5. William Easterly, "Introduction: Can't Take It Anymore?" in *Reinventing Foreign Aid*, ed. William Easterly, 1–43 (Cambridge, MA: MIT Press, 2008), 10.

6. Meadows, 169.

7. Peter Checkland and John Poulter, *Learning for Action* (New York: Wiley, 2006), 63.

8. Meadows, 169–170.

9. Meadows, 178.

10. For a related approach, see Cynthia Sampson et al., eds., *Positive Approaches to Peacebuilding: A Resource for Innovators* (Chagrin Falls, OH: Taos Institute Publications, 2010).

11. Michael Woolcock and Lant Pritchard, "Solutions When Solutions Are the Problem: Arraying the Disarray in Development," in *Reinventing Foreign Aid*, ed. William Easterly, 147–178 (Cambridge, MA: MIT Press, 2008), 171.

12. Willemijn Verkoren, "Debating Complexity," *The Broker*, July 28, 2008, www.thebrokeronline.eu/en/Magazine/articles/Debating-complexity.

13. Ben Ramalingam et al., "Exploring the Science of Complexity: Ideas and Implications for Development and Humanitarian Efforts," ODI Working Paper 285 (London: ODI, 2008), 67.

14. Easterly, "Introduction: Can't Take It Anymore?" 24.

15. This raises questions about whose values count. For example, do the values of Western donor's count the same as those of the people of a country that receives aid? Being a

participant in the system gives you the opportunity to affect the system based on your values. Is everyone an equal participant in the system? No, there will be people trying to influence the system for selfish economic gain (e.g., war profiteers from both inside and outside a war-affected country)—it is not a question of who has the moral right to shape the development of the system but an acknowledgment that in reality, be it morally right or not, participants in the system will be trying to affect the system, and those trying to produce a system that evolves toward a state of sustainable levels of coexistence and healthy processes of change have the same right to try to effect systems change. Who will prevail is up to the system and those in it to decide.

16. Meadows, 181.

17. Mark D. Cannon and Amy C. Edmondson, "Failing to Learn and Learning to Fail (Intelligently): How Great Organizations Put Failure to Work to Improve and Innovate" (working paper, Harvard Business School, February 5, 2004), 7. Available at http://hbswk .hbs.edu/item/5434.html (accessed October 10, 2010).

18. Amy Edmonson, lecture at the World Bank Managerial Leadership Program, University of Maryland, September 21, 2010.

19. Cannon and Edmondson, "Failing to Learn and Learning to Fail (Intelligently," 29.

20. Peter T. Coleman, "Conflict, Complexity, and Change: A Meta-Framework for Addressing Protracted, Intractable Conflicts—III," *Peace and Conflict: Journal of Peace Psychology* 12, no. 4 (2006): 344–345, and Meadows, *Thinking in Systems,* 177.

21. Easterly, 22.

22. For example, if you multiply 0.85 by 0.85 ten times, you get 0.1968, which rounds up to 0.20.

23. Alan Fowler, "Connecting the Dots," *The Broker,* April 7, 2008, www.thebrokeronline .eu/en/Magazine/articles/Connecting-the-dots.

24. Diane Hendrick, *Complexity Theory and Conflict Transformation: An Exploration of Potential and Implications,* Working Paper 17 (Bradford, UK: University of Bradford, 2009), 50.

25. Meadows, 178.

26. Meadows; Fowler.

27. Martin Rupiya and Jemima Njeri, "An Evaluation of the Post-Savimbi Peace Process in Angola Since February 2002: The Victor's Peace Treaty," Institute for Security Studies, July 2004, www.issafrica.org/pubs/Books/civmilzambiaaug04/Rupiya2.pdf.

28. For perspective, Peter Senge estimates that a typical time frame for incubating basic innovations, such as the use of airplanes for commercial travel, is thirty years. Peter Senge, *The Fifth Discipline: The Art and Practice of the Learning Organization* (New York: Doubleday, 1990), 6.

29. John Paul Lederach, *Building Peace: Sustainable Reconciliation in Divided Societies* (Washington, DC: US Institute of Peace, 1997), 37–55.

30. Meadows, 183.

31. Robert Ricigliano, "Networks of Effective Action: Implementing an Integrated Approach to Peacebuilding," *Security Dialogue* 34, no. 4 (2003): 445–462.

32. Meadows, 11.

33. Easterly, 2.

34. T. Moss, G. Pettersson, and N. van de Walle, *An Aid-Institutions Paradox? A Review Essay on Aid Dependency and State Building in Sub-Saharan Africa,* Working Paper 74 (Washington, DC: Centre for Global Development, 2006), and Easterly, "Introduction: Can't Take It Anymore?" 269.

35. Workshop on Communication and Negotiation, Kabul Afghanistan, May 2007.

36. See Fowler, "Connecting the Dots."

37. Verkoren, "Debating Complexity."

38. Easterly, "Introduction: Can't Take It Anymore?" 11.

39. Meadows, 14.

40. Global Partnership for the Prevention of Armed Conflict, "About us," Global Partnership for the Prevention of Armed Conflict, www.gppac.net/page.php?id=1485 (accessed October 2010).

41. Interview with Tjip Walker by author, Washington, DC, February 23, 2010.

42. Ibid.

CHAPTER 5

1. Conflict Prevention and Post-Conflict Reconstruction (CPR) Network, *Peace and Conflict Impact Assessment (PCIA) Handbook,* Version 2 (N.p., 2005). See also organizations noted in note 4 of this chapter.

2. John Prendergast, *Frontline Diplomacy* (Boulder, CO: Lynne Rienner Publishers, 1996), 39.

3. Mary B. Anderson, *Do No Harm* (Boulder, CO: Lynne Rienner Publishers, 1999).

4. These organizations include the Africa Peace Forum, the Center for Conflict Resolution, the Consortium of Humanitarian Organizations, the Forum on Early Warning and Early Response, International Alert, and Saferworld. The entire resource pack, titled "Conflict Sensitive Approaches to Development, Humanitarian Assistance, and Peace Building: Tools for Peace and Conflict Impact Assessment," is available online at www.conflictsensitivity.org/resource_pack.html.

5. See Mark Hoffman, *Peace and Conflict Impact Assessment Methodology* (Berlin: Berghof Foundation, 2004); Alexander Austin, Martina Fischer, and Oliver Wils, eds., *Peace and Conflict Impact Assessment: Critical Views on Theory and Practice,* Berghof Handbook Dialogue Series 1 (Berlin: Berghof Research Center for Constructive Conflict Management, 2003); Kenneth Bush, "A Measure of Peace: Peace and Conflict Impact Assessment (PCIA) of Development Projects in Conflict Zones," Working Paper 1 (Ottawa, Canada: International Development Research Centre, Peacebuilding and Reconstruction Program Initiative, 1998).

6. Maria Lange and Mick Quinn, "Conflict, Humanitarian Assistance and Peacebuilding: Meeting the Challenges" (London: International Alert, 2003), 20.

7. Ibid., 20.

8. The response to the famine and conflict in Somalia in the late 1980s is a classic example of the difference in these two modes of thinking. The linear analysis said that importing grain to Somalia was a good idea because feeding starving Somalis would counter the humanitarian tragedy there, which, in turn, was a prerequisite for peace. A more dynamic, systems analysis saw that importing free grain to Somalia might worsen the conflict by both strengthening warlords (who controlled the main port, confiscated the grain, and sold it to buy more arms) and destroying the market price for grain.

9. For example, ICAF looks at drivers of conflict and mitigating factors or sources of resilience.

10. Jonathan Goodhand, Tony Vaux, and Robert Walker, *Conducting Conflict Assessments: Guidance Notes* (London: UK Department for International Development, 2002), 5.

11. Introduction to "Conflict Sensitive Approaches to Development," 6.

12. See Michael Lund, *Preventing Violent Conflicts* (Washington, DC: US Institute of Peace Press, 1996), 21.

13. Mary B. Anderson and Lara Olson, *Confronting War: Critical Lessons for Peace Practitioners* (Cambridge, MA: Collaborative for Development Action, 2003), 15.

14. Ibid., 46.

15. Cynthia Gaigals and Manuela Leonhardt, "Conflict Sensitive Approaches to

Development Practice," An International Alert–Saferworld–IRDC Report, International Development Research Centre, International Alert, 2001.

16. The Fletcher School of Law and Diplomacy, *Advanced Seminar in Development and Conflict,* DHP P227, class lecture, Fletcher School of Law and Diplomacy, March 6, 2010.

17. In theory it is possible that some factors might have more than one effect (e.g., both escalatory and ameliorating), but generally factors tend to have one dominant impact.

18. US Department of State, Office of the Coordinator for Reconstruction and Stabilization, *Interagency Conflict Assessment Framework* (Washington, DC: USAID, 2009).

19. In the ICAF, these factors are known as resilience (US Department of State, *Interagency Conflict Assessment Framework,* 4–5.)

20. See Chapter 3, note 22.

21. Nadime Rouhana and Daniel Bar-Tal, "Psychological Dynamics of Intractable Ethnonational Conflicts: The Israeli-Palestinian Case," *American Psychologist* 53, no. 7 (July 1998): 761–770.

CHAPTER 6

1. Peter Morgan, "The Idea and Practice of Systems Thinking and Their Relevance for Capacity Development" (report for the European Centre for Development Policy Management, Brussels, Belgium, March 2005), 16. See also Elisabeth Bumiller, "We Have Met the Enemy and He Is PowerPoint," *New York Times,* April 26, 2010, A1.

2. Special thanks are due to Nigel Pont, then Mercy Corps country director in Afghanistan, for agreeing to this exercise. This experience also served as the basis for a chapter I wrote for a book titled *The Non-Linearity of Peace Processes: Theory and Practice of Systemic Conflict Transformation,* ed. Norbert Ropers and Daniela Korppen (Boulder, CO: Lynne Rienner Publishers, forthcoming).

3. Note that these notations are meant to capture the current nature of the causal relationship and that over time, a parallel relationship might reverse depending on changes in the feedback loop. For example, a relationship that is currently "+/+" could become "–/–" if the initial factor was to decrease instead of increasing. The same can be said for opposite relationships; for example, a "+/–" relationship could change to a "–/+" relationship over time. After drawing an initial loop, a parallel causal relationship can be noted with a "p" instead of the "+/+" or "–/–" symbols. Similarly, an "o" can be used to denote an opposite causal relationship.

4. Roger Fisher, William L. Ury, and Bruce Patton, *Getting to Yes* (New York: Penguin Books, 1991).

5. You can also use a "sticky wall" (cloth is hung on a wall and sprayed with a tacky material) and larger sheets of paper. The sticky wall allows analysts to arrange and rearrange the paper as they develop their diagram.

6. Diana Chigas, "Advanced Seminar in Development and Conflict," DHP P227, class lecture, Fletcher School of Law and Diplomacy, March 6, 2010.

7. Peter Senge, *The Fifth Discipline: The Art and Practice of the Learning Organization* (New York: Doubleday, 1990); Donella Meadows, *Thinking in Systems: A Primer* (White River Junction, VT: Chelsea Green Publishing, 2008).

CHAPTER 7

1. Quoted in Richard Nixon, *Six Crises* (Garden City, NY: Doubleday, 1962).

2. See also Tim Murithi, *The Ethics of Peacebuilding* (Edinburgh: Edinburgh University Press, 2009).

3. W. Andy Knight, "Conclusion: Peacebuilding Theory and Praxis," in *Building Sustainable Peace*, ed. Tom Keating and W. Andy Knight, 355–382 (Tokyo: United Nations University Press, 2004), 372.

4. Kristoffer Liden, "What Is the Ethics of Peacebuilding?" (lecture prepared for the kickoff meeting of the Liberal Peace and the Ethics of Peacebuilding project, Oslo, Norway, January 18, 2007), 6. Available at www.prio.no/Research-and-Publications/Publication/?oid=62734 (accessed April 26, 2010).

5. Dan Heath and Chip Heath, "Analysis of Paralysis," FastCompany.com, November 1, 2007, www.fastcompany.com/magazine/120/analysis-of-paralysis.html (accessed April 20, 2010).

6. Heath and Heath, "Analysis of Paralysis."

7. Mark D. Cannon and Amy C. Edmondson, "Failing to Learn and Learning to Fail (Intelligently): How Great Organizations Put Failure to Work to Improve and Innovate" (working paper, Harvard Business School, February 5, 2004), 7. Available at http://hbswk.hbs.edu/item/5434.html (accessed October 10, 2010).

8. Department for International Development (DFID), "Tanzania," DFID, www.dfid.gov.uk/where-we-work/africa-eastern—southern/tanzania (accessed May 14, 2010). See also DFID, "Tanzania Country Assistance Plan," DFID, http://webarchive.nationalarchives.gov.uk/+/http://www.dfid.gov.uk/consultations/tanzania-part4.asp (accessed January 2007).

9. My intention is not to single DFID out for criticism. If anything, DFID has one of the more progressive and thoughtful planning cultures among international donor organizations.

10. See J. Sternin and R. Choo, "The Power of Positive Deviancy." *Harvard Business* (January–February 2000): 14–15.

11. Chip Heath and Dan Heath, *Switch: How to Change Things When Change Is Hard* (New York: Broadway Books, 2010), 28.

12. Heath and Heath, *Switch*, 28–32.

13. Peter T. Coleman, *The Five Percent: Finding Solutions to Seemingly Impossible Conflicts* (New York: PublicAffairs, 2011), 73.

14. Coleman, 138.

15. Because the ICAF process does not explicitly look at the impact of a system on the level of peace in the society, we did not include the level of peace as an output in the systems map. Stability is probably the closest variable to the level of peace, though these two concepts are not equivalent.

16. Note that in the Economic Red Scenario systems map diagram, there is greater use of modifiers like "more" or "fewer," which goes against the general advice to frame factors as nouns that can be scaled up or down. Because these scenarios are meant to depict specific future states, where things might be better or worse, it is more acceptable to use modifiers than in a general systems diagram.

17. Interagency Conflict Assessment of Cambodia, "Cambodia: Adjustment or Instability?" (study conducted at the request of the US Embassy in Phnom Penh, March 2009), 15–16. See also World Bank, *Sustaining Rapid Growth in a Challenging Environment: Cambodia Country Economic Memorandum* (Phnom Penh: World Bank Poverty Reduction and Economic Management Sector, Unit East Asia and Pacific Region, 2009).

18. Indeed, any ethical commandment more specific than a general respect for human rights, plus the existence of a healthy ethical debate among the peacebuilders involved, is what I would consider a form of ethical imperialism.

19. The ideas in this section were first developed for the chapter Robert Ricigliano, "Planning for Systemic Impact," in *The Non-Linearity of Peace Processes: Theory and Practice of Systemic Conflict Transformation*, ed. Norbert Ropers and Daniela Korppen (Boulder, CO: Lynne Rienner Publishers, forthcoming).

20. As of 2005, Afghanistan had thirty-four provinces and a total of 398 districts. Each district comprises many villages.

21. The detail complexity map is often better for assessing the relative impacts of multiple factors on another factor because it shows more of the causal relationships than the dynamic complexity map, which sacrifices showing the number of causal relationships in order to better illuminate feedback loops within a system.

22. Ricigliano, "Planning for Systemic Impact."

23. This section is based on Ricigliano, "Planning for Systemic Impact."

24. Jeremiah S. Pam, "The Paradox of Complexity: Embracing Its Contribution to Situational Understanding, Resisting Its Temptation in Strategy and Operational Plans," in *NATO at War and on the Margins of War,* ed. Christopher M. Schnaubelt (NDC Forum Paper 14, NATO National Defense College, July 2010), 26–45.

25. Coleman, *The Five Percent,* 23.

CHAPTER 8

1. The group was known as the Returned Peace Corps Volunteers (RPCV) for Peace in Congo and included Steve Smith, Chic Dambach, and John Garamendi, who were all former Peace Corps volunteers. Despite my inclusion in the group, I unfortunately am not an RPCV.

2. I should note that our view that "fixing" the national-level negotiations would lead to peace in the DRC was based on vague assumptions about the importance of these negotiations to creating the needed structural and attitudinal (not just transactional) changes that, in turn, would lead to sustainable peace in the DRC. The lack of clear analysis as to how the national-level negotiations fit into systemic change in the DRC certainly weakened the impact that any "successes" in the negotiation process would have on peacebuilding in the DRC more generally.

3. Donella Meadows and J. Robinson, *The Electronic Oracle* (New York: Wiley, 1985), 178.

4. Working with the "war profiteers" was going to be impossible, either because of the covert nature of most of these profiteers or because it would be politically impossible. In addition to the Mayi-Mayi militias, there were several Hutu militias operating in eastern DRC but working with them was also outside of our means as a team.

5. We spent the rest of the first day negotiating with the group about an acceptable way to move forward, and after reaching an accommodation, we had a very productive five-day session. At the end, the group members realized that they were much more skilled in negotiation than they initially believed and left the session much more willing, and probably better able, to negotiate with the white authorities in their townships.

6. This framework was inspired by the 7 Element Negotiation Framework developed by the Harvard Negotiation Project (HNP). I worked for HNP from 1986 to 1990 and was affiliated with the group until 2000. See the Program on Negotiation website at www.pon.harvard.edu/hnp/theory/tools/7elements.shtml.

7. Peter T. Coleman, "Characteristics of Protracted, Intractable Conflict: Toward the Development of a Metaframework—I," *Peace and Conflict: Journal of Peace Psychology* 9, no. 1 (2003): 1–37; Peter T. Coleman, "Characteristics of Protracted, Intractable Conflict: Toward the Development of a Metaframework—II," *Peace and Conflict: Journal of Peace Psychology* 10, no. 3 (2004): 197–235; Peter T. Coleman, "Conflict, Complexity, and Change: A Meta-Framework for Addressing Protracted, Intractable Conflicts—III," *Peace and Conflict: Journal of Peace Psychology* 12, no. 4 (2006): 325–348; S. Williams and R. Ricigliano, "Understanding Armed Groups," in *Choosing to Engage: Armed Groups and Peace Processes,* ed. R. Ricigliano (London: Conciliation Resources, 2005), 14–17.

8. "Measurement of Social Capital," Social Capital Research, www.socialcapitalresearch.com/measurement.html.

9. For more information on the connection between mind-set, actions, and results, see Chris Argyris, Robert Putnam, and Diana McLain Smith, *On Organizational Learning* (Cambridge, MA: Blackwell Publishers, 1993); D. Schön, *Organizational Learning: A Theory of Action Perspective* (Reading, MA: Addison-Wesley, 1978); Chris Argyris, Robert Putnam, and Diana McLain Smith, *Action Science* (San Francisco: Jossey-Bass, 1985); Peter Senge, *The Fifth Discipline: The Art and Practice of the Learning Organization* (New York: Doubleday, 1990).

10. Roger Fisher, William L. Ury, and Bruce Patton, *Getting to Yes* (New York: Penguin Books, 1991); David Lax and James Sebenius, "The Power of Alternatives or the Limits to Negotiation," in *Negotiation Theory and Practice,* ed. J. William Breslin and Jeffery Z. Rubin (Cambridge, MA: Program on Negotiation at Harvard Law School, 1991), 97–114.

11. I participated as part of a team from the Harvard Negotiation Project and the Conflict Management Group that led separate trainings for the negotiation teams from each side along with other ministers (in the case of the NP) or members of the National Executive (in the case of the ANC). Both trainings covered the issue of changing each side's negotiation frame. Key members of this team were Professor Roger Fisher and Bruce Patton of Harvard Law School, Diana Chigas of the Conflict Management Group, and Charles Barker of Conflict Management Incorporated.

12. Presentation by Roger Fisher, Cambridge, Massachusetts, Harvard Law School, June 9, 1998.

13. Roger Fisher, *Getting to Yes,* DVD (Lakewood, WA: Richardson Company Training Media, 1993).

14. Unfortunately, funding was cut for follow-up to the program and potential implementation of their relationship management plan, so a promising idea died on the vine. However, the Iraqis, the United States, and its coalition partners were able to reduce violence after 2006.

15. See a related concept of shifting from blame to joint contribution in Douglas Stone, Bruce Patton, and Sheila Heen, *Difficult Conversations: How to Discuss What Matters Most* (New York: Viking, 1999).

16. For the related concept of creative tension, see Senge, *The Fifth Discipline,* 150–155.

17. Interview with Azarius Ruberwa, then secretary-general of the RCD, Milwaukee, Wisconsin, October 17, 2007.

18. Martti Ahtisaari, "Lessons of Aceh Peace Talks," *Asia Europe Journal* 6, no. 1 (2008): 13.

19. Nelson Mandela, "Address to the People of Cape Town" (address on the occasion of Mandela's inauguration as state president, Cape Town, May 9, 1994).

20. Robert Ricigliano, *Choosing to Engage Armed Groups in Peace Processes,* Accord Issue 16. (London: Conciliation Resources, 2005).

21. Clem McCartney, "From Armed Struggle to Political Negotiations: Why? When? How?" in *Choosing to Engage: Armed Groups and Peace Processes,* ed. R. Ricigliano, 30–35 (London: Conciliation Resources, 2005), 32.

22. McCartney, "From Armed Struggle to Political Negotiations."

23. International pressure succeeded in getting the combatant parties to the talks but was not able to shift the negotiation frame from a disempowered one—we have no choice but to fight—to one where key leaders on each side felt that they truly had a choice between fighting and negotiating an end to their conflict. Although the negotiations ended with an agreement between the DRC government and the MLC rebel movement, the agreement was not implemented, and our team got word immediately after the process that the government did not want the agreement and felt forced into it.

24. McCartney, 33.

25. Saw David Taw, "From Choosing to Engage: Strategic Considerations for the Karen National Union," in *Choosing to Engage: Armed Groups and Peace Processes,* ed. R. Ricigliano, 40–43 (London: Conciliation Resources, 2005), 43.

26. Positions are demands. They are a combination of one or more interests, one way of satisfying those interests, and a purportedly unflinching commitment to that option. The positions of different parties are often irreconcilable, whereas interests, even opposing interests, can often be satisfied through a range of options.

27. Fisher, Ury, and Patton, *Getting to Yes*; Kevin Avruch, "The Poverty of Buyer and Seller," in *The Negotiator's Fieldbook,* ed. A. Schneider and C. Honeyman (Chicago: American Bar Association Books, 2006), 81–86.

28. Robert Ricigliano, "A Three-Dimensional Model of Negotiation," in *The Negotiator's Fieldbook,* ed. A. Schneider and C. Honeyman, 55–60 (Chicago: American Bar Association Books, 2006), 59.

29. Suresh Sethi and Gerald Thompson, *Optimal Control Theory* (Berlin: Springer, 2005), 4.

30. Fisher, Ury, and Patton, *Getting to Yes.*

31. Ibid.

32. Having a realistic sense of your alternatives to negotiation does not guarantee that you will be more willing to negotiate. It may turn out that, if my negotiation alternative is in fact better than any possible negotiating outcome, then it would be foolish to negotiate. For example, if my current job pays more than an identical job with a new employer, it would be pointless for me to engage in discussions with that potential employer to do similar work.

33. Fisher, Ury, and Patton.

34. Office of Conflict Management and Mitigation, *Conducting a Conflict Assessment: A Framework for Strategy and Program Development,* USAID, Washington D.C., April, 2005.

35. See Joseph Kony in Uganda and Charles Taylor in Karadži̧.

36. Steve Stedman, "Spoiler Problems in the Peace Process," *International Security* 12 (1997): 5–53.

37. Roger Fisher and Scott Brown, *Getting Together* (New York: Penguin Books, 1989).

38. Orrin Hatch, "The Ted Kennedy I Knew," *Politico,* August 26, 2009, www.politico .com/news/stories/0809/26482.html.

39. Michael R. Beschloss and Strobe Talbott, *At the Highest Levels: The Inside Story of the End of the Cold War* (Boston: Little, Brown and Company, 1993), 278–280.

40. For example, Stone, Patton, and Heen, *Difficult Conversations.*

41. Public presentation, University of Wisconsin, Milwaukee, March 1, 2005.

CHAPTER 9

1. See Chapter 3 for a description of participatory development.

2. This has been the case with all the transactional interventions with which I have been associated.

3. Roger Fisher and Keith Fitzgerald, "Facilitated Joint Brainstorming: Generating Options to Overcome Deadlock" (unpublished paper, Harvard Negotiation Project, Harvard Law School, Cambridge, Massachusetts, 1999).

4. Diana Chigas, "Negotiating Intractable Conflicts: The Contributions of Unofficial Intermediaries," in *Grasping the Nettle: Analyzing Cases of Intractable Conflict,* ed. Chester A. Crocker, Fen Osler Hampson, and Pamela Aall (Washington, DC: US Institute of Peace Press, 2005), 123–160.

5. R. Ricigliano, A. Chasen, and T. Johnson, "Problems Without a Process," *Harvard Negotiation Law Review* 4 (1999): 83.

6. Christopher Mitchell, "The Process and Stages of Mediation: The Sudanese Cases," in *Making War and Waging Peace,* ed. David R. Smock (Washington, DC: US Institute of Peace Press, 1993), 139–159.

7. William Ury, *The Third Side: Why We Fight and How We Can Stop* (New York: Penguin, 1999).

8. Peter Senge, *The Fifth Discipline: The Art and Practice of the Learning Organization* (New York: Doubleday, 1990), 150–155.

9. Confidential interview, Sun City, South Africa, March 2002.

10. See Ronald Fisher, ed., "Conflict Resolution Training in Divided Societies," special issue of *International Negotiation Journal* 2, no. 3 (1997).

11. Donald Mackenzie, *Myths of Babylonia and Assyria* (London: Gresham Publishing Company, 1915), 494.

12. John Paul Lederach is one of the leading scholar-practitioners to pioneer elicitive methods of conflict transformation. See John Paul Lederach, *Preparing for Peace: Conflict Transformation Across Cultures* (Syracuse, NY: Syracuse University Press, 1995).

CHAPTER 10

1. See Global Peace Index, "About the GPI," Vision of Humanity, www.visionofhumanity .org/about (accessed July 26, 2010).

2. Interview with Zoe Cooprider, July 14, 2010, Washington, DC.

3. Interview with Steve Killelea, September 10, 2010, Washington, DC.

4. Interview with Steve Killelea.

5. See the description of the Global Symposium of Peaceful Nations at the website for the Alliance for Peacebuilding at www.allianceforpeacebuilding.org/?page=workgspnabout& hhSearchTerms=peaceful+and+nations (accessed July 26, 2010).

6. See "Reflecting Peace Practice," CDA/Collaborative Learning Projects, www.cdainc .com/cdawww/project_profile.php?pid=RPP&pname=Reflecting Peace Practice (accessed July 27, 2010).

7. Interview with Peter Woodrow, Cambridge, Massachusetts, July 16, 2010.

8. Mary Anderson, Peter Woodrow, and Diana Chigas, *Encouraging Effective Evaluation of Conflict Prevention and Peacebuilding Activities: Towards DAC Guidance,* Development Co-Operation Directorate, OECD/DAC, DCD(2007)3.

9. Interview with Peter Woodrow.

WORKS CITED

Ahtisaari, Martti. "Lessons of Aceh Peace Talks." *Asia Europe Journal* 6, no. 1 (2008): 9–14.

Akol, Lam. "Operation Lifeline Sudan: War, Peace and Relief in Southern Sudan." *Conciliation Resources Accord* 16 (2005): 52–55.

Alden, Chris. *Mozambique and the Construction of the New African State: From Negotiations to Nation Building.* New York: Palgrave, 2001.

Alexander, Michele, and Shana Levin. "Theoretical, Empirical, and Practical Approaches to Intergroup Conflict." *Journal of Social Issues* 54, no. 4 (1998): 629–639.

al-Ghazzali, Muhammad. Theology Revived. 1058–1128 CE.

Alliance for Peacebuilding. "The Global Symposium of Peaceful Nations." Allianceforpeacebuilding .org. www.allianceforpeacebuilding.org/?peaceful_nations. Accessed July 26, 2010.

Anderson, Mary B., and Lara Olson. *Confronting War: Critical Lessons for Peace Practitioners.* Cambridge, MA: Collaborative for Development Action, 2003.

———. *Do No Harm.* Boulder, CO: Lynne Rienner Publishers, 1999.

Annan, Kofi. Press Release SG/SM/6335 AFR/16 SC/6421. September 25, 1997.

Argyris, Chris, Robert Putnam, and Diana McLain Smith. *Action Science.* San Francisco: Jossey-Bass, 1985.

———. *On Organizational Learning.* Cambridge, MA: Blackwell Publishers, 1993.

Assembly of Western European Union, Security and Defense Assembly. *Draft Resolution on Assessing the Impact of Armed Conflict on the Environment.* A/2003. 2008.

Austin, Alexander, Martina Fischer, and Oliver Wils, eds. *Peace and Conflict Impact Assessment: Critical Views on Theory and Practice.* Berghof Handbook Dialogue Series 1. Berlin: Berghof Research Center for Constructive Conflict Management, 2003.

Avruch, Kevin. "The Poverty of Buyer and Seller." In *The Negotiator's Fieldbook,* edited by A. Schneider and C. Honeyman, 81–86. Chicago: American Bar Association Books, 2006.

Bar-Tal, Daniel. *Shared Beliefs in a Society.* Thousand Oaks, CA: Sage Publications, 2000.

Berns, Jessica, and Mari Fitzduff. *Why Coexistence Is Important and Why a Complementary Approach.* Waltham, MA: Coexistence International, 2007.

Beschloss, Michael R., and Strobe Talbott. *At the Highest Levels: The Inside Story of the End of the Cold War.* Boston: Little, Brown and Company, 1993.

Bloomfield, D., and N. Ropers. "Dialogue and Social Integration: Experience from Ethno-political Conflict Work." Paper presented at the United Nations Expert Group Meeting titled "Dialogue in the Social Integration Process: Building Peaceful Social Relations—by, for, and with People," New York, November, 21–23, 2005.

Bumiller, Elisabeth. "We Have Met the Enemy and He Is PowerPoint." *New York Times,* April 26, 2010, A1.

Bureau for Democracy, Conflict, and Humanitarian Assistance, Office of Private and Voluntary Cooperation. *USAID-PVO Dialogue on Working in Conflict.* Washington, DC: USAID, 2003.

Burke, W. Warner, and George H. Litwin. "A Causal Model of Organizational Performance and Change." *Journal of Management* 18, no. 3 (1992): 523–545.

Burns, T., and G. M. Stalker. *The Management of Innovation.* London: Tavistock, 1961.

Burton, J. *Conflict: Resolution and Prevention.* New York: St. Martin's Press.1990.

Bush, Kenneth. "A Measure of Peace: Peace and Conflict Impact Assessment (PCIA) of Development Projects in Conflict Zones." Working Paper 1. Ottawa, Canada: International Development Research Centre, Peacebuilding and Reconstruction Program Initiative, 1998.

Cairns, Ed, and Micheál Roe. *The Role of Memory in Ethnic Conflict.* Basingstoke, UK: Palgrave Macmillan, 2003.

Checkland, Peter, and John Poulter. *Learning for Action.* New York: Wiley, 2006.

Chigas, Diana. "Negotiating Intractable Conflicts: The Contributions of Unofficial Intermediaries." In *Grasping the Nettle: Analyzing Cases of Intractable Conflict,* edited by Chester A. Crocker, Fen Osler Hampson, and Pamela Aall, 123–160. Washington, DC: US Institute of Peace Press, 2005.

Clemens, Walter C., Jr. "Complexity Theory as a Tool for Understanding and Coping with Ethnic Conflict and Development Issues in Post-Soviet Eurasia." *International Journal of Peace Studies* 7, no. 2 (2002). Available at www.gmu.edu/academic/ijps/v017_2/Clemens.htm.

CNA Corporation. *National Security and the Threat of Climate Change.* Alexandria, VA: CNA Corporation, 2007.

CNN. "Audit: U.S. Lost Track of $9 Billion in Iraq Funds." CNN. January 30, 2005. http://edition.cnn.com/2005/WORLD/meast/01/30/iraq.audit.

Coate, Roger, and Jerel Rosati. "Human Needs in World Society." In *The Power of Human Needs in World Society,* edited by Roger Coate and Jerel Rosati, 1–20. Boulder, CO: Lynne Rienner Publishers, 1988.

Coleman, Peter T. "Characteristics of Protracted, Intractable Conflict: Toward the Development of a Metaframework—I." *Peace and Conflict: Journal of Peace Psychology* 9, no. 1 (2003): 1–37.

———. "Characteristics of Protracted, Intractable Conflict: Toward the Development of a Metaframework—II." *Peace and Conflict: Journal of Peace Psychology* 10, no. 3 (2004): 197–235.

———. "Conflict, Complexity, and Change: A Meta-Framework for Addressing Protracted, Intractable Conflicts—III." *Peace and Conflict: Journal of Peace Psychology* 12, no.4 (2006): 325–348.

———. *The Five Percent: Finding Solutions to Seemingly Impossible Conflicts.* New York: PublicAffairs, 2011.

Collaborative Learning Projects. "What Is Effective Peace Building?" CDA/Collaborative Learning Projects. www.cdainc.com/cdawww/project_profile.php?pid=RPP&pname=Reflecting Peace Practice. Accessed July 27, 2010.

Colletta, Nat, and Michelle Cullen. *Violent Conflict and the Transformation of Social Capital.* Washington, DC: World Bank, 2000.

Collier, P., L. Elliott, H. Havard, A. Hoeffler, M. Reynal-Querol, and N. Sambanis. *Breaking the Conflict Trap: Civil War and Development Policy.* Oxford: Oxford University Press, 2003.

Collier, Paul. "Economic Causes of Civil Conflict and Their Implications for Policy." Policy Research Paper 2355. Washington, DC: World Bank, 2000.

Conflict Prevention and Post-Conflict Reconstruction Network. *Peace and Conflict Impact Assessment (PCIA) Handbook.* Version 2. N.p., 2005.

Crocker, Chester, Fen Osler Hampson, and Pamela Aall, eds. *Grasping the Nettle.* Washington, DC: US Institute of Peace Press, 2005.

———, eds. *Herding Cats.* Washington, DC: US Institute of Peace Press, 1999.

———. Introduction to *Herding Cats,* edited by Chester Crocker, Fen Osler Hampson, and Pamela Aall, 3–17. Washington, DC: US Institute of Peace Press, 1999.

———, eds. *Turbulent Peace.* Washington, DC: US Institute of Peace Press, 2001.

de Coning, Cedric. "Civil-Military Coordination Practices and Approaches Within United Nations Peace Operations." *Journal of Military and Strategic Studies* 10, no. 1 (2007): 1–35.

———. *Coherence and Coordination in United Nations Peacebuilding and Integrated Missions.* Security in Practice 5. Oslo: Norsk Utenrikspolitisk Institutt, 2007.

Demichelis, Julia. *NGOs and Peacebuilding in Bosnia's Ethnically Divided Cities.* Washington, DC: US Institute of Peace, 1996.

Department for International Development (DFID). "Overview of DFID Strategy in Tanzania." DFID. www.dfid.gov.uk/where-we-work/africa-eastern—southern/tanzania. Accessed May 14, 2010.

———. "Tanzania Country Assistance Plan." DFID. http://webarchive.nationalarchives.gov.uk/+/http://www.dfid.gov.uk/consultations/tanzania-part4.asp.

Deutsch, Morton. "Justice and Conflict." In *The Handbook of Conflict Resolution: Theory and Practice,* edited by Morton Deutsch and Peter T. Coleman, 44–68. San Francisco: Jossey-Bass, 2000.

Diamond, Louise. *Peacebuilding.* Arlington, VA: Institute for Multi-Track Diplomacy, 1993.

Doyle, Michael W., and Nicholas Sambanis. "International Peacebuilding: A Theoretical and Quantitative Analysis." *American Political Science Review* 94, no. 4 (2000): 779–801.

Dudouet, Veronique, Beatrix Schmelzle, and David Bloomfield, eds. *The Berghof Research Center for Constructive Management Seminar Report.* Berlin: Berghof Research Center for Constructive Conflict Management, 2005.

———, eds. *Transitions from Violence to Peace.* Berghof Report 15. Berlin: Berghof Research Center for Constructive Conflict Management, 2006.

Easterly, William. "Introduction: Can't Take It Anymore?" In *Reinventing Foreign Aid,* edited by William Easterly, 1–43. Cambridge, MA: MIT Press, 2008.

Eide, Espen Barth, state secretary, Norwegian Ministry of Defense. Speech given at the Finnish Institute of International Affairs, Helsinki, Norway, May 29, 2006.

Fisher, Roger. *Getting to Yes.* DVD. Lakewood, WA: Richardson Company Training Media, 1993.

Fisher, Roger, and Scott Brown. *Getting Together.* New York: Penguin Books, 1989.

Fisher, Roger, and Keith Fitzgerald. "Facilitated Joint Brainstorming: Generating Options to Overcome Deadlock." Unpublished paper. Harvard Negotiation Project, Harvard Law School, Cambridge, Massachusetts, 1999.

Fisher, Roger, William L. Ury, and Bruce Patton. *Getting to Yes.* New York: Penguin Books, 1991.

Fisher, Ronald, ed. "Conflict Resolution Training in Divided Societies." Special Issue of *International Negotiation Journal* 2, no. 3 (1997).

Fitzduff, Mari. *Beyond Violence.* Tokyo: United Nations University Press, 2002.

———. *Community Conflict Skills: A Handbook for Anti-Sectarian Work.* Cookstown, Ireland: Community Conflict Skills Project, 1988.

———. "Meta-Conflict Resolution." *Beyond Intractability,* edited by Guy Burgess and Heidi Burgess. Boulder: Conflict Research Consortium, University of Colorado, 2004. www .beyondintractability.org/essay/meta-conflict-resolution. Accessed August 23, 2007.

Fletcher School of Law and Diplomacy. *Advanced Seminar in Development and Conflict.* DHP P227, class lecture, Fletcher School of Law and Diplomacy, March 6, 2010.

Fowler, Alan. "Connecting the Dots." *The Broker.* April 7, 2008. www.thebrokeronline.eu/ en/Magazine/articles/Connecting-the-dots.

Gaigals, Cynthia, and Manuela Leonhardt. "Conflict Sensitive Approaches to Development Practice." An International Alert–Saferworld–IRDC Report, International Development Research Centre, International Alert, 2001.

Galtung, Johan. *Transcend and Transform.* London: Pluto Press, 2004.

———. "Violence, Peace and Peace Research." *Journal of Peace Research* 6, no. 3 (1969): 167–191.

Galtung, Johan, and Carl G. Jacobsen. *Searching for Peace.* London: Pluto, 2000.

Global Partnership for the Prevention of Armed Conflict. "About Us." Global Partnership for the Prevention of Armed Conflict. www.gppac.net/page.php?id=1485. Accessed October, 2010.

Global Peace Index. "About the GPI." Vision of Humanity. www.visionofhumanity.org/about. Accessed July 26, 2010.

Goodhand, Jonathan, Tony Vaux, and Robert Walker. *Conducting Conflict Assessments: Guidance Notes.* London, UK Department for International Development, 2002.

Gross Stein, Janet. "Image, Identity and Conflict Resolution." In *Managing Global Chaos,* edited by Chester Crocker, Fen Hampson, and Pamela Aall, 93–111. Washington, DC: US Institute of Peace Press, 1996.

Harris, Richard. "Reef Conservation Strategy Backfires." National Public Radio. November 18, 2009. www.npr.org/templates/story/story.php?storyId=120536304.

Hatch, Orrin. "The Ted Kennedy I Knew." *Politico.* August 26, 2009. www.politico.com/ news/stories/0809/26482.html.

Heath, Dan, and Chip Heath. "Analysis of Paralysis." FastCompany.com. November 1, 2007. www.fastcompany.com/magazine/120/analysis-of-paralysis.html. Accessed April 20, 2010.

———. *Switch: How to Change Things When Change Is Hard.* New York: Broadway Books, 2010.

Hendrick, Diane. *Complexity Theory and Conflict Transformation: An Exploration of Potential and Implications.* Working Paper 17. Bradford, UK: University of Bradford, 2009.

Hoffman, Mark. *Peace and Conflict Impact Assessment Methodology.* Berlin: Berghof Foundation, 2004.

Human Security Centre. *Human Security Brief 2006.* Vancouver: Liu Institute for Global Issues, University of British Columbia, 2006.

Interagency Conflict Assessment of Cambodia. "Cambodia: Adjustment or Instability?" Study conducted at the request of the US Embassy in Phnom Penh, March 2009.

Kanter, Rosabeth Moss, Barry A. Stein, and Todd D. Jick. *The Challenge of Organizational Change.* New York: Free Press, 1992.

Kassalow, Jordan S. *Why Health Is Important to US Foreign Policy.* New York: Milbank Memorial Fund, 2001.

Katz, Daniel, and Robert Kahn. *The Social Psychology of Organizations.* New York: Wiley, 1978.

Knight, W. Andy. "Conclusion: Peacebuilding Theory and Praxis." In *Building Sustainable Peace,* edited by Tom Keating and W. Andy Knight, 355–382. Tokyo: United Nations University Press, 2004.

Kreimer, A., J. Eriksson, R. Muscat, M. Arnold, and C. Scott, *The World Bank's Experience with Post-Conflict Reconstruction.* Washington, DC: World Bank, 1998.

Kriesberg, Louis. "Coordinating Intermediary Peace Efforts." *Negotiation Journal* 12, no. 4 (1996): 303–314.

Lange, Maria, and Mick Quinn. "Conflict, Humanitarian Assistance and Peacebuilding: Meeting the Challenges." London: International Alert, 2003.

Lawrence, Paul R., and Jay W. Lorsch. *Organization and Environment.* Homewood, IL: Richard D. Irwin, 1969.

Lax, David, and James Sebenius. "The Power of Alternatives or the Limits to Negotiation." In *Negotiation Theory and Practice,* edited by J. William Breslin and Jeffery Z. Rubin, 97–114. Cambridge, MA: Program on Negotiation at Harvard Law School, 1991.

Lederach, John Paul. *Building Peace: Sustainable Reconciliation in Divided Societies.* Washington, DC: US Institute of Peace, 1997.

———. *The Little Book of Conflict Transformation.* Lancaster, PA: Good Books, 2003.

———. *Preparing for Peace: Conflict Transformation Across Cultures.* Syracuse, NY: Syracuse University Press, 1995.

Liden, Kristoffer. "What Is the Ethics of Peacebuilding?" Lecture prepared for the kickoff meeting of the Liberal Peace and the Ethics of Peacebuilding project. Oslo, Norway, January 18, 2007. www.prio.no/Research-and-Publications/Publication/?oid=62734. Accessed April 26, 2010.

Lund, Michael. *Preventing Violent Conflicts.* Washington, DC: US Institute of Peace Press, 1996.

———. "What Kind of Peace Is Being Built? Taking Stock of Post-Conflict Peacebuilding and Charting Future Directions." Paper prepared for the tenth anniversary of *Agenda for Peace* for the International Development Research Centre, Ottawa, Canada, January 2003.

Mackenzie, Donald. *Myths of Babylonia and Assyria.* London: Gresham Publishing Company, 1915.

Maiese, Michelle. "Dehumanization." In *Beyond Intractability,* edited by Guy Burgess and Heidi Burgess. Boulder: Conflict Research Consortium, University of Colorado, 2004. www.beyondintractability.org/essay/dehumanization. Accessed April 23, 2008.

Mandela, Nelson. "Address to the People of Cape Town." Address on the occasion of Mandela's inauguration as state president, Cape Town, May 9, 1994.

Mansuri, Ghazala, and Vijayendra Rao. "Evaluating Community-Based Community-Driven Development: A Critical Review of the Evidence." Development Economics Research Group and the Social Development Anchor of the World Bank. September 2003. www.cbnrm.net/pdf/mansuri_g_001_cddfinal.pdf. Accessed September 2003.

Mason, T. David, M. Crenshaw, C. McClintock, and B. Walter. "How Political Violence Ends: Paths to Conflict Deescalation and Termination." Paper presented at the meeting of the American Political Science Association, Chicago, Illinois, August 30 to September 2, 2007.

Maynard, Kimberly A. "The Role of Culture, Islam and Tradition in Community Driven Reconstruction." A Study on the International Rescue Committee's Approach to NSP presented to the International Rescue Committee, New York, 2007.

McCartney, Clem. "From Armed Struggle to Political Negotiations: Why? When? How?" In *Choosing to Engage: Armed Groups and Peace Processes,* edited by R. Ricigliano, 30–35. London: Conciliation Resources, 2005.

Meadows, Donella. *Thinking in Systems: A Primer.* White River Junction, VT: Chelsea Green Publishing, 2008.

Meadows, Donella, and J. Robinson. *The Electronic Oracle.* New York: Wiley, 1985.

Mitchell, C. R. *The Structure of International Conflict.* New York: St. Martin's Press, 1981.

Mitchell, Christopher. "The Process and Stages of Mediation: The Sudanese Cases." In *Making War and Waging Peace,* edited by David R. Smock, 139–159. Washington, DC: US Institute of Peace Press, 1993.

Montgomery, Michael, and Stephen Smith. "The Few Who Stayed: Defying Genocide in Rwanda." American Radio Works. http://americanradioworks.publicradio.org/features/rwanda/segc2.html. Accessed March 17, 2010.

Moore, C. W. *The Mediation Process: Practical Strategies for Resolving Conflict.* San Francisco: Jossey-Bass, 1986.

Morgan, Peter. "The Idea and Practice of Systems Thinking and Their Relevance for Capacity Development." Report for the European Centre for Development Policy Management, Brussels, Belgium, March 2005.

Moss, T., G. Pettersson, and N. van de Walle. *An Aid-Institutions Paradox? A Review Essay on Aid Dependency and State Building in Sub-Saharan Africa.* Working Paper 74. Washington, DC: Centre for Global Development, 2006.

Murithi, Tim. *The Ethics of Peacebuilding.* Edinburgh: Edinburgh University Press, 2009.

Nadler, D., and M. Tushman. "A Diagnostic Model for Organizational Behavior." In *Perspectives on Behavior in Organizations,* edited by Richard J. Hackman, Edward E. Lawler, Lyman W. Porter, and Patricia S. Nave. New York: McGraw-Hill, 1977.

Nan, Susan Allen. "Complementarity and Coordination of Conflict Resolution Efforts in the Conflicts over Abkhazia, South Ossetia, and Transdniestria." PhD diss., George Mason University, 1999.

———. "Shifting from Coherent to Holistic Processes." In *Handbook of Conflict Analysis and Resolution,* edited by Dennis Sandole and Sean Byrne. New York: Routledge, 2009.

Nitze, P., S. Rearden, and A. Smith. *From Hiroshima to Glasnost.* New York: Grove Press, 1989.

Northrup, Terrell A. "The Dynamic of Identity in Personal and Social Conflict." In *Intractable Conflicts and Their Transformation,* edited by Louis Kriesberg, Terrell A. Northrup, and Stuart J. Thorson, 55–82. Syracuse, NY: Syracuse University Press, 1989.

Opotow, Susan. "Aggression and Violence." In *The Handbook of Conflict Resolution: Theory and Practice,* edited by Morton Deutsch and Peter T. Coleman, 509–532. San Francisco: Jossey-Bass, 2000.

Parry, Emyr Jones, permanent representative of the United Kingdom Mission of Greater Britain and Northern Ireland. Security Council Open Debate on Post-Conflict Peacebuilding. May 26, 2005. www.ukun.org. Accessed October 2, 2007.

Pascale, R. T., and A. G. Athos. *The Art of Japanese Management.* New York: Simon & Schuster, 1981.

PBS. "The Triumph of Evil." *Frontline.* January 26, 1996. www.pbs.org/wgbh/pages/frontline/shows/evil/interviews/gourevitch.html.

Peters, Thomas, and Robert Waterman. *In Search of Excellence.* San Francisco: Harper & Row, 1982.

Prendergast, John. *Frontline Diplomacy.* Boulder, CO: Lynne Rienner Publishers, 1996.

Putnam, Robert D. "The Prosperous Community." *American Prospect* 4, no. 13 (March 21, 1993), www.prospect.org/cs/articles?article=the_prosperous_community. Accessed September 1, 2010.

Ramalingam, Ben, Harry Jones, Toussaint Reba, and John Young. "Exploring the Science of Complexity: Ideas and Implications for Development and Humanitarian Efforts." Overseas Development Institute Working Paper 285. London: ODI, 2008.

Ramsbotham, Oliver, Tom Woodhouse, and Hugh Miall. *Contemporary Conflict Resolution.* Cambridge, MA: Polity, 2005.

Ricigliano, Robert. "A Three-Dimensional Model of Negotiation." In *The Negotiator's Fieldbook,* edited by A. Schneider and C. Honeyman, 55–60. Chicago: American Bar Association Books, 2006.

———. "Can't Get There from Here: The Need for Networks of Effective Action to Promote More Effective Peacebuilding." In *Towards Better Peacebuilding Practice: On Lessons Learned, Evaluation Practices, and Aid and Conflict,* edited by A. Galama and P. van Tongeren, 213–219. Utrecht: European Centre for Conflict Prevention, 2003.

————. "The Chaordic Peace Process." *Journal for the Study of Peace and Conflict* (2003–2004): 1–11.

————. *Choosing to Engage Armed Groups in Peace Processes.* Accord Issue 16. London: Conciliation Resources, 2005.

————. "Networks of Effective Action: Implementing an Integrated Approach to Peacebuilding." *Security Dialogue* 34, no. 4 (2003): 445–462.

————. "Planning for Systemic Impact." In *The Non-Linearity of Peace Processes: Theory and Practice of Systemic Conflict Transformation,* edited by Norbert Ropers and Daniela Korppen. Berlin: Berghof Foundation for Peace Support, forthcoming.

Ricigliano, R., A. Chasen, and T. Johnson. "Problems Without a Process." *Harvard Negotiation Law Review* 4 (1999): 83.

Rotberg, Robert I. "The New Nature of Nation-State Failure." *Washington Quarterly* 25, no. 3 (2002): 85–96.

Rothman, Jay. *Resolving Identity-Based Conflict in Nations, Organizations, and Communities.* San Francisco: Jossey-Bass, 1997.

Rouhana, Nadime, and Daniel Bar-Tal. "Psychological Dynamics of Intractable Ethnonational Conflicts: The Israeli-Palestinian Case." *American Psychologist* 53, no. 7 (July 1998): 761–770.

Rubin, Jeffrey. *Dynamics of Third Party Intervention.* New York: Praeger Publishers, 1983.

Rupiya, Martin, and Jemima Njeri. "An Evaluation of the Post-Savimbi Peace Process in Angola Since February 2002: The Victor's Peace Treaty." Institute for Security Studies. July 2004. www.issafrica.org/pubs/Books/civmilzambiaaug04/Rupiya2.pdf.

Ryan, Michael. Teleconference with the University of Wisconsin, Milwaukee's Global Studies Summer Institute. August 6, 2002.

Sachs, Jeffrey D. *The End of Poverty.* New York: Penguin, 2005.

Schein, Edgar H. *Organizational Culture and Leadership.* San Francisco: Jossey-Bass, 1992.

Schön, D. *Organizational Learning: A Theory of Action Perspective.* Reading, MA: Addison-Wesley, 1978.

Senge, Peter. *The Fifth Discipline: The Art and Practice of the Learning Organization.* New York: Doubleday, 1990.

Sethi, Suresh, and Gerald Thompson. *Optimal Control Theory.* Berlin: Springer, 2005.

Shalizi, Hamid, and Peter Graff. "Taliban Ready if Afghan Government Fails, Analyst Warns." Reuters. August 31, 2009. www.reuters.com/article/idUSTRE57U17020090831.

Smith, Dan. *Getting Their Act Together: Towards a Strategic Framework for Peacebuilding.* Oslo: International Peace Research Institute, 2003.

Stedman, Stephen John, Donald Rothchild, and Elizabeth M. Cousens. *Ending Civil Wars.* Boulder, CO: Lynne Rienner Publishers, 2002.

Stedman, Steve. "Spoiler Problems in the Peace Process." *International Security* 12 (1997): 5–53.

Stein, Janet Gross. "Image, Identity and Conflict Resolution." In *Managing Global Chaos,* edited by Chester Crocker, Fen Hampson, and Pamela Aall, 93–112. Washington, DC: US Institute of Peace Press, 1996.

Sternin, J., and R. Choo. "The Power of Positive Deviancy." *Harvard Business* (January–February 2000): 14–15.

Stone, Douglas, Bruce Patton, and Sheila Heen. *Difficult Conversations: How to Discuss What Matters Most.* New York: Viking, 1999.

Suhrke, A., and I. Samset. "What's in a Figure? Estimating Recurrence of Civil War." *International Peacekeeping* 14, no. 2 (2007): 195–203.

Taw, Saw David. "From Choosing to Engage: Strategic Considerations for the Karen National Union." In *Choosing to Engage: Armed Groups and Peace Processes,* edited by R. Ricigliano, 40–43. London: Conciliation Resources, 2005.

Tongeren, Paul, Malin Brenk, Marte Hellema, and Juliette Verhoeven. *People Building Peace II: Successful Stories of Civil Society.* Boulder, CO: Lynne Rienner Publishers, 2005.

Tschirgi, Neclâ. "Post-Conflict Peacebuilding Revisited: Achievements, Limitations, Challenges." Paper presented at the War-Torn Societies Project International/International Peace Academy Peacebuilding Forum Conference, New York, October 7, 2004.

UN General Assembly. "A More Secure World." Prepared by the High-Level Panel on Threats, Challenges and Change as a follow-up to the outcome of the Millennium Summit. Fifty-Ninth Session, Official Records, 2004. A/59/565.

UN Secretary-General. "In Larger Freedom: Towards Freedom, Security and Human Rights for All." A/59/2005. 2005.

———. "Note of Guidance on Integrated Missions." January 17, 2005.

———. "Note of Guidance on Integrated Missions." February 9, 2006.

Ury, William. *The Third Side: Why We Fight and How We Can Stop.* New York: Penguin, 1999.

US Department of State, Office of the Coordinator for Reconstruction and Stabilization. *Interagency Methodology to Assess Instability and Conflict (IMIC).* Washington, DC: US Department of State, 2006.

———. *Interagency Conflict Assessment Framework.* Washington, DC: USAID, 2009.

Verkoren, Willemijn. "Debating Complexity." *The Broker,* July 28, 2008. www.thebrokeronline .eu/en/Magazine/articles/Debating-complexity.

von Bertalanffy, Ludwig. *General System Theory.* New York: George Braziller, 1968.

Weisbord, M. "Organizational Dialogue: Six Places to Look for Trouble With or Without a Theory." *Group & Organizational Studies* 1, no. 4 (1976): 430–447.

Williams, S., and R. Ricigliano. "Understanding Armed Groups." In *Choosing to Engage: Armed Groups and Peace Processes,* edited by R. Ricigliano, 14–17. London: Conciliation Resources, 2005.

Woodrow, Peter. "Strategic Analysis for Peacebuilding Programs: A Modest Proposal." Draft on file with author. 2002.

Woolcock, Michael, and Deepa Narayan. "Social Capital: Implications for Development Theory, Research, and Policy." *World Bank Research Observer* 15, no. 2 (2000): 225–249.

Woolcock, Michael, and Lant Pritchard. "Solutions When Solutions Are the Problem: Arraying the Disarray in Development." In *Reinventing Foreign Aid,* edited by William Easterly, 147–178. Cambridge, MA: MIT Press, 2008.

World Bank. *Sustaining Rapid Growth in a Challenging Environment: Cambodia Country Economic Memorandum.* Phnom Penh: World Bank Poverty Reduction and Economic Management Sector, Unit East Asia and Pacific Region, 2009.

World Bank, Social Development Department, Environmentally and Socially Sustainable Development Network. *Community-Driven Development in the Context of Conflict-Affected Countries: Challenges and Opportunities.* Washington, DC: World Bank, 2006.

World Health Organization (WHO). *Official Record of the World Health Organization.* Volume 2. Geneva: WHO, n.d.

Yom, Sean L., and Basel Saleh. "Palestinian Violence and the Second Intifada: Explaining Suicidal Attacks." Paper presented at the annual meeting of the New England Political Science Association, Portsmouth, Maine, April 30, 2004.

INDEX

⟜⟞

3P Human Security (3D Security), 13
7S Framework, 29

ABC Conflict Triangle, 48, 49
ability to change, key actors and, 182–183
access, to structures meeting human needs, 43
ACCORD project, 46, 194–195
action-reaction escalation cycle, 44, 100, 129–130
adaptability: systemic planning and, 174; working with systems and, 64
adversarial strategy, in negotiation, 185–186
advocacy, networking and, 170
affinity diagramming, 110, 111, 218
Afghanistan, 4; causal loop diagramming in assessment of, 109–112, 116, 117–118, 122, 123, 125–126, 128; change as nonlinear process in, 64–65; conflict resolution training in, 214; holding election in, 24–25; key people and conflict in, 47; peacebuilding funding in, 7; reforestation project in, 71–72; success of reconstruction projects in, 54–55; US counterinsurgency strategy in, 12

African National Congress (ANC), 186, 191, 199–200
African Union (Organization of African Unity), 180
Ahtisaari, Martti, 189–190
aid agencies: donor demands *vs.* service needs and, 71–72. *See also under* third-party
Akol, Lam, 36
Alliance for Peacebuilding, 20, 180, 237–238
altering initial conditions, 65
ameliorating dynamics, 104
ameliorating factors, 94
ameliorating reinforcing feedback loops, 115
amplifier effect, 165–166
analysis, danger of paralysis by, 139, 142–143
analytical habits, avoiding bad, 82, 88–90
ANC. *See* African National Congress (ANC)
Anderson, Mary: Do No Harm movement and, 74, 239; on focus of peacebuilding programs, 51; on foreign aid, 84; on goals of peace practitioners, 14;

ABOUT THE AUTHOR

Robert Ricigliano is the director of the Institute of World Affairs and teaches at the University of Wisconsin, Milwaukee. He is also a former executive director of the Conflict Management Group and served as an associate director of the Harvard Negotiation Project at Harvard Law School. He has worked on peace processes with government officials, armed groups, and community activists all over the world.